D1320236

Defense, Controls, and Inflation

Defense, Controls, and Inflation

A CONFERENCE SPONSORED BY

THE UNIVERSITY OF CHICAGO LAW SCHOOL

Edited by

AARON DIRECTOR

THE UNIVERSITY OF CHICAGO PRESS

THE UNIVERSITY OF CHICAGO PRESS, CHICAGO 37
Cambridge University Press, London, N.W. 1, England
W. J. Gage & Co., Limited, Toronto 2B, Canada

FOREWORD

THE current mobilization program raises issues which are of obvious importance to law and economics. These issues concern the effectiveness of alternative measures to achieve economic mobilization as well as the influence of these measures on the more permanent objectives of public policy.

The conference held at White Sulphur Springs, West Virginia, on April 5–8, 1951, was planned to achieve a discussion of these issues and to clarify the areas of agreement and difference. It was sponsored by the University of Chicago Law School. The following committee was in charge of the conference: Walter J. Blum, Milton Friedman, Wilber G. Katz, Edward H. Levi, W. Allen Wallis, and Aaron Director, chairman.

I am indebted to Mr. Ward S. Bowman and Mr. Harry Kalven, Jr., of the Law School staff, and Mr. Milton Friedman, of the Department of Economics, for their considerable assistance in preparing the Introduction.

The University of Chicago Law School is grateful to the William Volker Fund of Kansas City for a grant to cover the expenses of the conference and for further financial assistance toward publication of the transcript.

AARON DIRECTOR

UNIVERSITY OF CHICAGO LAW SCHOOL

v

28555

TABLE OF CONTENTS

LIST OF PARTICIPANTS

GARDNER ACKLEY, Office of Price Stabilization, Washington, D.C.

THURMAN W. ARNOLD, Arnold, Fortas & Porter, Washington, D.C.

LAIRD BELL, Bell, Boyd, Marshall & Lloyd, Chicago, Illinois

THE HONORABLE WALLACE F. BENNETT, United States Senate, Washington, D.C.

ROY BLOUGH, Economic Adviser to the President, Washington, D.C.

WALTER J. BLUM, Associate Professor of Law, The University of Chicago, Chicago, Illinois

WARD S. BOWMAN, JR., Research Associate, The University of Chicago Law School, Chicago, Illinois

OTIS BRUBAKER, Director, Research Department, United Steelworkers of America, Pittsburgh, Pennsylvania

W. RANDOLPH BURGESS, Chairman, Executive Committee, The National City Bank of New York, New York, New York

THE HONORABLE EMANUEL CELLER, House of Representatives, Washington, D.C.

JOHN CHAMBERLAIN, *The Freeman*, New York, New York

BENJAMIN V. COHEN, Washington, D.C.

HERBERT C. CORNUELLE, The Volker Fund, Kansas City, Missouri

PHILIP CORTNEY, President, Coty, Inc., New York, New York

GARFIELD V. COX, Dean, The University of Chicago School of Business, Chicago, Illinois

OSCAR COX, Cox, Langford, Stoddard & Cutler, Washington, D.C.

ELI W. DEBEVOISE, Debevoise, Plimpton & McLean, New York, New York

AARON DIRECTOR, Professor of Economics, The University of Chicago Law School, Chicago, Illinois

MICHAEL V. DISALLE, Director of Price Stabilization, Washington, D.C.

JAMES H. DOUGLAS, JR., Gardner, Carton & Douglas, Chicago, Illinois

PEYTON O. FORD, Deputy United States Attorney-General, Washington, D.C.

DAVID E. FELLER, Assistant General Counsel, Congress of Industrial Organizations, Washington, D.C.

MILTON FRIEDMAN, Professor of Economics, The University of Chicago, Chicago, Illinois

MARTIN R. GAINSBRUGH, Chief Economist, National Industrial Conference Board, Inc., New York, New York

LLOYD K. GARRISON, Paul, Weiss, Rifkin, Wharton & Garrison, New York, New York

RICHARD B. GOODE, Assistant Professor of Economics, The University of Chicago, Chicago, Illinois

GEORGE E. HALE, Wilson & McIlvaine, Chicago, Illinois

ROBERT L. HALE, Professor of Law, Columbia University, New York, New York

BERNARD F. HALEY, Professor of Economics, Stanford University, Stanford, California

ALVIN H. HANSEN, Professor of Economics, Harvard University, Cambridge, Massachusetts

ROY HARROD, University Lecturer in Economics, Christ Church College, Oxford, England

FRIEDRICH A. HAYEK, Professor of Social and Moral Science, The University of Chicago, Chicago, Illinois

HENRY HAZLITT, *Newsweek,* New York, New York

LEON HENDERSON, Research Institute of America, Washington, D.C.

H. STRUVE HENSEL, Carter, Ledyard & Milburn, New York, New York

CHARLES J. HITCH, The RAND Corporation, Santa Monica, California

JOHN JEWKES, Professor of Economic Organization, Merton College, Oxford, England

HOMER JONES, Federal Reserve System, Washington, D.C.

HARRY KALVEN, JR., Associate Professor of Law, The University of Chicago, Chicago, Illinois

WILBER G. KATZ, James Parker Hall Professor of Law, The University of Chicago, Chicago, Illinois

MEYER KESTNBAUM, Hart, Schaffner & Marx, Chicago, Illinois

FRANK H. KNIGHT, Morton D. Hull Distinguished Service Professor of Social Science and Philosophy, The University of Chicago, Chicago, Illinois

FRED LAZARUS, JR., Federated Department Stores, Inc., Cincinnati, Ohio

HAROLD LEVENTHAL, Price Stabilization Agency, Washington, D.C.

EDWARD H. LEVI, Dean, The University of Chicago Law School, Chicago, Illinois

BERNARD D. MELTZER, Professor of Law, The University of Chicago, Chicago, Illinois

EUGENE MEYER, *The Washington Post,* Washington, D.C.

LLOYD W. MINTS, Associate Professor of Economics, The University of Chicago, Chicago, Illinois

LUDWIG VON MISES, Visiting Professor, Graduate School of Business Administration, New York University, New York, New York

H. GRAHAM MORISON, Assistant United States Attorney-General, Washington, D.C.

GEORGE M. MORRIS, Morris, KixMiller & Baar, Washington, D.C.

W. C. MULLENDORE, Southern California Edison Company, Los Angeles, California

THE HONORABLE JOSEPH C. O'MAHONEY, United States Senate, Washington, D.C.

PAUL A. PORTER, Arnold, Fortas & Porter, Washington, D.C.

WILLIAM WOOD PRINCE, The Union Stock Yard Company, Chicago, Illinois

EUGENE V. ROSTOW, Professor of Law, Yale University, New Haven, Connecticut

BEARDSLEY RUML, New York, New York

THEODORE W. SCHULTZ, Chairman, Department of Economics, The University of Chicago, Chicago, Illinois

CARL S. SHOUP, Professor of Economics, Columbia University, New York, New York

ROSCOE T. STEFFEN, John P. Wilson Professor of Law, The University of Chicago, Chicago, Illinois

HERBERT STEIN, Committee for Economic Development, Washington, D.C.

HERMAN W. STEINKRAUS, Bridgeport Brass Company, Bridgeport, Connecticut

GEORGE STIGLER, Professor of Economics, Columbia University, New York, New York

GEORGE W. STOCKING, Professor of Economics, Vanderbilt University, Nashville, Tennessee

THEODORE TANNENWALD, JR., Counsel to the Special Assistant to the President, Washington, D.C.

J. CAMERON THOMSON, Northwest Bancorporation, Minneapolis, Minnesota

JACOB VINER, Professor of Economics, Princeton University, Princeton, New Jersey

W. ALLEN WALLIS, Professor of Statistics and Business Economics, The University of Chicago, Chicago, Illinois

LYNN A. WILLIAMS, JR., Vice-President, The University of Chicago, Chicago, Illinois

HENRY C. WINGATE, International Nickel Company, New York, New York

I
INTRODUCTION[1]

I T SEEMS useful to preface this transcript of the three-day conference on "The Economics of Mobilization" with a brief review of the issues raised, the conclusions reached, and agreement and disagreement expressed. A mobilization program is to be judged by three principal criteria: the rapidity and efficiency with which the required resources are allocated to the defense effort, the extent to which inflation is prevented, and the extent to which other inequities and hardships are minimized.

The major theme of the conference was the nature and extent of the controls which should be applied by the government. All agreed on the need for some form of action by the government. Moreover, there was agreement on a great many specific proposals: that expenditures for the current mobilization program should be covered by increased taxes and that the budget should be substantially balanced; that the base for the additional taxes would have to be broad, including increased taxes on low and middle incomes; that an easy-money policy should not be followed by the monetary authorities and that a Reserve policy of rigorously maintaining existing interest rates was inappropriate; that the monetary authorities should not purchase government securities for the purpose of maintaining existing interest rates and that affirmative measures should be taken to prevent increases in the stock of money; and that priorities may be appropriate in cases where market imperfections

1. This Introduction was prepared by members of the Law School and sent to all participants. To expedite matters, we asked not for suggested changes but for comments which could be used as footnotes to specific points. Of those participants who responded, some merely indorsed the statement as an accurate summary of the discussion, one even going so far as to say that it was "too fair." But others were of the opinion that we had failed at several points to grasp the substance of their views. While they did not in all cases direct their comments to specific statements, we have put their comments where they seemed most in point.

prevent the government from getting resources for the defense effort by bidding them away from other purchasers.

In addition to the agreement on the above specific proposals, there was also agreement that a mobilization program should be judged by the consequences of indefinite continuance. There was hope and, indeed, some belief that the emergency would be of short duration, but no one held that policy should be based on this hope. It was agreed that general fiscal and monetary control could be continued indefinitely without interfering with long-run objectives of public policy but that widespread allocations and direct wage and price controls could not. No one held that direct controls would be desirable permanent institutions.[2] At the same time there was considerable feeling, which was given strong stimulus by the report on the British situation, that public irritation against widespread direct controls would necessitate their eventual removal. Hence the imposition of such controls during the emergency would in fact not involve a permanent commitment to central planning.[3]

2. MR. STEIN: I do not think this paragraph adequately explains the frame of reference with respect to the duration of the mobilization program. As I see it, the proponents of direct price-wage controls generally assume that there will be a hump period in the mobilization program and that the hump period will not last more than three of four years. I do not think they would accept the proposition that the desirability of direct controls in dealing with the problems of the hump period should be judged by the desirability of their indefinite continuation, if by "indefinite" we mean permanent. On the other hand, while accepting the hump hypothesis, I do not think the desirability of adopting direct controls in the emergency can be argued without reference to longer-run implications. Many of the assertions made in support of emergency controls would, if valid, also support permanent controls. The argument that monopoly business and labor organizations will push up prices in a free market and the argument that we cannot tolerate "rationing by the purse" are examples. I am personally less worried by the actual harm that would result from a year or two of price control than by the long-run consequences of the kinds of statements one apparently has to make and believe about the American economy in order to justify controls even for a year or two.

3. MR. G. E. HALE: I was slightly disappointed that the Introduction did not touch upon the long-term effects of direct controls upon free institutions. While I recognize that the discussion of that aspect of mobilization was telescoped and perhaps contained little of permanent interest, the subject seems so vital that some mention in the Introduction would appear appropriate. Indeed, it might be possible to effect some linkage between

This widespread consensus on some of the major issues should not obscure the important fact that there was disagreement on a number of other central issues. Perhaps the chief disagreement was whether direct controls were needed as a supplement to or substitute for the market system supplemented by vigorous monetary policy and an approximately balanced budget.[4]

---

the impact of direct controls upon free markets and the argument that direct controls are made necessary by the absence of competition.

4. MR. ACKLEY and MR. DiSALLE: We believe that the whole focus of the conference and the summary give undue prominence to monetary controls. The issue is stated to be "direct controls" versus "monetary controls." In particular, fiscal policy is not specifically set forth as a major alternative. Many people confuse fiscal and monetary policies. Most fiscal policies have monetary consequences, but the two are clearly separable; and in our opinion fiscal policies are more important than monetary policies. Obviously, however, the monetary policies we use should operate in the same direction as our fiscal policies.

MR. MISES: There is no agreement whatsoever concerning the fundamental issue. There is, on the one hand, the official doctrine. It passes over in silence the problem of the increase in the quantity of money in circulation and deposits subject to check, the phenomenon that until a few years ago would have commonly been called "inflation." It applies the term "inflation" to the inevitable consequences of this increase, viz., the general tendency of the prices of all goods and services to rise. It ascribes this tendency not to monetary factors but to the selfish machinations of businessmen. It thinks that all that is needed to prevent prices from rising is to decree and to enforce maximum prices. There are, on the other hand, the quantity theory of money and the theory about the necessary consequences of fixing maximum prices below the height at which the unhampered market would have determined the market price. The supporters of the first doctrine want to stop what they call inflation by price control. The second group wants to stop inflation by preventing the government from increasing the quantity of money in circulation and bank deposits subject to check. There is no compromise possible between these two opposite points of view.

MR. LEVENTHAL: I have the general reaction that the Introduction presents, more in its tone than in any specific statement, a report of the conference which slants it in favor of those advocating reliance solely on indirect controls. For example, the conference reports the general agreement on the necessity of "indirect controls" (itself a misnomer) and then focuses on the question, "Why direct controls?" in such a way as subtly places the burden of proof upon anyone who argues for additional controls.

MR. BRUBAKER: The Introduction shows substantial bias in favor of the exclusive use of monetary controls throughout its discussion of most of the points raised in the conference. In my opinion, the conference was pre-

Some felt that there was no occasion for direct controls except possibly for some limited priorities. Others argued that they were required to promote the transfer of resources, to prevent inflation, or to prevent inequities. Still others felt that they were required simply to assure the public that the government was taking its responsibilities seriously.[5]

The following summary concentrates attention on the unresolved issues in the hope that an attempt to sharpen these important issues of public policy by relating them to three important criteria of a mobilization progam—efficiency, prevention of inflation, and equity—may serve to delimit areas of apparent disagreement and make further discussion of them more significant.

I. EFFICIENCY OF MOBILIZATION

Mobilization involves the efficient and rapid marshaling of the human and natural resources required for national defense.[6] Under current conditions, with high levels of employment and production, there is little slack in the economy. Consequently,

---

dominantly opposed to any sole, or even major, reliance on money manipulation as a means of controlling inflation or furthering our defense effort. I find it impossible to understand why advocates of monetary "controls" and a "free" market—a sharp inconsistency in itself—are so sure direct controls cannot succeed because no one is smart enough to make the complicated decisions which are required in a system of direct controls. Surely, if the conscious decisions which constitute the "market" itself can be made by mere men, so could other distribution decisions.

5. MR. HITCH: My view is that there is no general categorical answer to this question; that the need for direct controls (or expenditure rationing, which is hard to classify as direct or indirect) depends upon the magnitude and speed of mobilization.

6. MR. MORISON: The attorney-general, in his second report to the President and the Congress under the Defense Production Act of 1950, which was submitted on April 30, 1951, pointed out that a primary objective of the act and the directives of the President is to attain our defense requirements within the framework of our competitive enterprise system. He emphasized that this objective can be met only by broadening the base of our procurement program so as to utilize all of our production facilities, small as well as large.

The attorney-general's second report under the Defense Production Act emphasized the need for the introduction into our mobilization program of the essential element of over-all central planning, which "will make possible considered decisions in the execution of the nation's procurement

the mobilization job involves primarily the shifting of resources from other uses to the defense sector. According to current estimates, the defense program at its peak will require approximately 20 per cent of the national income. It is not apparent, however, that the argument would be much affected by substantial increases in this estimate.

Will the market allocate resources rapidly enough?—Since time is of the essence, debate here centers on whether resources can be allocated to the defense program more rapidly by relying on the market alone or by supplementing the market with some system of controls. The advantage of a free market in allocating resources in normal times was generally recognized. Scarce means are rationed among competing ends by this method more efficiently and more sensitively. The most effective inducement for shifting men and materials to needed areas is to make work in those areas relatively more attractive. The case for the market with respect to mobilization is that the government can obtain all the defense goods it needs by outbidding others.

There was a strong challenge to this position. Priorities for strategic defense requirements were said to be indispensable, because some prices, especially for important defense items like steel, either would not respond to higher government bids or would not respond rapidly enough to meet the requirements of the mobilization program. The principal factors offered to account for the slow response of the market were lack of effective price competition in the markets and large backlogs of orders or contractual commitments. In addition, the expectation of a very short mobilization period may well cause some pro-

---

program so that we can best utilize existing and potential industrial capacity to meet military requirements and achieve a balanced expansion of our economy."

Central procurement planning for our defense and essential civilian requirements will avoid, the attorney-general pointed out, the undue concentration of production and production facilities in the hands of a few dominant enterprisers and will thereby directly promote the objective of the Defense Production Act to meet our defense requirements within the framework of our competitive enterprise system. Such planning, the attorney-general noted, will also contribute materially to the strategic dispersal of production facilities as a defense against air attack.

ducers to prefer to retain steady customers in the private sector even though higher prices might temporarily be obtained for defense work.

Some advocates of priorities stressed that their points were not applicable to a long period of mobilization in which market factors would have time to adjust and that these controls should be limited solely to strategic defense requirements and then only to those industries in which the above sticky characteristics were fully manifested. It should be noted that, although there seemed to be considerable agreement that there were some areas in which market reactions would be slow, there was little discussion and no evident agreement as to how widespread those areas were.

Inasmuch as the principal reason given by some advocates for priority control was the fact that market prices would not rise or rise fast enough, these advocates took special pains to point out that price and wage controls would be wholly inappropriate. They envisaged supplementing market forces by priorities alone, leaving prices completely free. The introduction of this one limited type of control would not entail as an aftermath the addition of all sorts of collateral controls to support it. It was thought that the limited priorities would be required only for what was described as the initial step-up part of the mobilization program, which is not likely to last for more than two years.

The above case for some priority controls does not depend on the existence of inflation. The presence of inflation would strengthen the case for such controls, as still larger price rises would be required to enable the government to bid resources away from other purchasers.

Other proponents of priority control did not limit their case to areas where the market was not fully competitive. They argued that the market mechanism could not be relied upon to bring about substantial changes in the allocation of resources rapidly enough and that the price changes which would be required were not desirable. These advocates of priority control consequently favored a much wider use of priorities as well as price and wage controls. Some among them, however, favored such wider use only for the period when defense production was being increased and conceded that such control would not be required to maintain a given level of defense production once that level was attained.

Does reliance on the market make the procurement cost for the government so high as to call for price controls?—Reliance on the market either alone or supplemented solely by priorities requires that the government bid as high as necessary to obtain the resources it requires. It has been argued that this is too expensive a method of procurement. Though little explicit attention was given to this issue at the conference, it was implicit in some of the positions taken and accounts for some of the support given to price control.

The issues here involved can be suggested by noting that higher monetary costs to the government are undesirable if they involve the use of more real resources to obtain a given amount of defense production, if they reduce the efficiency of use of other resources, or if they have undesirable effects on the distribution of the costs of the defense program through such consequences as windfall gains to some and high burdens to others. But, equally, price or other controls may reduce the money cost to the government and yet involve the use of a larger volume of resources to obtain a given amount of defense production, may reduce the efficiency of use of other resources, or may have undesirable consequences on distribution of the cost of the program.

II. PREVENTION OF INFLATION

There was virtual unanimity that mobilization increases the danger of inflation, that inflation is a serious evil, and that some form of government action was urgently required to prevent the mobilization situation from producing an inflation. The disagreement centered upon the best forms of government action. The widespread agreement on the desirability of two types of government action has been mentioned: that the government should be on a pay-as-you-go basis during the mobilization emergency and that the Federal Reserve policy of maintaining present low interest rates on government bonds was inflationary and should not be continued. Attention was repeatedly called to the fact that in contrast to World War II experience the business community was today solidly behind an increased tax program. But there was deep disagreement about the use of additional monetary measures to the exclusion of other devices for inflation control.[7]

The controversy centered on the position, strongly held and strongly challenged, that additional monetary measures by themselves were the best method of preventing inflation. Those who stressed monetary control urged that the Federal Reserve authorities should sell securities and thereby contract the money supply by whatever amount necessary to prevent prices from rising—and this irrespective of the effect on interest rates. The alternative urged was the use of direct controls, either general direct controls on wages, prices, and credit or some combination of selective controls.

The advocates of monetary controls urged not only that the monetary controls would work without aid from the direct controls but that direct controls, even if vigorously and effectively enforced, would, except for its possible effect in reducing the deficit, merely delay inflation. The converse challenge was that

---

7. MR. HALEY: I doubt whether the issue between the advocates of monetary controls and direct controls was as clearly joined as it might have been. The former appeared to maintain that, no matter how inadequate, say, for political reasons, fiscal policy might be, it would be feasible to make up for this deficiency by a sufficiently rigorous monetary policy. Those who disagreed and who believed that there might be circumstances under which price controls or rationing, or both, might be useful doubted whether it would be any more possible *politically* to make monetary policy effective than it would be to make fiscal policy effective. Both groups would have agreed, I believe, that monetary policy under the assumed conditions probably would result in very high interest rates and that this would create political obstacles to the continuance of the policy. But in the discussion there was not adequate examination of (1) the effectiveness of high interest rates for discouraging less essential private investment and for encouraging saving and (2) the alleged serious economic consequences for the economy as a whole of very high interest rates.

There was, I think, a third group who felt that the issue was discussed at too high a level of abstraction to be very interesting. They had mental reservations to begin with about the implicit assumption that there was some one *best* method of preventing inflation. They felt, furthermore, that too much time was devoted to debating a position which was so far isolated from political considerations as to be not very useful. I shared this view.

monetary controls alone were clearly not sufficient and that direct controls would make a substantial contribution to prevention of inflation.[8]

A. THE ALLEGED WEAKNESSES OF MONETARY CONTROLS

Will monetary controls be ineffective because of the existence of large quantities of liquid assets?—It was contended that monetary controls alone, even if the budget were substantially balanced, could not stop inflation because of the potential increase in expenditures without an increase—and even with a decrease—in the stock of money. Much emphasis was given to the large volume of "savings bonds" for which the government is obligated to give cash on demand and to the large volume of other government securities which could readily be converted into money. While it was implicitly assumed that current policies of meeting these demands with new money would be continued, the argument was also independent of this assumption. It was contended that attempts by the Reserve authorities to limit or decrease the quantity of money would be doomed to failure, since the contraction of the money supply would be offset by an increased rate of use of money.

The proponents of monetary control gave a summary answer —any increase in the rate of use of money could be offset by a sufficient decrease in the supply of money. This might involve a substantial rise in the rate of interest, but there would be some interest rate at which inflation would be effectively counteracted by the proposed Federal Reserve action, whatever the other consequences of raising the interest rate that much might be.

8. MR. BURGESS: This whole presentation seems to me to state the dilemma too sharply. There is a whole range of anti-inflationary steps which are neither monetary controls nor, strictly speaking, direct controls. These include the cutting of nonessential government expenditures, national, state, and local; the reduction of investment by various means, including capital issues committees and voluntary co-operation; and a campaign to induce saving. The solution seems to me neither monetary controls nor direct controls by themselves but a broad program including these and various other means of influencing human action. The discussion at the conference covered this broad range and did not confine itself to the dilemma with which this Introduction is preoccupied.

The possible effectiveness of monetary policy in controlling inflation was not systematically explored. It seems probable that the critics of the monetary approach were not urging that it would not work at some "price" but rather that the consequences of very high interest rates would not be acceptable.

Will monetary control be ineffective because it will require prohibitively high interest rates?—The advocates of monetary control believed that a great increase in interest rates would not follow from reliance on monetary measures to prevent inflation. The critics believed that there was at least a very strong presumption that large increases in interest rates would result. Advocates of monetary control seemed not to be concerned with high interest rates. In any event, they were willing to state their case, for purposes of analysis, as though high rates could be expected.

It was argued that the sharp increase in interest rates would be a pronounced deterrent to investment, but the advocates of monetary control contended that this was not a disadvantage. They held, in fact, that this would actually be in line with the goals of those who were proposing direct controls to reduce private investment. In so far as high interest would equally deter investment in the defense sector where the investment was desired, the relative profitability of defense investment in a free market would be adequate to attract the investment needed at the higher rates.

Another objection was that high interest rates on government securities would mean a revaluation of these securities in the market and, further, that this effect would be pervasive, causing a readjustment not only of government securities but of all capital assets. There appeared to be rather widespread fear of the consequences of a sudden and sharp change in capital values throughout the economy because of possible individual hardship raising equity consideration and because of concern for the embarrassment that might be caused banks and insurance companies by substantial shrinkage of asset values.

Those who rejected the monetary approach because of the high interest rates which might follow did not regard the danger of inflation as the lesser evil. Their position, rather, was that monetary measures should be supplemented by direct controls, thus avoiding dangerously high interest rates.

Will monetary controls be ineffective because undue unemployment will result?—If inflation is prevented by monetary measures, price rises would be compensated for by price declines. It was said that such price declines were not likely to occur in many areas, at least in the short run, because of stickiness in money wages and prices resulting from market imperfections. If prices in such instances do not decline, a substantial amount of unemployment might result. On the other side it was contended that any mobilization scheme will draw workers from the civilian sector, and a limited amount of temporary unemployment, which makes that movement easier and faster, is not too high a price to be paid for the necessary shift.

The seriousness of the unemployment problem depends upon one's evaluation of the nature of a large number of market structures. It is generally thought unlikely that there will be a general lack of demand for workers during mobilization. In fact, the opposite situation is usually cited. Still, even temporary unemployment in certain sectors is certainly not a desired end of mobilization policy. The use of direct controls was urged to meet this difficulty. Publication of defense-job opportunities as well as other aids to increased mobility of labor were also suggested as appropriate measures for short-run unemployment.

Will monetary controls be ineffective because they will not work rapidly enough?—A further objection to reliance on monetary policy was derived from the uncertainty about the rapidity of the impact of any measures of such policy. Two answers were given to this objection: (1) it is not clear that the monetary method is any slower than alternative means of inflation control and (2) the primary problem here is the effectiveness of measures to stop inflation with finality rather than the speed with which they might work.

Will monetary controls be ineffective because for "political reasons" they cannot be used as fully as required?—One other line of attack was that monetary controls substantial enough to be effective would be political impossibilities. It should be noted that it was not contended that the Federal Reserve authorities now lack adequate legal power to take the necessary steps but that public pressures generated by a fall in capital values will cause the Board not to take the necessary steps or to cause Congress to intervene. The argument was buttressed by reference to the history of monetary policy in the United States. Critics and proponents of monetary control agreed that at several critical stages in the country's financial history when prices were rising rapidly the Reserve Board's action was of a kind that fostered the price rises rather than checked them. On no occasion has the Board taken sufficiently vigorous counter-inflationary measures. While the record clearly does not support the contention that the history of monetary policy shows that it does not work, it is, on the other hand, disquieting evidence that the political point may be well taken. Finally, it might be added that in so far as gestures by the government are important to morale during a national crisis, monetary measures have singularly little political glamour. Of course the political fate of monetary policy depends on the cultivation of an informed public opinion.

B. THE ALLEGED WEAKNESS OF DIRECT CONTROLS[9]

Will limited direct controls be ineffective in preventing inflation?—There was considerable feeling that the situation did not call for general controls in all areas but rather for selective

9. MR. HALEY: The Introduction seems to be deficient in that, although it offers a very complete statement of the case for monetary controls and of the counterarguments to criticisms of this method of control, it offers, in my opinion, a less adequate statement of the positive case that was advanced for direct controls other than priorities and allocations —specifically the case for price controls. For example, I have been unable to find reference to the important political consideration that organized labor might be willing to exercise self-restraint in its demands for higher wages if effective price controls were maintained.

MR. LEVENTHAL: There is a failure to state the case for the use of direct controls in its, let us say, most appealing form—that fiscal and monetary controls must be regarded as basic elements in a sound government program to combat the problem of inflation but that relying solely on these forms of programs would yield many undesirable consequences and that it is the part of wisdom not to push any one program coldly and analytically to its logical extreme but instead to rely upon a combination of programs, each having some role to play in supporting the others.

controls especially tailored for particular situations and that the problem of social policy was to devise such new and appropriately limited controls. Control of consumer credit, of prices, and of sensitive wages and the use of such devices as depreciation allowances in the tax system to regulate undesired private investment were cited as examples of desirable types of limited control.[10] Proponents of controls indicated that the sources of inflation could be identified and that inflation could accordingly be stopped by dealing with these sources directly. The advocates of monetary control objected that the use of selective controls would only divert spending to other sectors.

Will a general scheme of direct price controls be effective to stop inflation?—A comprehensive system of price control fully enforced would by definition prevent a rise in prices while the controls were enforced. It is perhaps surprising to note that the possible emergence of black markets and product deterioration under a system of general price controls received almost no attention in the conference discussion. The critics of such controls did not choose to rest their case on difficulties of this order but on the distortions in the allocation and use of resources which they feared might follow from the replacement of the market.

Will the general scheme of direct price controls merely defer inflation to the period when controls are removed?—There was in this connection some discussion whether inflation later was better than inflation now. Even if price controls did nothing but defer the inflation, was that not useful to morale during the crisis period?[11] Even on this issue when so narrowly joined the

10. Mr. G. E. Hale: There should have been more discussion of the possibility of so altering the income tax as both to discourage consumption and to avoid the necessity of direct controls. I have in mind, of course, an increase in tax rates with a credit for savings. The savings credit itself might have to be adjusted to mobilization requirements. My own feeling is that some proposal of the foregoing type offers the most hopeful prospect of maintaining free institutions during a protracted period of semiwar effort.

11. Mr. Leventhal: Did not one of the labor people make the point in favor of direct price controls, as contrasted with reliance solely on fiscal and monetary controls, that they permit the workers to increase the amount of savings? There is much to be said from the point of view of

opponents of direct controls contended that if it had to be a choice between evils they would prefer their inflation now, since it would then not be necessary to forego the very important advantages of relative price changes.

The main argument, however, was whether the direct controls actually reduced the inflation which would subsequently occur when controls were lifted.[12] There was the opinion that inflation resulting from so-called price-wage spirals which were not related to more basic monetary causes could be prevented[13] by controls and that the inflationary effects of removing controls could be greatly mitigated by keeping the controls on after the mobilization crisis was over until production in the private sector began to catch up with the demand. This position was challenged by the advocates of monetary policy who claimed that price controls only delay inflation, because there must be a monetary concomitant of inflation, and that there is nothing in the direct control mechanism or in the subsequent restoration of the premobilization level of civilian output which removes this basic factor. In any event, it was clear that the appropriate timing of removal of price controls provided a useful test question for both positions.

Are direct controls undesirable because they prevent relative

---

psychological incentive which would have a very favorable effect on productivity, if the workers work, meet their bills, and save money rather than work and merely meet their bills.

12. Mr. LEVENTHAL: If I recall correctly, it was argued that the deferral of inflation is important even if deferral cannot be contained to the perfect moment when it will mean no price increase. Even if controls are lifted in a time of insufficiency of supply, so that there is a strong increase in prices, the resulting inflation will in any event be smaller in amount in view of the fact that it has been deferred. Thus if there has been a doubling of prices due to the "inflation" following World War II, there would have been a tripling of prices, reflected in the 1949 price level, if the inflation had taken place during World War II and then been compounded, etc.

13. Mr. HITCH: Not "prevented" but slowed down. If one realistically assumes a fairly elastic supply, the amount of money created during mobilization and therefore the amount of inflation we ultimately experience will be reduced by any measures which slow down increases in prices and incomes. The choice is not merely between inflation now and later but also between more and less inflation.

adjustment of prices in the private sector?—It was agreed that one consequence of direct control would be that they would prevent the utilization of relative price adjustments. While the function of such adjustments was generally recognized, some argued forcefully that the suspension of this function would not be too high a price to pay for the advantage of direct controls. They further argued that the large adjustments which might occur because of the shortages in the civilian sector would be undesirable because of the resulting inequities in distribution.[14]

14. MR. ACKLEY and MR. DiSALLE: We believe that the summary of the discussion of direct controls neglects a number of crucial points.

The advocates of indirect controls, and of monetary controls in particular, treat the economy in very mechanistic terms. The economy does permit certain mechanical analogies—viz., our use of the term "market mechanism"—but the economy basically consists of people. The market is unquestionably an efficient mechanism for resource allocation when changes in demand (or productive techniques) are slow or are of relatively small magnitude. The market may not be an efficient mechanism for dealing with very large and very rapid changes in demand. If we ask the market mechanism to assume the entire load of resource redirection, the task might conceivably be accomplished but, like any machine carrying an overload, with great inefficiency and substantial destruction to the parts of the machine. We must remember, however, that the parts of the machine in this case are people and that people do not like to be pushed around.

To be more specific. Even if fiscal and monetary controls were applied with sufficient rigor to hold stable the general price level, prices of the most critical and scarce goods would nevertheless rise sharply. This rise in price would provide sure incentive for the hoarding of scarce goods, thus seriously impairing the efficiency of the mobilization program. A moderate rise in the relative prices of the particularly scarce goods might have a favorable effect on resource use (and such selective increases can be permitted under controls), but the very sharp rise which would ensue without controls would mean profiteeering for those fortunate enough to be engaged in the production of such goods and hardship to those unfortunate enough to depend upon such goods. We must not forget that both supply and demand may be very inelastic, particularly on the part of some producers and some users. This can create powerful social pressures and unrest. Once again, we are dealing with people, not supply-and-demand schedules.

Advocates of indirect controls assume that sufficient restriction of demand through such controls would restrain pressure for wage increases, even in a full-employment economy. No such pressure would operate to restrain wage increases in the industries producing the particularly scarce

III. FAIR SHARING OF MOBILIZATION COSTS[15]

Fair and just allocation of the burdens of a mobilization program is an objective on which one would scarcely expect to find disagreement. Discussion of what constitutes fair distribution of the rewards and penalties in a defense mobilization program becomes to a considerable extent a restatement of general convictions about the equity of the distributive process at any time. The very strong and almost unanimous conviction

---

goods, whose largest buyer is the government. Wage increases in these areas would surely spread throughout the economy, unless prevented by so heavy a dose of fiscal and monetary medicine as to create substantial unemployment. And people do not like to be unemployed. (Perhaps they could avoid unemployment by moving, accepting wage cuts, or not trying to get wage increases which others have received; but people unfortunately behave in a very human way.)

Most absurd were the statements of those who argued that, even if the general level of prices could not be controlled through indirect means, the advantages of market allocation were greater than the cost of inflation. Surely it cannot be argued that the market operates efficiently in allocating resources when all prices are galloping upward, when anyone can make profit on anything if he merely withholds it from use, when the speculator rather than the producer is rewarded. It is not even clear that the government could win out in a race of competitive bidding when one recalls that government procurement must of necessity be surrounded by substantial "red tape." And the argument ignores the plight of the fixed-income recipient, the interruption to production and social unrest arising from the necessity for constant revision of wage contracts, the effects of inflation in impairing willingness to make long-term contracts, the permanent damage to the social fabric from the destruction of middle-class assets.

We believe that indirect controls, both fiscal and monetary, must have a major role in inflation control. But if the magnitude of the mobilization is great, direct controls are needed, too.

15. MR. BRUBAKER: I find it difficult to understand why such a low place is given to equity considerations in the summary, almost as though equity were something of which one should be ashamed or for which one should feel it necessary to apologize. Certainly, efficiency and inflation control are entirely proper goals in a mobilization program, but any such program will fail miserably of its purpose in a democratic economy unless equity considerations are given not only a place but the major and controlling place. This problem of the economics of mobilization is not one to which we can or should give the usual academic treatment if we are interested in practicalities and equities which comprise the political framework in which the program must function.

that inflation should be prevented rests of course on equity considerations.[16] Some of the objections to reliance on monetary policy can also be viewed as matters of equity. This was the thrust of the argument that monetary policy with market imperfections would result in unemployment—at least temporarily. Similarly the case against high interest rates which might follow an appropriate monetary policy was in part based on the hardships which might fall on some holders of securities.

Is it fair that compulsory controls should be imposed on some groups and not on all?*—One example of this issue will suffice. It was suggested that voluntary control by bankers over credit expansion would be more effective than stringent compulsory control. This gave rise to the complaint[17] that it would involve giving the banking industry greater freedom than others were permitted to enjoy.†

While discussion of price control emphasized its role as a

16. MR. G. V. Cox: This is the only sentence in the entire Introduction which disturbed me. A good many thoughtful people believe it rests also on considerations of productive efficiency. Inflation that becomes severe encourages the buying of materials ahead of productive needs and the withholding of goods from the market. It undermines agreements not to strike and forces frequent renegotiation of contracts. It sharpens conflict between special interest groups. Even the varying rates of moderate inflation which the United States has suffered in the last decade have impaired the adequacy of cost-accounting figures as bases for business decisions. It has also weakened the incentive to work in order to save.

17. MR. BURGESS: This fallacious charge with respect to the banking industry was answered fully in the conference. Banking is now perhaps the most controlled industry in the United States, and the voluntary program was designed not to replace but to supplement such controls as the regulation of instalment credit, building credit, loans on securities, and the regulation of bank reserves.

* Another somewhat comparable point above fairness relates to representation on policy-making boards.

† A closely related point was ably presented at the conference. The difficulties of wage stabilization and avoidance of work stoppages under current conditions were stressed. It was pointed out that the difficulties were likely to be much greater than during the last war. The mobilization emergency was apt to extend for a number of years. Wage stabilization depends on the existence of widespread stabilization in other fields as well. If these general measures are inappropriate over an extended period, then wage stabilization measures will be ineffective. Under these circumstances, voluntary arrangements among industry, labor, and agriculture were suggested.

means of preventing inflation, there was also support for price control on the assumption that inflation was otherwise prevented. Thus it was urged that free-market rationing by purse was not acceptable during an emergency characterized by substantial reductions in the supply of civilian goods. The resulting high prices for some of these goods will deny lower- and middle-income families access to the goods which they are in the habit of consuming. This issue was not fully explored at the conference. Consideration of it would involve discussion of the need for a specific alternative system of rationing and whether, given such a system, price control is also required. It would also involve the more fundamental question of whether the underlying issue is not the fairness of the distribution of income and wealth.

What would be a fair allocation of the tax burden?—There are as many proposals for taxes to meet the costs of mobilization as there are kinds of taxes. One's views about this matter tend to reflect general views on the relative equities of varying kinds of taxes at any time. Sales taxes, for example, were objected to as regressive. Special excise taxes were suggested by those persons who felt that consumption of certain items was not important or necessary and could properly be reduced in time of emergency. No attempt was made to resolve the impossible problem: What is a necessity?

There was general agreement that the amount of revenue required to meet the costs of mobilization is such that the tax base would have to be rather broad and that this might suggest some lowering of income-tax exemptions.[18] On the other hand, reliance on income taxes was objected to as likely to involve so much progression as to impair incentives.[19] Considerable

18. MR. BRUBAKER: I strongly oppose any reduction of present individual exemptions, as I know a number of other conference participants did. The discussion on this particular point, as on many others, was totally inadequate to warrant any such conclusion as indicated in the Introduction.

19. MR. SHOUP: It seems to me that it should also be noted that an increase in the income tax has likewise a simultaneous effect in the opposite direction, increasing the incentive to work.

attention was given to the question of closing various tax loopholes. Particular attention was directed along this line to upward revisions in the capital gains tax.

Finally, a particular use for excise taxes was suggested to counteract large windfall gains accidentally arising under rapid mobilization. The conference was very critical[20] of excess profit levies because of the extreme ambiguity of the concept "excess."[21]

IV. CONCLUSION

If this summary of the conference is accurate, it confirms the sense of wide agreement on many issues.[22] But it also points up the existence of unresolved disagreement. Although there is some disagreement disclosed as to various measures tested under each of the three criteria for a mobilization program—efficiency, prevention of inflation, and avoidance of inequities—it is clear that a paramount issue emerges: Whether appropriate monetary policy can control inflation and whether the costs involved in its use prohibit reliance on it.[23] This issue, which is of necessity very complex, was not resolved at the White Sulphur Springs meetings. It is hoped that the publication of the

20. MR. BRUBAKER: It is a rank misstatement of my opinion to say that the "conference was very critical of excess profits levies." Not only were many of us at the conference not critical of excess profits taxes but we were convinced that those presently existing are much too loose. There was no opportunity offered at the conference to discuss this matter at any length.

MR. SHOUP: This seems to me to be too strong a statement. At least, I am on record as supporting the use of an excess profits tax during the present period of large expenditures for defense.

21. MR. HITCH: More important criticism is the undesirable effects on allocation of resources and incentives to economy.

22. MR. BRUBAKER: The Introduction suggests that there was "general agreement" on the need for a broad base for any increase in income tax, including some lowering of some present individual tax exemptions.

23. MR. HALEY: I believe that it was somewhat unfortunate that this was persistently regarded as the "paramount" issue by those responsible for directing the conference—and that as a consequence other equally important issues had to receive less attention than they merited.

transcript will promote further discussion of it and of the companion issues of public importance raised at the conference.[24]

24. MR. MULLENDORE: I have examined the statement of issues inclosed with your letter and have only this to suggest: I endeavored (I think unsuccessfully) to raise the issue as to whether we are not now in a very serious economic condition. The conference did not devote itself to the question, but Martin Gainsbrugh, Henry Hazlitt, and I did try to present some facts and some conclusions which would indicate not only that we are about to overspend but that we have been overspending and overtaxing for many years.

I raised the issue by asking the question: "Is this a sound prosperity which we have been experiencing since 1945?" As you know, I think it is a phony prosperity; that the country is in a dangerously unsound condition with a debt burden which it cannot now carry, to say nothing of the problem which will be created if we add to that debt burden. I think that, even before Korea, the fundamentals of the free market had been seriously impaired by the advance of socialism in many areas and by managed currency and the very serious inflation which had already been built into our economic system.

It seems to me that unless we discussed this question of "Where are we now?" we could not intelligently discuss the question, "Where do we go from here?"

MR. HENSEL (from a memorandum submitted April 19, 1951): The economics of mobilization were discussed, in my opinion, in terms of generalities and somewhat abstract economic laws and theories. Consequently, upon reflection, I have become more concerned with what was *not* said and *not* considered than with what was discussed at the conference.

The statement that, by the end of 1951, defense mobilization will be consuming 20 per cent of our national product seems to me too much of a generality for practical use in making plans or determining policies. It is obvious that defense activities will take a much larger proportion than 20 per cent of certain materials and much less of others.

Perhaps the generality of an over-all 20 per cent is sufficient for a consideration of monetary and fiscal policies, but I have difficulty understanding it as a workable concept when dealing with allocations, priorities, price-fixing regulations, and wage restrictions. There is no doubt that we all agree that every effort should be made to limit controls as much as practicable, but it seems to me well within the realm of possibility that we may need varying types of controls with respect to various materials; for example, one type of control for tungsten and chrome, another type of control for steel, aluminum, and copper, another type of control for carbon black, etc. Similar comments may also be made, I think, with respect to price and wage regulations.

I would be more inclined to regard the conclusions discussed on the last day of the conference as background material rather than as a plan for action—until we have a pretty fair bill of the materials needed for the defense effort (e.g., broken down into units of steel, tungsten, wool, etc.) and at least some analysis of the skills to be drafted into the armed services. Then we can turn to our basic effort, that is, to channel those particular materials and skills into the military service, with full realization, however, that compromises even on military estimates of so-called requirements will have to meet civilian demands to deal with public psychology and human emotions and to maintain foreign alliances and strengthen our allies. These compromises will not all be the same, and I do not see how they can be forecast in general terms.

There is one more observation which can be made with respect to the need for a more detailed analysis of the defense program. One extremely vital control, which, as best I can remember, was mentioned only once, is the continuous analysis and questioning of military spending. That continuous check cannot be left to military men and cannot be performed by the Bureau of the Budget. The Defense Department, in my opinion, needs a group of skeptics to maintain a continuous audit and review of the military spending programs.

In addition, the forthcoming mobilization is quite different from the war mobilization in 1941. Before World War II, we were short of everything needed by the military. The current program, on the other hand, will be a selective one. This selective mobilization will create dislocations just as severe as encountered in 1941—but different. That difference will clearly determine the extent and the types of allocations and priorities and perhaps shape some features of taxation and wage policies.

It is also hard for me to believe that the Korean situation and even our mobilization plans have had much mechanical effect on today's inflation. Prices have risen substantially, in my opinion, largely because of the impact of Korea and the mobilization of public psychology. If that is correct, should we not seriously consider countermeasures which are purely psychological, and is that not the real justification of the price-control regulations of today?

Restrictive monetary policies and general high-level taxation undoubtedly strike at the general tendencies toward inflation or help to create a climate unfavorable to inflation. Some of the suggested policies are undoubtedly long overdue, but I fear that, in addition, we are going to need some specific remedies. It is also difficult for me to think of taxation in general terms. I can understand that taxation must be heavy, but, from the standpoint of the impact of taxation on our economy, it seems to me equally important that we determine what kind of taxes, how high and on what transactions the incidence will fall, and the probable public reaction to such taxes.

I am convinced that certain direct controls will be imposed, no matter how much we dislike them and no matter how completely it can be shown that they are economically dangerous. Some of such controls will be dictated by the mechanics of varying situations. Some will be in response to public clamor. The most we can determine at present is that we should try to have as few as are deemed practicable in the light of all the varying circumstances as they develop from day to day.

II

FIRST SESSION, FRIDAY MORNING
APRIL 6, 1951

THE ROLE OF MONETARY POLICY

Outline for Discussion

Total payments for goods and services during any period can be expressed in two equivalent ways: as equal to (1) the stock of money times its rate of use during that period; (2) the volume of output times its average price. Any assertion that prices will rise is therefore equally an assertion that the stock of money will rise, or that its rate of use will rise, or that output will fall.

I. Can inflation be avoided simply by preventing an increase in the supply of money or by reducing the supply to offset an increase in the rate of use?

   A. Are changes in the rate of use of money likely to occur with mobilization? With mobilization and an announced noninflationary policy? Are changes likely to be significant?

   B. Would a reduction in the supply of money to offset an increase in its rate of use be frustrated by a further increase in the rate of use?

   C. Could the attempt to prevent inflation by monetary means be successful only if it were carried to the point of producing a decline in employment and output?

II. To what extent does the possibility of an effective monetary policy depend on the associated fiscal policy?

   A. Is it necessary that the government should cover all its current expenditures by taxation?

   B. If not, what is the limit of the amount which, without inflation, the government can borrow from individuals and commercial banks?

III. What are the implications of a tight monetary policy for the effectiveness of mobilization?

   A. How does a tight monetary policy compare with such other methods of preventing inflation as high taxes and direct controls?

      1. It may be argued that the pervasiveness of monetary policy, its automatic functioning, speed of operation, and administrative simplicity are favorable to mobilization as compared with taxation or direct controls.

      2. It may be argued that a tight monetary policy will prevent producers of military supplies from getting their share of bank credit while higher taxes or direct controls would not.

      Is this because the existing credit structure is such that it is harder to obtain new or additional funds than to maintain existing lines of credit?

   B. How does a tight monetary policy compare with inflation?

      1. Is inflation the best means of shifting resources because it maintains incentives?

      2. Is inflation to be preferred because it maintains employment with rigidity of particular prices and wages against declines?

      3. If inflation is preferred for any of the above reasons, is it appropriate only during the period when the mobilization program is expanding and not once the high level is reached?

IV. Is the resort to direct controls for preventing inflation favored because it is assumed that the supply of money will in fact be permitted to increase as has been our experience in similar periods in the past?

 V. Is the resort to nonmonetary means for preventing inflation a consequence of the public policy of keeping down interest rates? Is this policy of such importance as to justify sacrificing the advantages of a noninflationary monetary program?

A. Is keeping down interest rates a relevant objective?
   1. Is the argument for it that it keeps down interest payments on the public debt? But if inflation is to be avoided, keeping down interest rates will mean a higher level of taxation or more stringent direct controls. Are these preferable to higher interest payments?
   2. May not the objective of low interest rates prevent achievement of any effective noninflationary program?
   3. If this happens do the gains to the Treasury justify the costs of inflation?
B. Is the program of keeping down interest rates favored because a rise in rates now will make it difficult to lower them again when it becomes appropriate to do so?
C. Can we have both the program of keeping down interest rates and a noninflationary monetary program with existing institutional arrangements? Can the effect of Reserve purchases of securities (to prevent a rise of interest rates) be offset by increasing reserve requirements? Will the only effect of this be to reduce *interest payments* while the *interest rates* on nonbank-held debt remain unaffected? Is the proposal to establish special interest-bearing security reserves for this purpose justified except as a means of providing banks with additional earnings?

VI. Can some inflation be justified as a means of putting special burdens on groups not important for the mobilization program? If so, is this objective sufficiently important to justify weakening the bias against inflation?

CHAIRMAN LEVI: In behalf of the Law School, my colleagues, and the committee, I bid you welcome to this conference and thank you for your willingness to participate in it, and we express our appreciation again to the Volker Fund for its grant to the Law School which has made this conference possible.

The issues to be discussed at this conference are complicated ones and important ones, and the purpose of this conference, as we have stated, is to achieve a discussion of these issues. It will be, I think, difficult to achieve such a discussion because, quite properly, among us there are varied views on these subjects and, in addition, we are numerous. Therefore, I beseech your indulgence for the various chairmen of these sessions and ask you to help observe a few ground rules.

The ground rules will be that at the beginning of each session there may be some general statements pertaining to the issues to be discussed. You will find at your place an outline of a possible discussion, and we ask you to try to observe this outline. We have tried in this outline to state the possible views of the subject. In some cases, these views may not be correctly stated and other important views may have been omitted; and, as we go down the outline together, we ask you to make the arguments that should be made for and against the position stated and to insert where you think it necessary a better statement of the view or the omitted view.

There will be, for the gentlemen of the press, a period, not today but later in this conference, when questions can be asked of the participants; and I should state that this conference is being taken down, and it is our hope that, following the form of the outline, the discussion will be such that this conference can be published as a book.

There will be microphones available in this room, but the formality of the room is such already that we had hoped that it would not be necessary to use these microphones. If you find it necessary to do so, they are here.

We will begin the first session, on "The Role of Monetary Policy," with a statement by Mr. Mints.

MR. MINTS: I will attempt to make what few comments I have very briefly and perhaps in a somewhat dogmatic manner, at least in the sense that I will mostly state conclusions rather than reasons for the conclusions.

To begin with, it seems to me the first thing that we should recognize in regard to monetary policy is that monetary action is in the nature of the case pervasive. What I mean to imply by that statement is that we cannot use monetary action to affect particular segments of the economy, such as particular industries, particular occupations or commodities, etc. We have to use monetary policy on the assumption that it is going to have a very general influence, and then, if there is an influence in any particular direction, it is a reflection of that general influence.

From that I come to the conclusion that so far as monetary policy is concerned what we have to say pertains almost exclusively to the matter of inflation versus stable prices as a means of bringing about the necessary mobilization of resources. For that matter, what I shall say applies equally well to an outright war economy.

In this connection, I think there are three problems that are of primary significance. First, the allocation of resources to the production of war goods. How can that best be brought about? Second, the problem of inducing all able persons to enter occupations, productive occupations, and to put forth their best efforts therein. The third problem is that of managing the whole program with a minimum of injustice. We cannot avoid all injustice, perhaps, but at least we can do something to minimize it.

Let me briefly comment on each of these three points.

First, the allocation of resources. I think, in all honesty, we must conclude that the answer here is inconclusive. We cannot be quite sure whether stable prices, with the corresponding taxes that are required to prevent an inflationary movement, will be better than inflation for the purpose of bringing about the necessary allocation of resources. I myself am inclined to the belief that it at least will be as good as an inflationary program.

Briefly, if we follow a noninflationary program, so far as the budget is concerned, it means that the budget must be substantially balanced. There might be some minor amount of borrowing, noninflationary borrowing, but I will not bother with that. The required taxes would reduce disposable incomes of consumers, thereby causing losses in some peacetime industries. Consequently, resources would be released for the war industries; and the rise in the demand on the part of the government for the output of the war industries would readily take up the workers so ejected from the civilian goods industries.

The second point, then, is to induce all able-bodied persons to enter occupations and to put forth their best efforts therein. Again, it seems to me that the tax program and stable prices are adequate and, in all probability, preferable; but, again, the answer is somewhat inconclusive—preferable, I mean, to a policy of inflation. To be sure, under inflation, those with fixed incomes, who might not otherwise do so, would be compelled, or at least induced, to enter productive occupations. That is to say, if there were not this inflation and no impingement upon their standard of living. But I do not see any reason why a tax program cannot be designed so as to bring about the same result, so that, again, it seems to me that from this point of view we get as good a performance of the economy from a tax program and stable prices as from an inflationary program.

In the third place, that of minimizing injustice. It seems to me that in this case the argument for stable prices is emphatically and unambiguously in favor of stable prices as opposed to inflation. I do not quarrel with the contention that those with fixed incomes should, of course, be compelled to bear their share of the mobilization program. But the difficulty with an inflationary program is that, after the period of inflation is over, those people who are not in the class that can enter productive occupations—the older persons—are not going to be able to re-establish their money incomes at a level corresponding to the higher price level. So the inflationary program not only compels them to bear their share of the burden while it continues but also condemns them to a lower standard of living for the remainder of their days. On that score, I think emphatically that we should favor stable prices, even though on the other two scores we cannot say that the answer is unequivocal.

What does this mean with respect to policy? It means, I think, that the federal budget should be substantially balanced. I am not going to enter into the question as to whether we should include some noninflationary borrowing here. I know there is some difference of opinion among the group congregated here in regard to that question. But, substantially, it should be balanced.

What I am really saying is that I think there is nothing distinctive about a monetary policy in time of mobilization and in time of peace. In either case, I think the policy should be one of stabilizing the price level, and I see no reason why the policy should not be instituted now as well as any other time. In fact, I see a strong reason why it should be instituted now, because now is precisely the time when we are going to run into inflation if we do not do something pretty emphatic about it.

In the short run, a stable price level means substantially a balanced budget. We are not interested in the long run in the possible mobilization period here, but, parenthetically, I might say that in the long run we probably would have to resort to continuing budget deficits of a restricted amount for the purpose of supplying the additional money that would be needed to prevent the price level from falling. But that is a problem that we do not need to bother with at the present time.

Now, the next question that I want to consider very briefly is that of the current and recent program of monetary policy with respect to the question of how it lines up with what I have been saying here. Even though the federal budget is substantially balanced, it still remains true that there is some function for the Federal Reserve System to perform. There may be a tendency for inflation to develop because of a rise in the rate of use of money or because of a rise in the volume of private loans of the banks, or it might be that the government could not precisely balance the budget.

The Federal Reserve System has the power to offset those developments if it so chooses. I mean it has the power now. It does not need additional power, as the Board has been inclined to tell us in recent years. That is to say, it has the power, if it is willing to forsake the bond-support program that it has been following since 1942. Whether it has forsaken that now, I take it, is a little bit of an open question. We do not know what the announcement of March 5, 1951, means in its entirety. I suspect it means nothing more than a slight reduction of the support level, but I pretend to no intimate knowledge in regard to that.

I am skeptical that we can depend on the Board to follow any such policy as I am suggesting; that is to say, of trying to offset developments which would otherwise bring about some inflationary development, and I do not rest my decision exclusively upon the basis of the performance of the System since 1942. I took the trouble to look through some particularly important periods in the history of the Reserve System since its organization, and I isolated seven of them at times when there was particular need for action. They run from June to June, simply because that is when we can get adequate data. They were 1920–21, 1929–31, 1937–38, and later periods following 1940—I do not remember the details. There were seven of the periods altogether.

Now, if the Reserve System is to operate in what I would call an "enlightened" manner—if it is to use as its guide to action such an index as the price level or any other index that goes up with boom and down with depression—then it is clear that the volume of earning assets of the Reserve System should rise as the index falls and should fall as the index rises. That is to say, as the price level goes down, the Reserve banks should buy in the open market, thus increasing their earning assets. As the price level rises, they should sell in the open market, so as to contract the stock of money.

How does the history of the Reserve System stand up in the light of this analysis?

Of the seven periods, in five the earning assets of the Reserve System went in the same direction as the price level. That is to say, as the price level rose, the earning assets of the Reserve System rose. As the price level went down, the earning assets of the Reserve System went down. In two periods the assets and the price index went in opposite directions, to be sure, but even in those cases I doubt that much credit should be granted to the Reserve System, because the price level moved in a much greater degree than the earning assets moved, and, consequently, we can say that their action was woefully inadequate, even though in the right direction.

I was going to talk about some of the arguments that have been put forth in defense of the bond-support program and what seemed to me to be the objections to them, but I think I have taken all the time that I should take.

CHAIRMAN LEVI: We will have another general statement at this session from Mr. Harrod.

MR. HARROD: Gentlemen, I hope you will excuse me, from a procedural point of view, if, while saying something about my views on this subject, I try to state very briefly my general view on how to combat inflation, in which monetary control is a part. I think that that will help our purpose.

May I begin by saying that my background of thought is very much hostile to physical controls, on the ground, primarily, that they are so inefficient. By physical controls I mean particularly price controls and the allocation of materials. I believe those methods to be essentially inefficient and obstructive to the flexible working of the economy.

I think that perhaps we here in this country, and everywhere, are too much influenced by the fact that Britain had to adopt such methods very quickly in 1939–40. She did so because she had to act in a very great hurry, in a rapid step-up, and there was no time to think out more elaborate plans for having an economy which would run rather more freely in time of war.

Also, in the British case, it is important to remember that there was from the very beginning the limiting factor of the shipping shortage, which made an import program absolutely essential, and from the import program all other controls over the flow of materials, components, etc., sprang.

It may be that these physical controls will be necessary. Nonetheless, I think it would be very important in instituting physical controls here to give them a time limit. I suggest a time limit of two years, because it seems to me that that is the time of maximum danger of the inflation gathering momentum. I am assuming, of course, we are not to be involved in total war. If that happens, then the whole picture changes.

Assuming not total war but a maintenance of high defense expenditure, I submit that the crucial period is when we are stepping up the defense expenditure. Presumably, at the end of about two years, we reach a plateau; it is mounting up toward the top of that plateau that imposes the great strain. Once we get to the top of the plateau, then we may maintain our high defense expenditure, while the increased flow of production renders successive easements possible; we may then relax controls in many directions.

So that if, at the worst, physical controls are found necessary, I think it would be a good thing to visualize them—and to publicize that—as a two-year affair for the period of the ascent and not as a system that is to be kept in being so long as very high defense expenditure is necessary. But I am against these physical controls altogether if they can possibly be avoided.

The next thing I have to say is that I do not believe that monetary controls, in the sense that we have already begun to discuss them, can be very effective in preventing inflation. I do not believe that additional monetary controls as they can now be managed by the Federal Reserve, and with co-operation from other great banks, are strong enough; I do not believe that in history we can find an example of pure monetary control preventing an inflation of the sort with which we are threatened, because the forces are too strong.

I would suggest that monetary controls can always break an inflation if the inflation is something of the nature of a bubble due to speculative activity, etc. We can then tighten our credit and put up our interest rates, and we can always burst the bubble.

But the kind of inflation with which we are faced is not bubble inflation at all. It is due to a very real demand for defense and for capital outlay consequent to defense programs. In the face of those very real demands coming on top of a fully active economy, I believe that the monetary controls are not strong enough to be really effective.

Well, I am against physical controls, and I say that monetary controls by themselves are ineffective. But I certainly do not recommend inflation, because that is the worst evil of all. Open inflation is worse than physical controls, bad as those physical controls may be.

Now, having presented that dilemma, I will just say a very

few words—I do not want to take up too much time—about my own line of approach.

We are going to discuss at another session the fiscal method of preventing inflation. Mr. Mints has already said something about whether you have to balance your budget, or whether you can have a little bit of borrowing, which might easily become a little more, etc.

I should say that if you are going to rely on fiscal methods for preventing inflation, and on those only, you have to do what we have been doing in Britain for three or four years. You have to overbalance your budget and overbalance it by quite a lot—for two reasons.

If you look away from the budget to the balance of the whole economy, you have two further things to think of. As you step up your taxes—and you have to step them up mightily to cover this vast defense program—private and personal saving will undoubtedly be affected, and you will get less private and personal saving. That is one reason. On the other side, the whole of this expansionary situation is going to lead to a good deal of additional investment outlay, with all the different firms tooling up and getting ready to meet government orders which are going to flow out over the whole economy.

Quite apart from the actual outlay of the government, which on this heroic scheme of relying solely on fiscal controls, one would seek to cover by taxation, you have a double factor making for inflation: personal savings being reduced by high taxes and nongovernment investment expenditure being stimulated to meet the direct government expenditure. So I conclude that, however heroic you are on the fiscal side, you will still not succeed in preventing inflation by that alone. That brings me to the hub of the matter.

The fiscal side of things, the high taxation, is designed to release resources for defense expenditure by making the consumers consume less than they otherwise would; and that you have to do, of course. You can go a long way along that line. But I do not think that, with this step-up of expenditure at the pace we contemplate in these two years while we climb the plateau, you can get all you need out of cuts in consumer expenditure. You have also to budget for a decline in nondefense investment expenditure.

Now, you may say, "But that is precisely the object of our monetary control; tight credit policy and high interest rates are designed to reduce investment expenditure."

I have given my reasons for supposing that the banking credit policy will not be strong enough to stem the flow of investment expenditure; and this brings me to a point that I should like to put to the meeting, that the alternatives envisaged in this very able summary of matters before us on the table, physical controls on one side and monetary controls on the other, do not cover the ground. I think there is a third method we have still to think out, namely, a stronger method of reducing investment expenditure in parallel with taxes which reduce consumer expenditure. I believe there is a constructive task here that we can achieve.

Can we not think out some method that has the pervasiveness, which Mr. Mints mentioned, of monetary policy—unlike physical controls—but is something additional to monetary policy?

This is where I am going to end. I am going to make a constructive proposal. It is very daring for me to come here and make a constructive proposal. I do not know whether I could arouse a little interest in it.

My suggestion is that we want to amplify, or to reinforce, the monetary policy of strict credit by some kind of tax incentive to people not to make investment expenditures during the next two years; not to make investment expenditures, let us say, for purposes not directly connected with the arms effort.

I should say that through your corporate tax, income tax, etc., an adjustment could be made on the side of depreciation allowances by which firms undertaking investment expenditures would not get back for two years their normal depreciation allowances on the tax. New capital outlay undertaken here and now for the next two years, except in relation to the arms effort, would not qualify in the way of normal law for depreciation allowances.

I believe that people in these days are tremendously influenced in their conduct by anything that affects the tax assessment. Tax assessment is a far more vital factor than interest rates in influencing decisions of people as to what they are going to do. I have the impression that the present tax setup rather encourages people to make investment expenditures that are not strictly necessary.

I want the taxes to do the opposite, anyhow for the next two years. I stress my two years, because I think otherwise people would say, "This is hopeless from the point of view of American business, which is essentially expansionary. People will never stand for that sort of thing."

If you say, "This is for two years only; we are going to make a severe tax deterrent to capital expenditure, which will be something stronger than a high interest rate," and if you combine that with ordinary taxation on the consumer, I think that you could, for the next two years, get away with a system that allows the essentials of a free economy to remain without having any excessive amount of inflation.

CHAIRMAN LEVI: I now refer you to the outline in front of you, "The Role of Monetary Policy": "I. Can inflation be avoided simply by preventing an increase in the supply of money or by reducing the supply to offset an increase in the rate of use?" Then these questions are asked as to the rate of use: "A. Are changes in the rate of use of money likely to occur with mobilization? With mobilization and an announced noninflationary policy? Are changes likely to be significant?" Would someone like to speak on this point at this time?

MR. ARNOLD: I am not going to speak to the point. I simply raise the question for enlightenment. Talking about inflation, just what do we mean? There is a vast difference between the inflation in Germany and in Italy and in France and the decline of the value of our dollar, and yet we seem to be lumping the whole thing as one phenomenon. What is it, and how much inflation, with our tremendous productive capacity, can we expect, and what kind of inflation are we talking about? I would like to have someone enlighten me on that.

CHAIRMAN LEVI: Mr. Mints, would you like to enlighten Mr. Arnold?

Mr. Mints: I do not know that I can enlighten Mr. Arnold. I can state what my position is in regard to inflation. I do not think our tremendous productive capacity has anything at all to do with the question. What I mean by inflation is simply a rise in some particular index in the price level. I am quite aware that there have been other definitions of inflation, but even the other definitions do not diverge too far from that particular one.

Mr. Arnold: How much rise?

Mr. Mints: Any rise. Of course, if we have a considerable rise, then we have more inflation than if we have a little rise.

Mr. Arnold: You spoke of eliminating injustices. There is a vast difference between the injustice of the German inflation and the injustice of the inflation we have had so far.

Mr. Mints: We do not concede that.

Mr. Arnold: And you are not concerned with that. You think that our policy should be to prevent any further devaluation of the dollar?

Mr. Mints: Yes.

Chairman Levi: Now I refer the conference again to the questions asked in Item I, A, and ask if anyone wishes to speak to this point.

Mr. Burgess: Governor Meyer and I are the two people in the conference who have had long years of service with the Federal Reserve System. As such, I know we are strongly tempted to lock horns with Professor Mints. I will try to forego that because of conservation of time.

Those of us who have worked with the System are firmly convinced of the power of money as a major development in economic changes, perhaps the most powerful of all. I am delighted to see the economists turn back to a study of money as compared with fiscal policy because of my belief that it is more effective and more controllable than fiscal policy.

While believing that money policy is very influential, I would like to enter a dissent from the complete belief in the document put out by five or seven Chicago professors, which I think vastly overstates the case for money policy. I was distressed that the pamphlet took so little account of the velocity of circulation, though I am glad that your statement here does. I call attention to the fact that, while in the past year production has increased 15 per cent or thereabouts, prices have risen, say, 8 or 10 or 12 per cent, and the cost of living some 5 or 6 per cent; that the volume of money has risen 6 per cent; and that velocity has risen from 10 to 15 per cent. That is, this inflation has been financed not primarily by the money created during the period but by money created before that time which has been used more freely by the possessors of it.

This leads me to suggest that we have to look at the longer-term influence rather than the immediate one. We cannot turn the spigot on and off and hope to have it operate. We have been pitching our economy on an inflationary plane ever since the war, and that carries over into this period. The money policy of today may affect the economics of four and five years from now or even longer. "The fathers have eaten sour grapes, and the children's teeth are set on edge."

It was notably true in the twenties that we pitched our money to an easy-money policy in the early twenties, partly as a favor to our British friends and the rest of the world in the hope that expansion here would make their recovery easier. When 1928 and 1929 came, we tried to reverse it and found it almost impossible to do it because we had built up a huge volume of money that then proceeded to be used.

That leads me to a second limitation which is that the economic situation is at times very much more sensitive to a change in money than it is at other times. In the earlier twenties the change of one-half of 1 per cent in the rediscount rate or the sale or purchase of two hundred million dollars of government securities appeared to change the trend of prices and business from time to time: 1928 and 1929 were impervious to those changes.

Applying that to the present time, I think the recent change in money comes at a time when the situation is highly sensitized to it, and it may produce more results than it would at other times. That is developed in our *National City Bank Bulletin* of April 1, 1951, that we distributed. Let me say it comes at a time when many people are overinventoried, when there is a bubble, as Professor Harrod has said, that may be in process of being pricked.

The effectiveness, of course, lies in the holdings of government securities. The banks find themselves in a position where additional loans can be made only at the price of a sale of government securities at a loss. We do not like to sell government securities at a loss. It comes also at a time when many banks are heavily loaned, perhaps overloaned, when the country banks are coming to us to try to get us to take over part of their portfolio. It is a tight situation, I assure you, gentlemen.

Even more tight is the situation of the insurance companies which come into this period heavily overcommitted for mortgages and corporate bonds, perhaps committed for their income six months to a year ahead. They counted on selling government securities. They now sell them at a loss, and they have locked up a substantial number in the new 2¾ per cent bonds which are attractive. So I think it is fair to say that the average insurance company has cut its mortgage program for taking new mortgages by as much as 50 per cent and that they are screening their corporate loans very much more vigorously than they were, so that that will impinge not only on short-term money but on long term.

While we may have pricked an inventory bubble, however, the long-term effectiveness in dealing with inflation I believe to be essentially a problem of investment. We simply cannot finance in this country twenty-four billions of new capital proposals, along with this defense program, and carry on at the same time a private building program at the pace we have been doing, without inflation, no matter if we put the interest rate up to 5 per cent in the banks.

I agree with Professor Harrod that there we have a force that we cannot deal with solely by money policy. We have to plug some of the leakages of this tremendous investment program. We have to deal with that in some way or another.

State and municipal expenditures are between three and four billion dollars a year. That certainly can be cut back, and we can do that partly by co-operation, pulling the governors and mayors together and agreeing on some sensible standards.

The building program, if it has not been reached by Regulation X—and I doubt if it has—I believe has got to be cut back. Control is now in the government's hands, because most of it is done under government guaranties.

CHAIRMAN LEVI: Turning back to the outline, then, again looking at Item I, A, assuming that the first question, "Are changes in the rate of use of money likely to occur with mobilization?" has been answered in the affirmative so far, I call your attention to the next question, "With mobilization and an announced noninflationary policy?" I ask if anyone wishes to speak to that? If not, I suppose that it should be assumed that this is also answered in the affirmative.

MR. ROSTOW: I should like to invoke Mr. Arnold's precedent of not speaking altogether to the point. I should like to put a question equally to Mr. Harrod and to Mr. Burgess. Is it their feeling that direct cuts in the rate of private nonwar investment expenditure, imposed through one or another of the available direct techniques, are so necessary that they would be opposed to the most vigorous possible use of banking policy as an instrument for reducing the supply of money and its private expenditure?

After all, in the last six or eight months, we have seen an extraordinary expansion of bank loans, while the national budget was in balance, or rather at a considerable surplus. As Mr. Burgess points out, and I fully agree with him, at the present time the banking system is pretty well loaned up. Many other factors should make the banks markedly sensitive to central bank controls. Now, is it their feeling about the inherent weakness of monetary policy that leads them to oppose the most vigorous possible use of Federal Reserve powers at this time?

MR. HARROD: I would only say that I do not think of my proposition as an alternative but as complementary to the use of a restrictive monetary policy. Mr. Burgess knows much more about that. I should not go so far, however, as to support "the most vigorous possible use" of monetary policy. If we may imagine, say, a 5 per cent short-term rate; that would not be desirable.

I would only add that, so far as the British case is concerned, as we are all in this together, I think banking policy is much more difficult on our side because of the greater size of our national debt. I think it really does close the door pretty effectively to anything in the way of a drastic high-interest-rate policy. Our national debt is, roughly, equal to two and a half years' income. I think yours is, roughly, equal to one year's income. Two and a half years' income is pretty tough.

Mr. Burgess: I would quite agree with that answer. I would find it difficult to take the suggestion, "the most vigorous possible." I think we ought to deal with this thing vigorously and effectively and apply the remedy where the most effective points are.

Now, up until the time of getting rid of the pegs, that was obviously the point of impact. A ridiculous policy was being followed, and it is a great relief that it has been broken. I take a good deal of comfort out of it. It means more perhaps than many people think. It is a return to a policy applied a decade ago when we thought in terms of orderly markets and not in terms of pegged markets.

Now, it is pretty powerful medicine. If we push that too far —let us say if we put our discount rate at 4 per cent—we are going to have a very difficult problem to deal with in our government markets. We are also going to bring the businessman and others who cannot get credit in flocks to Senator O'Mahoney.

Mr. Mints: May I ask a question of both Mr. Harrod and Mr. Burgess? How can people invest if they cannot get the money or if they are not willing to use money that they already have? Or, a somewhat different question but it gets at the same thing—how do they imagine that inflation is going to take place if we do not increase the stock of money and if we do decrease it when the rate of use of money rises?

Mr. Harrod: Mr. Burgess has already mentioned velocity of circulation which is a very important thing, and I believe....

Mr. Mints: We all agree to that, you know.

Mr. Harrod: We all agree, but then the increasing velocity

of circulation might mean that we would require a restriction in the volume of money greater than anybody would in practice contemplate. Furthermore, I do not believe it is only that. The people are not going to be held back from these investments. They have portfolios of securities which they can sell out. They will find a means. When there is investment that is nationally needed and they see the profit there, they will find a way of making that investment, unless we have some other method of discouraging it.

MR. MINTS: Does not that mean simply that the central bank should sell still more securities? Do you mean to say there is a limit beyond which the central bank cannot go?

MR. BURGESS: Yes; we have to have a market for them when we sell them.

MR. MINTS: There is always a market at a price; there is no difficulty on that score.

MR. BURGESS: I beg your pardon. I sat there and tried to sell them, and there was no market at any price when they thought it was going on down farther.

CHAIRMAN LEVI: I see that we are following the outline. I should like to ask Mr. Harrod whether he has now spoken on Item I, C, on the outline.

REPRESENTATIVE CELLER: Before we come to that, may I ask Mr. Burgess a question, please? Senator O'Mahoney has made reference to the social pressure for investments in building construction. It may be all very well in theory to say that we should curtail building operations on the part of governments, federal, state, and municipal; but we are faced with situations in many metropolitan areas where we have people living in miserable habitations. How can Washington and the state capitals and the municipalities successfully resist the pressure and demand for expenditures of funds for new construction? It may be very well in theory, but we have to go a little bit beyond that.

MR. BURGESS: I recognize that problem, Mr. Celler. I have recently canvassed the building situation with someone who knows it pretty thoroughly. A certain amount of this demand is a demand for housing at very low charges and very easy pay, and we could cut down on that considerably, probably to the advantage of the building industry. The building industry, I understand, is in very considerable danger of overbuilding on low-cost housing. The leakages on that are not simply the government-guaranteed program. Regulation X is not working too well. There is the question of the purchase of mortgages by Fanny May. They could be pulled down or at least the premiums reduced at which they purchase mortgages, and they could sell more of what they have.

Then the question of that recent bill before the Congress. I think that was quite properly cut back from its original contemplation. I realize the pressures, but there is the impact of inflation. I think the building boom of the past few years has been more responsible for the present inflation than any other single item.

MR. MINTS: No, it has been the increase in the stock of money or the increased rate of use of the stock of money.

CHAIRMAN LEVI: Getting back to Item I, C, which we seem to have been discussing indirectly, "Could the attempt to prevent inflation by monetary means be successful only if it were carried to the point of producing a decline in employment and output?" can we take it, Mr. Harrod, that your answer to that is "Yes"?

MR. HARROD: I do not think it could be successful by itself at all.

MR. TANNENWALD: I would like to state a corollary of that which all of the gentlemen who have spoken thus far seem to ignore, and that is they have concerned themselves only with the role of monetary policy in holding the line. But if, as many of us feel in the present day, the only way we are going to win this struggle that we are now in is through an expanding economy both here and abroad, what do they feel is the role of monetary policy in helping to achieve that expanding economy? The whole tenor of this discussion has had a restrictive philosophy which troubles me in terms of how we achieve an expanding economy.

MR. CORTNEY: Mr. Chairman, I am afraid that there is a tendency to relate too closely the supply of money to changes in prices. I do not think it can be established so closely over short spans of time as it is assumed in the discussion. I believe the quantity of money will influence the trend of prices, depending also on other economic conditions. I am afraid that there is a terrible oversimplification of the issue of formation of prices, and, furthermore, confusion comes in all the time in the discussion between money and credit, which is not the same thing at all. I do not believe that, in some of these discussions where you have concluded that A and B are answered in the affirmative, they can be answered in the affirmative. It is not so simple as that. It is not a "Yes" or a "No." The answer is much more complicated.

CHAIRMAN LEVI: Do you think that Item I, A, B, and C, cannot be answered "Yes" or "No" but must be answered in terms of there being other factors which must be taken into account?

MR. CORTNEY: Sure.

MR. KESTNBAUM: Since we have apparently reached the end of the discussion of the first point of Item I, I think it is appropriate to come back to the question that Mr. Arnold raised because it has something to do with the answer to all these questions. It might appear to be a truism to say that if we have a monetary inflation it could perhaps be curbed by monetary measures, but I do not believe that anyone here would suggest that we now have a purely monetary inflation. Professor Mints seems to hold that position, but I think he himself would agree that there are many other factors: the fear of further inflation, the feeling that a higher price level is inevitable, some growing lack of confidence in our money, and the recognition of the fact that we are now paying the penalty for prior errors. We have been building up the basis for inflation for a great many years, and we are now discovering that this is an aspect of the problem which we did not not recognize and that we would be grateful now for a little more restraint in prior years.

I should like to suggest at some point a discussion of the factors that determine the character of this inflation. I believe that no two inflationary movements are exactly alike, that this one is unique, and that, when we come to examine proposed remedies, we must try to see what will meet this particular kind of situation. While it is undoubtedly true that restricting the quantity of money would retard inflation to the extent that it is purely monetary, it would not change the underlying situation, it would not change the basic psychological factors, and we could not apply drastic monetary measures without doing violence to certain sections of the economy.

Of course the Federal Reserve can sell government securities on the open market at whatever price they will bring, but I cannot imagine that anyone believes we can finance a huge defense program in the face of a sharp drop in the price of government securities. It simply cannot be done.

The problem of controlling inflation is made difficult by the fact that we must expand our economy to meet the needs of a defense program and that we must accommodate ourselves to the pressure for higher living standards on the part of various groups in our society and also meet the needs of the business system not only for profits as such but for profits out of which to repay the huge amounts that have been borrowed in recent years. Business has financed a great deal of its expansion through borrowed money. Severe restrictive measures applied at this time could paralyze the economy.

Therefore, I suggest that monetary measures as part of a general scheme of control are useful and necessary, but I thoroughly agree with Mr. Harrod that they cannot by themselves operate to prevent the particular kind of inflation which we have in this country today. It would be useful here to try to answer the question which Mr. Arnold has raised, because a sound analysis of the nature of this inflation might indicate the means which should be used to curb it.

CHAIRMAN LEVI: I should like now to refer the conference to the questions under Item II of the outline, namely, "To what extent does the possibility of an effective monetary policy depend on the associated fiscal policy? Is it necessary that the government should cover all its current expenditures by taxation? If not, what is the limit of the amount which, without inflation, the government can borrow from individuals and commercial banks?" Does anyone wish to speak to this point?

SENATOR O'MAHONEY: Our British friend has stated that Britain's public debt is two and a half times the national income of Britain. The United States national debt is roughly equal to our national income. This difference may be in part a corollary of the fact that Britain has progressed further toward socialism than we have. I say "progressed further" in deference to my good friend, Eugene Meyer. The first time I met Mr. Meyer in Cheyenne, Wyoming, he was a representative of a government corporation. He came to Wyoming after World War I to help the cattle industry to recover from the 1921 deflation which began under Secretary of the Treasury Houston and continued under his successor, Andrew W. Mellon. His trip to Wyoming represented but a minor episode in his busy career, yet it forcefully illustrates the general principle that, when the economic conditions become so bad as to require remedial action, the people turn to the government to do the job no matter what party is in power.

The problem which we are examining tonight goes far deeper, it seems to me, than monetary policy. A large number of other factors are involved, psychological, political, economic, and social. Consumer behavior often springs surprises on the experts. No one can be sure what people want to do with the money they get. Until the answer to that question can be found, no sure way can be found, it seems to me, to halt inflation by simple adjustments in monetary policy. The Federal Reserve Board in 1921 did not prevent the relatively minor panic of that year. The Federal Reserve Board did not prevent the big panic of 1929. Yet in both of those years it was free to act without direction from either Congress of the executive branch of the government.

Fundamentally, what people want to do with their money causes both inflation and deflation. Until we are able to provide sure guidance for the mass action of people, we are not going to be able to come up with a plan which will guarantee success one way or the other. People's confidence or lack of confidence in the national currency can cause, and at times has caused, the velocity of circulation of money and bank deposits to change so rapidly and so much as to make achievable manipulations of the total quantity of money or credit by monetary authorities about as effective as a broom sweeping against the tide.

CHAIRMAN LEVI: I should like to ask Mr. Kestnbaum whether it would be appropriate to relate the point which he has raised to the phrase "announced noninflationary policy" in Item I, A.

MR. KESTNBAUM: That is what I have in mind. That we intend to have a noninflationary policy is a statement of high purpose, but I think that we have not yet worked out a national policy calculated to bring that about.

MR. ARNOLD: I would like to say that my whole belief is that one of the reasons for inflation is the fear of inflation and that economists generally are advocating measures which, as Mr. Celler can tell us, no politician believes can be taken, and the man on the street does not believe they can be taken; and so we have this pronouncement, " We are going to get inflation if we don't do this," and the man on the street knows that such a rigid program cannot be followed.

CHAIRMAN LEVI: This is a reference, Mr. Arnold, to Item I, C, is it?

MR. ARNOLD: Yes.

MR. MINTS: May I make a comment there? I think what Mr. Kestnbaum and Mr. Arnold are saying is in very large degree the same thing as I am trying to say when I say that an increase in the rate of use of money is responsible in part for the inflation. That is because of the expectation of price rises, so that I am not omitting from my own thinking the sort of thing that you two men are referring to.

CHAIRMAN LEVI: Now, doing what I have been doing, looking at the outline again, I ask if anyone wishes to speak specifically to Item III, A, 2, that is, "It may be argued that a tight monetary policy will prevent producers of military supplies from getting their share of bank credit while higher taxes or direct controls would not. Is this because the existing credit structure is such that it is harder to obtain new or additional funds than to maintain existing lines of credit?" Does anyone wish to make this precise argument?

MR. THOMSON: Item III, A, 2 ought not to go unanswered.

The Committee for Economic Development has indicated its position, and I think that business organizations generally have gone along on the proposition that as to fiscal 1952 the proposed federal expenditures should be met through a balanced budget. That means an increase in taxation. Borrowing from banks is inflationary in general and ought to be avoided. Additional federal funds as required should be borrowed from individuals and fiduciary institutions rather than banks.

A sound monetary policy depends upon a co-ordinated fiscal policy. I am sure we have not enough information to appraise the expansion of bank loans in the last six months from the standpoint of its inflationary effects. We need a better understanding of the techniques that are being used and their anticipated effect on various segments of the economy, as well as particular institutions. We should not have expected the Federal Reserve policy to be effective in the United States as it should be, for the simple reason that the Federal Reserve has until recently been prevented from acting and that their function as a monetary authority has not been thoroughly understood by even the banking fraternity.

In the last thirty days monetary policy has been put in the position to work as it could not have worked before (1) by passage of legislation for the refunding of the "E" bonds, (2) by the start of voluntary credit controls, (3) by the issuing for the first time in quite a while of a bond that is suitable for long-term investors, and (4) by the agreement that the Federal Reserve is to operate to an extent we do not know fully yet but to a large extent through a flexible support policy.

I do not believe that we can give a categorical answer to Item III, A and B. All these factors have to be taken into account and co-ordinated at the governmental level with other policies of government. The manner of government purchases, their timing, governmental policy in regard to encouraging housing and furnishing credit for same, the control of credit expansion for housing through savings and loan—all these things have to be taken into account.

SENATOR O'MAHONEY: I intended a while ago but omitted to call attention to the striking contrast between testimony given to the Banking and Currency (watchdog) Committee in the Senate the other day by C. E. Wilson, head of the Office of Defense Mobilization, and the great battle of words carried on previously between the Treasury and the Federal Reserve System before the same committee. According to Federal Reserve theory, we must rely on open-market operations to prevent inflation; we must limit accessibility to credit and prevent the banks from putting money into the hands of people who want to spend it. Mr. Wilson, on the other hand, urged upon the Banking and Currency Committee that RFC loans, or maybe Treasury loans, were necessary to finance the expanded defense work needed in this emergency. These two proposals, from a monetary point of view, seem contradictory.

The question to which I should like to call attention is the one reading: "Is it necessary that the government should cover all its current expenditures by taxation?" My answer is: "Yes, if we don't want to have government step into the picture and do the job that has to be done."

We have to defend ourselves and the free world. Either we do it by organizing the banks of the United States to make loans to the producers who need those loans to produce the commodities that are needed in the nation's crisis or we will have it done by government.

CHAIRMAN LEVI: At this point we would like to introduce a new device for such discussions. For each session we have a summarizer and critic of the discussion who is allowed to speak at least twice, once during the middle of the discussion and finally at the conclusion. For this session, Mr. Milton Friedman is asked to speak at this point as a summarizer and critic of the discussion so far.

MR. HANSEN: Could I make one comment on Item II, A? It would seem to me one criterion that would apply to II, A, is: How large is the volume of capital outlays? So long as they remain very large, we need an overbalanced budget. If we can cut the capital outlays to a very small figure, then the savings from business and other individuals can be applied to finance the defense expenditures. I would suggest that that is one of the criteria we might use in answering that question.

CHAIRMAN LEVI: Mr. Friedman.

MR. FRIEDMAN: This discussion is, of course, very difficult to summarize, and I trust you will bear with me if I seem to do less than justice to every interesting point that has been raised.

On the major problem of the role of monetary policy in combating inflation, most of those who have spoken have assumed that there would be a reasonably satisfactory fiscal policy, in the sense of a reasonable balance between government income and government expenditures. This raises a question that still remains largely undiscussed: What would be the situation with respect to monetary policy if there were not a satisfactory fiscal policy?

Two major positions about monetary policy have been expressed. One position, presented by Mr. Mints, and which, I may say, I share, is that monetary measures, given a reasonable fiscal policy, could be effective in stabilizing the level of prices whatever might happen to the rate of use of the existing stock of money. This position, if I understand it, is that any attempt on the part of the public at large to spend existing balances at a faster rate, occasioned by expectations of further price rises or other reasons, could be offset by a reduction in quantity of money on the part of the central bank through the sale of securities on the open market, and that in consequence the increased difficulty of getting credit would offset the increased willingness to spend existing balances.

The other major position has been taken by Mr. Burgess, Mr. Harrod, Mr. Kestnbaum, and several of the others who have spoken, that monetary policy can do some good but cannot, even associated with a decent fiscal policy, be expected to prevent completely the kind of inflation which is now occurring.

I am not sure quite how to describe the logic of this position. It seems to fall into two parts. There is, first, the position that monetary policy is not strong enough. This is the position of Mr. Harrod and, I think, of Mr. Burgess, that for some reason it is not possible to reduce the quantity of money as much as would be required to offset an increase in the rate of use of money. Why it is not possible to reduce the quantity of money sufficiently is a question that has been left unanswered, and I would like to suggest that it very badly needs an answer.

The second alternative in this position is, I think, the one expressed by Mr. Kestnbaum, that monetary policy is too powerful because, if it is in fact used to offset the increase in the rate of use of money, it will "paralyze the economy," if I may quote his words; that somehow there are undesirable implications of the strong use of monetary policy. I think that this is also the position that underlies a number of other comments referring to the existence of factors other than monetary factors in producing the inflation.

If I interpret them correctly, the argument is: Granted we could stop an inflation if we were willing to cut the supply of money enough, this would have effects in other directions that would be undesirable, and hence it would be preferable to take other measures to prevent inflation. I think that this comment also relates to the brief discussion of the role of fiscal policy, and particularly to Mr. Hansen's comment. It is implicit in this position that the interest rate is not the best means for controlling the amount of investment, and hence that a monetary policy which depends very largely on the use of the interest rate for this purpose is inappropriate and should be supplemented either by a fiscal policy which produces a surplus or by direct controls of investment or by the particular scheme for discouraging investment that Mr. Harrod outlined.

If this summary is correct, it suggests that our discussion might appropriately consider in the remaining time some of these other factors, some of these adverse effects, that it is claimed monetary policy would have and the means for dealing with them that would be less adverse than a tight-money policy. To be a bit more specific, two main adverse effects have so far been mentioned in the discussion. The first has to do with the difficulty on the part of government in refinancing its debt. It is urged that there are limits to the interest rate that it is appropriate to pay on government debt aside from the effect of the interest rate on investment. The second is the structure of investment. It is implied that interest rates will produce an erroneous or undesirable structure of investment. I think we need consideration of these points as well as specification of those other adverse consequences of a tight monetary policy.

MR. HAYEK: May I formulate two questions on points where the assumptions underlying much of the discussion have remained rather obscure to me? One is on the general issue of inflation. Is it argued that, unless we increase monetary demand faster than supply, we shall fail to provoke a maximum effort? My impression is that, once monetary demand rises faster than supply, it produces inefficiences likely to be greater than any additional stimulus. Then, I think, the underlying argument that we need monetary expansion in order to stimulate maximum effort actually turns into the opposite. That is the first question.

The second question I should like to ask is this: Is it argued that we cannot transfer any amount of resources which we want to divert to mobilization purposes by either taxation or borrowing for this purpose at the expense of nonmobilization purposes?

And this raises my third question, which really is a subquestion of the second, namely: Is it the main argument that, if we set up this new demand for mobilization purposes, it will give rise to such large induced investment demands that by no traditional means of monetary policy can these investment demands be curbed?

My impression is that most of the argument just tacitly assumes that the rate of interest which would be required for this purpose is impracticable solely because of the large volume of floating government debt. Really the point to which we have to turn now is Item V of the program; it is the crucial one on which everything else depends.

CHAIRMAN LEVI: The discussion at this point, then, is going in the direction of combining Item III, A, 2, and Item V, and my suggestion is that we turn to Item V, which is this: "Is the resort to nonmonetary means for preventing inflation a consequence of the public policy of keeping down interest rates? Is this policy of such importance as to justify sacrificing the advantages of a noninflationary monetary program?" Then Item A under that is: "Is keeping down interest rates a relevant objective? (1) Is the argument for it that it keeps down interest payments on the public debt? But if inflation is to be avoided, keeping down interest rates will mean a higher level of taxation or more stringent direct controls. Are these preferable to higher interest payments?"

Mr. BRUBAKER: Before we get too far away from Item III, since you say you are combining it with Item IV, I would like to make a very brief comment about the question of monetary policy and how it ties in with some of these other problems. I have refrained from speaking earlier because the framework of the earlier discussion was limited strictly to monetary policy and how it functioned. I notice the entire framework of the conference, as it was drawn up, is essentially in terms of one alternative: Shall we have inflation, or shall we have a tight monetary policy?

In the first place, I represent here one of the groups that has already been caught tight in the web of inflation. In the labor group we already have our wages frozen. We have almost no area of movement within which we can function as a labor group at the present time—in the wage field at least. We already have inflation in several other areas. I do not have to tell most of you that. We have it in prices—despite the best efforts of Mr. DiSalle and others. We have it, certainly to a degree, already in wages; though it came belatedly and though it has been stopped short. We already have it in credit supply, and, frankly, we do not like it. We do not care for the inflation, and we would be delighted to see whatever steps taken that are necessary to stop it.

We do not, however, have the confidence that Professor Mints and others seem to have in using monetary controls alone as the alternative to inflation. If monetary controls alone are the alternative, I would say to you frankly I think we are on the high road to the hell of inflation in a hurry—a road where there is no turning point.

There certainly are some other alternatives and some which we will probably discuss in the course of the conference. Certainly we have to have fiscal controls, and some rather rigid ones. We have no objection to the kind of overbalancing of the budget which has been mentioned here. I think that may be a very good suggestion as one alternative. We certainly have to have some direct controls, and we would be foolish to suggest that we do not need them at this time at least. We have to have controls over prices and wages, and, as you know, the group which I represent has stated publicly and jointly with other groups, government and industry, that it is willing to take part in those controls.

We have to have monetary controls. I would not argue that we do not. But if we are going to have monetary controls, I would like to see us get this discussion down to the level of some kind of controls that we think have some hope of working.

I am inclined to agree with Professor Mints on this score, that, as our monetary controls have worked in the past—or have functioned in the past, perhaps I should say, for they have not actually worked—to keep down the supply of money to the extent necessary to control inflation, they badly need supplementing.

I would like to suggest that we talk a little bit about a point which has been mentioned by Mr. Kestnbaum and others here today and one which John Clark, for instance, has been urging for some time, namely, that we already have in our system enough of the elements of credit inflation and monetary supply inflation that we cannot hope, simply by tinkering with interest rates, to stop that inflation. I think we are just kidding ourselves if we fail to recognize this fact. Goodness knows, most of the banks and insurance companies and loan associations have the money and the credit to expand the monetary supply if they want to expand it. And they will do an awful lot of expanding, no matter what the Federal Reserve Board does with the interest rates. If we are going to talk about controlling that credit, we might just as well get right down to talking about controlling the amount of money that banks can loan. If we want to talk about that, that is something else, and maybe it is getting down to the problem we have to face. I would like to urge that someone speak on that subject.

CHAIRMAN LEVI: I should like to ask Mr. Friedman at this point whether he will restate, as summarizer and critic, the question he thinks we should now discuss.

Mr. Friedman: It is very hard for me to get into the role of summarizer without making an initial comment about the comment we have just heard, because I think it is important to do so to see why the questions we have been talking about are important. It simply is not true that banks and other financial institutions have the cash with which to expand the credit supply. The fact is that there are no excess reserves in the System and that the possibility of being able to expand the money supply depends essentially on what is involved in Item V here, on their ability to sell government bonds to the Federal Reserve Bank and thereby get additional reserves, additional new money, printed money, with which to expand credit.

Mr. Brubaker: All I can say in answer to that, very briefly, is simply that I know the industry in which I am working is getting very substantial amounts of money from banks, from insurance companies, to do expanding of investment capital, if you will, as well as working capital. They are getting it today. The money is there. I will not argue with you whether the total amounts available in the System are so great that we do not have to worry about them. Frankly, I think they are.

Mr. Mints: Do you also know that there are other industries that are failing to get funds to the extent that these industries are getting funds?

Mr. Brubaker: Perhaps it is because they have not gone after them. Our industry claimed last year or the year before it could not get these funds either, but finally when they decided it wanted them, and finally after the government had made it so damned attractive to them to get funds for capital expansion, they went out and got them so easily that they have been surprised.

Chairman Levi: I now call the attention of the conference again to Item V, which is, "Is the resort to nonmonetary means for preventing inflation a consequence of the public policy of keeping down interest rates?" May I ask if anyone wishes to speak to this point?

Mr. Cortney: I am afraid that this question is not properly stated. The real issue is whether we shall have control on the amount of money which we can issue. The interest rate is only one of the consequences of the volume of money. I submit that stressing the question of interest rate is misleading both the initiated and the noninitiated. I am less worried about misleading the initiated, but I am very worried about misleading the noninitiated, by whom I mean the general public. One of the fundamental causes of inflation is precisely the power of the government to sell unlimited amounts of bonds to the Federal Reserve Board against cash. I submit therefore that the reference to interest rates on government bonds in Item V is misleading. In the debate between the Federal Reserve Board and the Treasury, the real issue is the volume of money.

MR. FELLER: I would like to supplement what has just been said, and I think in a misleading way. I think many of the questions here are stated in a misleading way. I think implicit in the statement of this question and other questions is that, when we talk about tight monetary policy, we are talking about a particular type of monetary control, and that is sale or purchase of government securities by the Open Market Committee of the Federal Reserve Board. Now, that has been an implicit assumption, and the reason I think it needs to be made express is that that is not the only method of controlling bank loans and thus controlling the total supply of money.

It has been suggested by Mr. Clark, who is vice-chairman of the President's Council of Economic Advisers, that, rather than go through the type of operation which Mr. Mints apparently regards as the exclusive method of monetary control, we simply put a freeze on the total amount of bank loans. Certain relaxations to accomplish certain purposes would be required, but it is a control which, compared with other types of direct controls, is fairly easy to administer, since we have relatively few banks that keep very good books and whose accounts are open to the public.

The reason I think it is important to inject this is that we seem to have a dichotomy between direct controls and monetary controls. I do not know whether Mr. Mints would call this a monetary control or a direct control. It would be a direct control of the making of loans and thus affect the supply of money.

The reason I mention that at this time is that in the summary

Mr. Friedman has very much changed the burden of proof from what it ought to be. He said that it has so far not been shown that changes in the velocity of money would more than compensate for changes in the supply of money which is made by the sale of government securities by the Federal Reserve Board.

MR. FRIEDMAN: Which could be made.

MR. FELLER: It seems to me, the burden of proof is the other way around. The velocity of money is just a kind of compendium expression for a lot of things, but it is very difficult to describe precisely. There are many ways in which balances can be held and many ways in which they can be transferred to other holdings in which the velocity of money is increased. When you have this kind of loose catch-all which you call the velocity of money, if you are going to advance a policy of reducing the quantity of money in this one particular way, then you have the burden of showing that there are no other ways in which loans can be made, which result in an increase in the velocity of money. Corporations do not hold their excesses in cash but invest them. You have the burden of showing that there is not all that elasticity in the system which I think there is, so that nothing but the most drastic reduction in the quantity of money, which would mean an exorbitant increase in interest rates and the cost of the public debt, would suffice to accomplish your purpose.

Now, that burden has not been met, in my view. I think it ought to be met. On the discussion so far, and, I think, on the history, we would have to say that the type of operation which Mr. Mints advocates has so far been proved not to be effective.

The other point I would like to make is that the assumption that we can persuade banks, which hold such a tremendous quantity of government bonds now, to hold what they hold now or more, by the type of operation which Mr. Mints suggests, is also not proved. I think Mr. Clark made a small analysis based on his own experience, and he is a banker. He says his bank buys every week $200,000 worth of short-term government notes. He says we can drop the price of government bonds by Federal Reserve action as much as we want, and the bank still has the facility to increase its reserves simply by failing to subscribe next week to $200,000 worth of government bonds. Now, I see some shaking of heads, so that may not be so, but in any event the statement was made that the bank still has the facility to increase its reserves, thus reducing its net portfolio of government bonds and increasing its cash portfolio when the bonds mature. When we are dealing with quantities like that, I think it is not proved yet that within the realm of practical reason—and I take it Mr. Mints would not want to drive government bonds to 50—that we can, by the type of operation he suggests, control the amount of money times the velocity.

MR. THOMSON: Banks started in 1951 with the anticipation that their loans, after leveling off, would go down from natural causes without any additional controls. Specifically, 50 per cent of the bank loans in the aggregate are covered by selective controls—Regulation X applying to mortgage credit; Regulation W covering consumer credit and provisions governing loans on securities. I think that the feeling of the bank fraternity is that Regulation X as to mortgage credit has not become effective because there were so many authorizations at the last minute and that, unless there is some new governmental policy as to defense housing or something of that kind, mortgage loans in the banks will go down. I told our board of directors that we would be lucky if our affiliated banks maintained their volume of mortgage credit during 1951.

As to consumer credit, we will have a drop-off in production of durable goods, and Regulation X has not had time to be fully effective yet. We have no information available at this time to base a judgment as to the inflationary effects of the increase in bank lending since Korea. We do know that car shortages have resulted in delay in liquidation of some agricultural loans, and there are other factors accounting for a temporary increase in bank loans. The present drop in the price of government bonds is a deterring factor to banks, insurance companies, and other lending institutions considering additional loans.

CHAIRMAN LEVI: We ought to get back to the outline because of the time, and I think we ought to go to Item V, A, 2, which is what I think the last speaker was talking about and ask if anyone wishes to speak on that.

MR. MULLENDORE: May I make an observation there which seems to me to be very practical in clearing up from the borrower's standpoint the question of interest rate? Interest rate, of course, is merely the rate per dollar, whereas what we really are interested in is the rental cost of capital. We find that, when we have to hire two dollars to buy the same bit of equipment that could previously be bought with one, a low interest rate is not the determining factor. The question is: How much do we have to pay for renting our capital? And it seems to me, therefore, that if we emphasize only interest rates, in the sense of per dollar borrowed, that it is likely to be misleading.

SENATOR BENNETT: I am Senator Wallace F. Bennett, and I am very much interested in what Mr. Brubaker and Mr. Feller have said. I should like to point out that if we are going to attempt to control the conditions under which banks loan money, we have to take the federal government out of the lending business, because everybody that is turned down at the bank will show up at the RFC or any one of the hundreds of agencies that the federal government operates now to try politically to make up for the hardheartedness of the banks. So we cannot control bank lending unless the government is prepared to prevent the borrower from getting in the back door and breaking down our whole process.

MR. BRUBAKER: If the government is determined to control the amount of capital that is issued, it could control the amount of government-lending agencies. . . .

SENATOR BENNETT: Have you been reading the Reconstruction Finance Corporation investigation stories?

MR. BRUBAKER: They surely can determine how much is loaned by the RFC.

SENATOR BENNETT: While the pressure on the banks is economic, the pressure on the government is political. I think all my confreres in Congress will admit it is much more difficult either in Congress, or as an administrator of the government agency, to resist a political pressure to loan money.

MR. KESTNBAUM: Knowing the chairman's addiction to following the outline, I should like to offer an idea that can perhaps advance this discussion on interest rates. It does seem to me that interest rates have been overemphasized in certain quarters, partly for historic reasons—the classical theory does not always operate well. The assumption that moderate changes in the interest rate will effectively control the volume of credit under present conditions seems to me unreasonable.

The suggestion that Senator Bennett made is certainly proper. If we could control the amount of money lent by the banks, it would be desirable. In fact, I think it is desirable to have some restriction on the total amount of lending. But we must bear in mind that what Senator O'Mahoney said is true.

The control of bank credit is difficult especially if government agencies are set up to facilitate credit for the expansion of defense facilities. To the extent that these agencies take over financing which might otherwise have been handled by the banks, the controls are short-circuited.

Furthermore, we must remember that there are "E" bonds which have been purchased at the rate of some five billion dollars a year which can find their way into the supply of credit if necessary. Those can be cashed. That money can move into savings, into other investments, or into consumer goods. There is still a large volume of savings in this country which, under more attractive interest rates, might be brought into the capital market.

It seems to me that there are many persons here who have the general view that no one of these controls can accomplish the kind of control that is needed here; that it will take a broad, well-thought-out national policy in which large sections of the community will have to co-operate if we are to guide our economy in the direction that is necessary. I for one want to say that with respect to bank credit my own belief is that the most effective way of controlling bank credit would be to put the responsibility on the banking system itself. I think it would be better handled. We would do less violence to the economy, and we would get better performance. I think the results would be more satisfactory than any attempt to impose limits or controls because, when we do, we put a premium on a line of credit.

We have learned one thing about controls. They require skill in their administration, and, whenever the people who are administering controls try to match wits with the people who are subject to controls, the people who are subject to controls usually win.

MR. DIRECTOR: I regret that the phrasing of Item V is causing some difficulty of interpretation. It was not designed to direct attention to any particular interest rate, nor, to put it even more concretely, was it directed to discussion of the desirability of high interest rates as a means of checking the demand for loans at banks. The main purpose of this question was directed to discussion of whether the objective of keeping down interest rates makes it impossible to prevent an increase in the supply of money.

MR. BLOUGH: I would like to rephrase that as a question: How high are we willing to see government interest rates go over the next two or three years? How low are we willing to see government bond prices go? Why are we not willing to see the bond prices go lower, or the interest rates go higher? It seems to me that the answer may be the key as to whether this monetary policy can be made to work in this period.

MR. HAYEK: Is there any limit to the rate of interest which it would not be worth while to incur? If a 12 per cent rate of interest is necessary, would it be too high if it prevented inflation? The costs of inflation are such that I do not see that any rise in the rate of interest should be offset.

MR. VINER: Let us assume that we do not know what the effect would be of the restriction of the volume of money on the price of government bonds but that we are very much concerned with such an effect and, for whatever reason, good or bad, we would not want it to go far. It would nevertheless then be a serious mistake to throw up our hands and say, "We cannot control the volume of credit." We can insulate the government debt from the impact of higher interest rates.

Ideas as to how this can be done have been circulating for years. I think some of them are relatively simple to administer, although they would require new legislation. One of the ways that I would suggest, which seems to me the simplest way, is to make reserve requirements hold against assets and not against liabilities of the banks and then to permit the Federal Reserve to set up different reserve requirements against long-term government bonds as compared to all other income-earning assets in the banks.

On that basis, we can make the reserve requirements zero on government bonds held by banks, or make it 10, or 5 per cent, or make it half or a quarter of the reserves on the other types of assets, as we find it necessary, in order to induce the banks to keep on holding these bonds. In that way, we can protect the market value of the bonds, and we can limit the interest burden of the public debt, while still having freedom to move in the direction of control of the aggregate volume of credit.

I want to make it clear, however, that I am not saying that if a dictator were running this country, he ought to do that. I am not sure. It may be that what he ought to do is to restrict by some method or other, definitely, the volume of bank credit without regard to whether it is government-created or private-created credit. But if public opinion and the government are so concerned about the market value of the government bonds, and/or the interest burden on the debt, that they will not accept a type of control which sharply lowers their market value, and if we do not know, as I believe we really do not know, what the effect of real tightening of credit would be on the market value of the bonds, then I say that we should consider a device such as the one I suggest.

There are at least three or four other proposals circulating, and they have been circulating for years, whereby we can protect the public debt against the impact of credit control and throw the burdens of credit control wholly on the nongovernmental side. I prefer the device I have suggested, but I do not insist upon it.

CHAIRMAN LEVI: I direct the attention of the conference to Item V, C, which asks, "Can we have both the program of keeping down interest rates and a noninflationary monetary program with existing institutional arrangements?" and I ask if anyone else wishes to speak to that point.

MR. BRUBAKER: I would like to ask a question on that point. I notice that the Federal Reserve Board, in conjunction with the banking fraternity, has attempted to work out a voluntary credit restriction program which they hope will induce the banks not to loan as much money as they have been lending. I realize that probably the Federal Reserve Board people here would have to defend that system in terms of its possibility of success. I would like to hear one of the other bankers who is in attendance give us a candid answer as to whether or not he thinks any bank which has the money to lend is going to pay much attention to this kind of voluntary restriction system— if it can lend money at a good rate and make a good profit on it.

Very frankly, our own answer to this question is that very probably they would be just as little disposed to practice that kind of system of self-restraint as would a business firm which has a product which it can sell at a higher price. Neither could we expect labor to refuse to try to get a wage increase if its costs are going up and it feels the need of a wage increase. I just wonder if anyone feels we can have even a little hope that this voluntary credit restriction plan will work.

Mr. Burgess: If that is addressed to the bankers, there are only two of us here, and the other banker present has spoken and taken his turn. I might say that this program of voluntary credit control originated with the bankers, although in form it appeared to come from the Federal Reserve Board, because that is the way the attorney-general wanted it to come. But it was at our initiation.

I believe it will be reasonably effective. Generally speaking, these conservative bankers do have consciences. I think it may be as successful as the program of voluntary restraint from pressure for wage increases that the British labor unions have exercised over a recent period. That was one of the outstanding achievements since the devaluation of the pound. British labor has been willing to stand without any substantial wage increases in spite of rising prices. I think the bankers may be as effective with their voluntary controls as that.

Mr. Brubaker: Do you think they are of a different stripe from the business people?

Mr. Burgess: I am not such a pessimist about human nature.

MR. LEVENTHAL: Are you not also influenced by the fact that voluntary controls may be effective because, if they are not effective, they might be made involuntary?

MR. BURGESS: That is one of the real arguments for this. May I also say that this set of controls can be made more effective and moved over toward more direct controls? There was a very effective Capital Issues Committee, for example, in World War I, staffed by people who were being controlled, which turned down nine hundred million dollars worth of capital issues and approved two and a half billion, or something of that sort, but did its job extremely well under the chairmanship of a banker. These voluntary committees can be incorporated into such a capital issue control, without too great difficulty, if we find that it does not work on its present basis.

MR. BRUBAKER: Let me follow the question, then, with another one. Do you think that, if we are going to have direct controls in the area of prices and wages, there is a reason why we should not have direct control in this monetary area in terms of direct controls on loans?

MR. BURGESS: We already have, Mr. Brubaker, something like 50 per cent of the loans—we have it in real estate, in securities, and in instalment credit.

MR. BRUBAKER: Excluding those, do you think there is reason why we should not have it?

MR. BURGESS: I think it is a very difficult thing to determine as the loans come up. It is a very difficult thing for somebody else to set up a set of categories without establishing a tremendous system of policing.

MR. BRUBAKER: Even in terms of controls of the gross amount of credit which can be issued? You see, we are in an area where we are called upon to do a great amount of sacrificing on the basis of some kind of equality of sacrifice in this emergency setup. We ask businessmen to control their businesses; we ask labor to control their wages; and, when Congress is not satisfied that this is being done properly, they slap direct controls on prices and say that, when they are controlled there, we will control wages at the same time, so that two major areas of our economy are already functioning under a direct control system, presumably because that is going to help to effectuate this equality of sacrifice. We are wondering why the equality-of-sacrifice doctrine should not go into the area of credit.

MR. BURGESS: My first answer is that it has, in terms of the area where controls have already been established. The second is that we want to do things that work. We are trying to do two things here. That is the principle that we need to bear in mind. We are trying, first, to finance the defense effort; second, we are trying to do it without inflation. That delicate balance is where our problems arise. I would say that 85 per cent of the loans that I have seen go through our bank have been directly related to doing a defense job and maintaining the production of an economy at a level 15 per cent higher than it was a year ago. Now, it is a delicate job to do, and I think it can be dealt with with the kind of setup that is being worked out.

MR. HAZLITT: The most desirable form of voluntary control in the field of credit would be simply to allow the interest rate to rise, and that can be done simply by the government's stopping the process of holding it down. And, answering Mr. Blough's question, the interest rate should be allowed to rise to a level sufficient to stop inflation, sufficient to stop further expansion of bank credit.

As to Mr. Viner's proposal, I think it would be a very dangerous thing to try to isolate government credit from the credit market. It would end up in direct controls, and it would end up in government lending, as a matter of fact, so that the only real choice that we have is to allow the interest rate to go up if we wish to preserve a free economy at the same time that we wish to stop inflation. That is going to have adverse effects on government bonds, and one of the reasons is because such a bad policy has been followed in the past. These bad effects are the result of that policy and nothing else.

CHAIRMAN LEVI: I should like, at this point, to ask Mr. Friedman to summarize and take the role of the critic. But, before he does so, I should like to remind you that the next discussion begins with a continuation of this discussion, so that there is some counterbalancing compensation for stopping, as you will have to do after Mr. Friedman's summary.

MR. HARROD: I have been sitting here feeling that what Mr. Friedman said halfway through demanded a certain rejoinder, but I have not made it. Since he is going to speak again, I should like to say that I did not agree with some of his interpretations of my views.

MR. FRIEDMAN: Would you mind saying what they are?

MR. HARROD: There was a double criticism. One was for lack of logic; and, second, he divided the skeptics into those who thought that an interest policy would be too weak and those who thought it would be so strong as to have outside bad effects. I should like to say that I do not think it is an issue that can be decided by logic but rather by history and experience, and my contention is that history does not show that a tight credit policy can prevent the development of inflation in the kind of situation where there is a real demand for goods and services, such as we have at the present time.

I do not agree with the attempt to put a wedge between various exponents of skepticism. Is there any contradiction between saying that a thing would be ineffective and saying that, if pushed very far, it would have very disturbing effects? It is two aspects of the same point. I would submit that a strict credit policy on lines that are familiar, on the traditional lines of the past, would be ineffective; but that if we really try to stop inflation and say, "We will carry this to a logical extreme," the Federal Reserve can sell all the government bonds they have. They could sell gold in the free markets of the world for a nice premium, etc. If they did all those things, pushing the policy to an absolute logical conclusion, we do not know whether they could stop inflation. They might.

But if they did that and got to the point at which the member banks were having to refuse loans all around and to withdraw loans from their customers who had perfectly good collateral, and we really carried the policy to that great extreme, we would get to a point at which we would introduce an element of confusion into the whole economy. My contention is that, if we carry the policy to a reasonable level, I am in favor of doing it, but that it is not, even when joined with a proper fiscal policy, going to stop our inflation. If we carry it beyond a reasonable level, we will introduce grave confusions in the whole economy.

While I am speaking, I would like to make one final point about this rate of interest. Great stress, in certain parts of the room, has been laid to a high rate of interest. I am not sympathetic to this—not beyond a certain point—because it seems to me that what we are fundamentally trying to do with a high rate of interest is to stop off investment expenditure in the order of ten billion dollars in this country.

If we really put through a very high rate of interest—12 per cent has been mentioned—we are disturbing values throughout the whole economy. We are disturbing the relation between capital values and all other values. I do not know what the capital of the United States is, but it is in the order of a thousand billion dollars. We are disturbing the relation of that capital, a thousand billion dollars, and the income yield of property, in order to check expenditure of ten billion dollars. It is altogether out of proportion. It is doing a gigantic thing in order to produce a relatively small result. That is why I would like this meeting to endeavor to explore other general methods, besides fiscal controls, such as Regulations W and X, which, looking across the Atlantic, seem to be excellent expedients.

I have thrown out the idea of a tax incentive to reduce expenditure. Can we not find some general pervasive method to reduce capital expenditure and not stick to the traditional rate of interest method, which, in my opinion, has a grossly exaggerated importance attached to it?

Mr. Friedman: Let me start by indicating what I think to be the area of real agreement. I think there is widespread agreement that a more rigorous and tighter open-market monetary policy than has so far been carried out in the United States would be desirable to counter inflation. Further, I think there is agreement that a particular, single, rigid rate of interest derived from past history is not sacrosanct and should not be allowed to interfere with further use of monetary policy. Beyond this, I think there is considerable disagreement, which I might try to summarize as follows.

There is one group that believes that open-market policy—

I use this phrase to meet Mr. Feller's point that "monetary policy" can be conceived of as including many types of controls we have not discussed—combined with reasonably adequate fiscal policy could prevent inflation, by its effect on the quantity of money, without direct controls and without any undesirable effects that would not characterize other policies as well.

There is a second group that believes that, while tighter monetary policy is desirable, it is not enough, even in conjunction with a reasonably adequate fiscal policy. Those who take this second position offer different reasons why monetary policy would not be enough. One reason is that velocity is extremely variable, that the rate of use of money can alter very easily, and hence that it would require extraordinarily large declines in the amount of money to offset any potential velocity increases.

In the main, however, it is felt that monetary policy is not enough, because it would have undesirable incidental effects. The major undesirable incidental effect mentioned is on the rate of interest on, and the price of, government securities. While some variation in the price of government securities is recognized as possible and desirable, it is argued that there is a point, as mentioned by Mr. Blough, beyond which it is better either to have inflation or to have alternative methods of stemming it. The other main category of undesirable incidental effects is on investment, particularly investment in war industries.

Among those who regard tighter monetary policy as inadequate, there are differences of opinion about the alternative policies that should be adopted to deal with inflation or with the undesirable incidental effects of tight money. One proposal, by Mr. Harrod, is for taxation deterrents on investment. A second proposal is for voluntary control over bank lending, similar to the plan now in operation. Unfortunately, one question was not considered in connection with this proposal that I think is basic, namely, whether voluntary controls, even if effective, are a desirable means of organizing a war effort. A third proposal is direct controls over the volume of bank lending. The proposal here is that there be either a freeze on total bank loans or the adoption of some similar device that will directly control bank lending as contrasted with the control of bank lending indirectly through a Federal Reserve policy of altering the total amount of funds available to lend. Fourth, a wide variety of other direct controls—such as allocations of materials—were mentioned as possibly having the effect of reducing the demand for credit and thus taking the pressure off monetary policy. Finally, Professor Viner suggested a plan for isolating the government debt and thereby offsetting or eliminating this one particular incidental effect of a tight-money policy that is widely regarded as undesirable.

III

THE ROLE OF FISCAL POLICY

Outline for Discussion

It can probably be taken for granted that there are alternative combinations of monetary and fiscal policies which can be utilized to prevent inflation; that a budget surplus must be offset by an easy-money policy and that a budget deficit must be offset by a tight-money policy.

I. Is a balanced budget (equality of cash receipts and cash expenditures) a reasonable proximate goal for a noninflationary mobilization program?

    A. Some groups favor a budget surplus. Is the argument here:

        1. That a budget surplus would permit adherence to the present easy-money policy of low interest rates?

        2. That a budget surplus would discourage consumption and permit a relatively easy-money policy which would stimulate private investment; that it is always desirable to have a larger volume of investment; and that the nature of the present program requires that investment should be stimulated all over the field so as to be available in case it is wanted later for a bigger program?

        3. That we can expect an increase in the rate of use of money (because people expect inflation, or because cash balances are already excessive as a consequence of suppressed inflation) and that a budget surplus is a better way of offsetting such an increase than a contraction in the supply of money?

4. That Congress is more apprehensive of the dangers of inflation than the Treasury and the Reserve System?
5. That Congress cannot trust the Treasury and Reserve System to follow a sufficiently noninflationary monetary policy?
6. That a budget surplus can prevent inflation while monetary policy cannot?
7. That although monetary policy could be as effective as a budget surplus in preventing inflation, the former would have undesirable consequences such as creating unemployment?

B. Some groups favor a budget deficit. Is the argument here:
1. That the resources used for the military program should be taken in large part from civilian investment; hence a tight-money policy is required to concentrate the contraction in the civilian sector of the economy on investment rather than on consumption?
2. That the taxes required to balance the budget would reduce productive efficiency more than the high interest rates required to offset a deficit; specifically that high taxes would
   a) Keep nonworkers from entering the labor market?
   b) Keep all workers from working longer hours?
   c) Keep workers from shifting to new occupations?
   d) Reduce the efficiency of all workers?
   e) Remove the incentive on the part of enterprises to economize labor, materials, and equipment?
3. That taxation is less effective in adjusting the resources contributed by individuals to their individual needs and capacities than borrowing at high interest rates which will be required to prevent inflation with a budget deficit?
4. That part of government expenditures will represent an addition to total civilian capital, and should therefore be covered by noninflationary borrowing rather than by taxation?

II. What tax increases would be most appropriate for a noninflationary mobilization program?

A. The personal income tax
   1. The chief argument for exclusive reliance on this tax is that income is the best measure of ability to pay; and the additional taxes can be distributed in whatever way is desired.
   2. The argument against such reliance is:
      a) The obviousness of the income tax impairs incentives to effort.
      b) An income tax is likely to be made very progressive, and the resulting high marginal rates will maximize disincentives.
      c) The income tax does not require the economizing of resources on the part of people financing consumption by sale of assets.

B. A general sales tax
   1. Is the chief argument for such a tax
      a) That it is hidden and likely to be nonprogressive and has relatively little disincentive effect; or
      b) That it provides people with a choice between saving and consumption and increases the relative attractiveness of saving?
   2. Is the chief argument against a general sales tax that it is regressive and discriminatory because it cannot be made comprehensive?

C. Spendings tax
   1. Is the chief argument for such a tax that, like the sales tax, it discriminates in favor of saving and, unlike it, can be made comprehensive and progressive?
   2. Is the only argument against it that it is administratively difficult to enforce?

D. Special excise taxes
   1. Is the chief argument for this tax that if the supply of any commodity is completely inelastic the tax on it has no effect on allocation, and if the commodity is one for which demand is abnormally high the tax prevents windfall gains?

E. Excess profits taxes
1. Is the main argument for such taxation that it prevents "profiteering"?
2. Is the argument against such taxation that it promotes waste of resources by eliminating the incentive to economize and discourages the required shift of resources?

F. Corporate taxes
1. Are the considerations listed in E above applicable to increases in corporate taxes of the usual kind?

G. Compulsory saving or returnable taxes
1. Are the chief arguments for these that they minimize disincentives; create a purchasing power reserve for later periods; redistribute property and thereby give everyone a stake in the capitalist system?

CHAIRMAN BLUM: This afternoon's session will generally follow the same formula as this morning's session. Presumably, you have in your hands an outline used for organizing the discussion. I have been asked to announce, for those of you who prefer to use microphones, that they are available, and it will simply be necessary for you to signal the boy who is sitting behind you, and they will be produced.

This afternoon there will be two opening statements, the first by Professor Goode, and the second by Professor Shoup.

MR. GOODE: I hope I can make my opening remarks rather brief and introduce the subject by saying that we now come to examine something that we took pretty much for granted this morning, the assumption that we shall have a strong and wise fiscal policy to supplement whatever we do in other areas. You may not feel that is a realistic assumption after we have had some discussion.

I believe that the main functions of fiscal policy in this period of mobilization are four in number. There are possibly others. Two of these functions I regard as relating primarily to the quantitative aspect of fiscal measures, that is, the appropriate amount of taxes, expenditures, and borrowing.

The first function is the traditional one of absorbing purchasing power in order to help close the inflationary gap. The other quantitative problem has to do with minimizing the increase in the public debt and the increase in liquid assets of the community. I suggest that we focus our attention primarily on these two problems.

The other two objectives I designate as qualitative. One of these is what I call "market equalization" in specific shortage areas which may call for excise taxes where there are limitations on possiblilities of expanding output or where there are direct controls on output. Finally, there is the use of taxation to support what has been termed the "stabilization compromise." This last objective may call, for example, for the use of taxation of profits to convince labor and other sections of the community that everybody is participating in carrying the burden of the mobilization program. In my opening statement, at least, I shall have little to say about these two qualitative objectives but shall center attention on the quantitative objectives of fiscal action at this time.

One point that I should like to make I almost hesitate to mention in this group. But I think it bears repetition because of the character of much of the public discussion of defense finance: The taxes and other fiscal measures that may be taken to absorb purchasing power do not actually impose burdens on the community as a whole. The burdens that we are called upon to shoulder are created by government expenditures and the mobilization program itself; taxes are only one way of allocating the burdens among individuals and groups in the community.

As for how much should be raised in taxes, I myself take the rough goal of balancing the government's budget. Now, I recognize great merit in the argument in favor of trying to achieve a surplus. All considered, however, my own judgment is that we shall do very well if we balance the government's budget and that balancing the budget is a feasible objective that we could set for ourselves in the field of taxation. I recognize that, if we do balance the government's budget, we shall not absorb all excess demand by that means. Certainly, we shall not absorb all excess demand if we have a lax credit policy at the same time.

I recognize that a very likely consequence of this course of action is that we shall have some inflation. How much inflation we have will depend, to some extent, on what we do in monetary policy and what we do with direct controls.

In my opinion, it is not clear that a moderate degree of inflation is entirely out of the question as a way of distributing some of the burdens of the defense program. Of course, there are those who point out that it is impossible to restrict inflation to a moderate amount, and that may well be so. Mr. Harrod asked this morning if there had ever been a time when monetary action had prevented inflation under circumstances such as we face. Although I am not a student of monetary history, I believe we should have to answer by saying there has never been such a time. I doubt that, under the circumstances we are considering, inflation has ever been wholly avoided by any program.

I think we must expect a little inflation. Perhaps we shall have more than we bargain for. It seems to me appropriate for the President to set as an objective prevention of any inflation, although we recognize that we shall probably fall short of this objective.

Let us now turn to the particular tax measures that can be used. I will state rather dogmatically my view of them, partly for the purpose of provoking discussion. I do not wish at this time to give any detailed arguments regarding the merits and demerits of the particular measures.

It does seem to me that we shall be able to accomplish our tax objective by using the conventional taxes, the familiar revenue measures. I believe that we should emphasize at the outset —an economist ought to emphasize, at least—that many dominant decisions in this area depend on ethical or equity judgments and not on considerations of technical economics in any sense. If I state some conclusions on such issues, they will be a reflection of my views of equity and the ethics of the situation. I think that is unavoidable. I recognize, however, that, as an economist, I have no claim to expertness in this area.

I suppose that most of us would think first of the individual income tax as a means of raising more revenue. This tax is generally regarded as the fairest of available revenue measures. It can be apportioned in accordance with our standards of ability to pay or social justice and also with regard to considerations of economic expediency. This view of the income tax, of course, rests on the assumption that it is a direct tax, that is, a tax that stays where it is imposed. We feel much less certain about the incidence of many other taxes. I am not sure that our confidence about the final resting palce of the individual income tax is entirely justified. But let us grant that there is much to be said for the popular view that most of the individual income tax is borne by the persons who file the returns, whereas we know less about who bears the corporation income and excess profits taxes, payroll taxes, and some of the excise taxes.

One limitation on the use of the individual income tax is its possible adverse effects on incentives to produce. I must say, however, that it seems to me that economists have not been able to settle the question of what effect the tax actually has on the incentive to work. Another limitation which may be more significant relates to the administration of the income tax. I fear that there is real danger of a breakdown in administration if we put too much emphasis on the income tax. We must remember that successful administration requires a large element of voluntary compliance on the part of taxpayers. In discussing the merits of the individual income tax, it seems to me, we nearly always assume that it is perfectly administered, whereas, in fact, we know that is not the case. Administrative problems may set a limitation on the tax. Nevertheless, in my own program, I put primary emphasis on the individual income tax for the immediate future and for a good while to come.

Corporate taxes may be useful for control of purchasing power and also to support the so-called stabilization compromise. With regard to the control of purchasing power, it seems clear that corporation taxes do somewhat restrict investment. They are a good supplement to a tight credit policy in that respect.

Another kind of effect of corporation taxes may be highly undesirable and may set a limitation on use of these taxes. Although corporate taxes restrict some kinds of investment, they encourage those kinds of investments which can be charged to current expense. That is the well-known wasteful expenditure argument which holds that businessmen are likely to be liberal if they feel they are spending the government's money to a large extent. That, I feel, we would all recognize as a limitation on corporate taxes. Partly because the rate of an excess profits tax would be higher than the rate of the regular corporation income tax, I lean toward use of the regular corporation income tax instead of the excess profits tax as a source for more revenue. Another reason for this preference is that I do not know how to define excess profits. This seems to me a rather serious shortcoming of the tax.

Turning now to the excise taxes, I want to dispose of these rather quickly in my present discussion by saying we could use excises to absorb purchasing power. We could also use them for specific control purposes. Looking at the absorption of purchasing power, I personally am skeptical about these taxes, because, first, it seems to me they discriminate unfairly against producers and consumers of the taxed commodities. Second, it seems to me that most of the taxes are regressive, a feature which I dislike. I see no great merit in most of these taxes, although, certainly, some of them are well established.

One argument that might be made for increasing the specific taxes on liquor and cigarettes is that the inflation which we have already experienced has reduced the real rates of these taxes by roughly 50 per cent since the present rates were imposed. If, for example, we mark up the tax on distilled spirits from nine dollars to twelve dollars a proof gallon, as the Treasury has proposed, the real rate in terms of actual purchasing power will still be less than it was when the nine-dollar-a-gallon tax was first imposed.

One question that I expect we shall want to argue at some length here is the place of a so-called general sales tax in the revenue program. Let me be explicit about my own view. I think that if we actually had to contrast the effects of extreme inflation with a sales tax, there would be no doubt that we should prefer a sales tax. But I do not believe that unchecked inflation and the sales tax are the present alternatives. It seems to me that we can reach the revenue goal of balancing the budget—on the basis of programs that have been made public—without resort to a sales tax. I personally do not like the sales tax because of its regressivity, and I am not convinced that we cannot do equally well with other means. Another objection to the sales tax is that it is difficult to integrate with price and wage controls. Therefore, the sales tax does not enter into my personal program at this time. I would, however, reserve it for use if we find we cannot, for economic or political reasons, raise enough taxes from other sources.

I will be through after a brief look at compulsory lending, often called compulsory savings. I can see no place for this in the present program, because I do not know what the maturity date ought to be. I do not see how we can ask people to lend to the government unless we can set some definite maturity date. The presumed economic advantage of compulsory lending over taxation is that its incentive effects are less damaging. If, however, we cannot set a definite and not too remote maturity date, that presumed advantage seems to me to disappear.

This unfavorable judgment does not apply to compulsory lending in the form of an expansion of the regular social security system, which would increase contributions in advance of benefits. Now is a good time to move toward a permanent improvement in the old age and survivors insurance system and in other social security programs.

I do not wish to outline a fiscal program in any further detail. In conclusion, however, I should like to say a few words about the tax program recommended by the Treasury Department on February 5, 1951. As you know, this program calls for a ten-billion-dollar increase in taxes made up of roughly four billion dollars additional from the individual income tax, three billion dollars from the corporation income tax, and three billion dollars from selective excise taxes. These recommendations are not precisely the measures that I should prefer; I doubt that they conform exactly to the preferences of any of us here. But the Treasury proposals do seem to me to offer a very good basis for the formulation of a sound tax bill this year. I believe that we shall need to go beyond the Treasury program and that it may be desirable to do so before the end of this year. In assessing the need for additional taxes, we should not make the mistake of becoming optimistic, because inflation increases the yield of existing tax rates.

In a tax program for a mobilization period such as that now envisaged, I repeat, it seems to me that we can place primary reliance on the individual income tax. Increases in the corporation income tax and in certain excises are also appropriate. I do not believe that it is wise or necessary to resort to a general sales tax or a special compulsory lending program at this time.

CHAIRMAN BLUM: Professor Shoup.

MR. SHOUP: To avoid repetition, let me say that I agree with practically everything that Mr. Goode has said, with the exception of two or three points.

I am inclined, perhaps, to emphasize more the justification for excess profits taxation as opposed to a further advance in the regular corporate tax rates, partly because I feel that, at these levels, the regular corporate tax rates have some danger of getting into prices; and, second, because I feel that, as a matter of common equity, we can do better by taking more away from profits that are higher now than they were in the last four years, if the alternative is to go up to 50, 55, or 60 per cent, even for concerns that are going downhill at the present time. While we cannot define excess profits exactly, we cannot for that reason say "No" to the measure, for if we adopted that attitude in taxation fully—and, of course, Mr. Goode, I know, was not going that far—we would not be able to do anything.

The problem of excessive or wasteful expenditures under high marginal rates on business exists, but I think it has been somewhat less serious than is generally supposed and could be made much less serious than it has been. Without attempting to assess the evidence of the past, let me point out that if we could extend the privilege of carry-back of losses, or of unused excess profits tax credit, to beyond one year and make it a two- or three-year carry-back, then the fact is that no businessman would ever be safe in assuming that the marginal rate of tax on this year's profits and loss is actually, in fact, 77 per cent. It might turn out to be zero or 47 per cent, when, in some future year, a carry-back was allowed. In that instance, it seems to me it would be to the advantage of every good business executive to keep almost as close a watch on expenses as he would in normal times. In any event, I am inclined to think that the procedures set up for economizing in business are not subject to such rapid deterioration as is sometimes assumed under the impact of tax rates.

One point that Mr. Goode, if I recall correctly, did not emphasize is the possibility of a tax on spending which would be levied on the individual, upon submission by him of a statement showing what he had spent in the last three months or a year. It would involve serious administrative difficulties. However, and this shows how all tax problems tend to link up, if, for the administration of the high income-tax rates, we were to insist upon a statement of net worth of the taxpayer at the beginning and the end of each year (the requirement would seem to me to be necessary in any administration of high income-tax rates), we might then be able to require net-worth statements further on down the income line; and, to the extent that that could be done, a spendings tax would, I think, be practicable. I would agree that it is something that should not be put into the tax program at this time. It is, rather, something to be held in reserve, but something that should be seriously considered before ever moving to a sales tax.

One further reason against the sales tax: I would prefer not to have inserted in the tax measure something which, through inertia, stands a good chance of staying there forever after the emergency is past. I do not think the excess profits tax poses any such danger. The sales tax, however, once in, would have a tendency to be there forever, and, for that reason, I should regard it as something close to a last resort.

A few comments on some of the implications of the statements in the program here. There seems to be a general tendency to imply that heavy taxation checks consumption rather than investment. First, if it checks consumption, it probably also checks investment indirectly, except investment induced or required by the government for the defense program. Presumably, business will be less eager to invest if consumption shows signs of crumbling under the tax burden.

Second, despite the degree to which money is available, the working capital effect of heavy corporate taxes is often decisive in deciding whether or not a firm shall undertake investments. Consequently, if we are really serious about further checking business investment by tax measures, we have powerful instruments at hand in further increases in the excess profits tax rate or in the corporation tax rate.

If I could take three or four minutes to discuss Mr. Harrod's proposal this morning, I would like to do so. It is a very stimulating thought, and I make these remarks not in opposition but rather in terms of testing or inquiring into the proposal.

What are the limitations to any such proposal? First, inventory accumulation as a form of investment would not be affected by this decelerated depreciation provision. Second, in practice, may we suppose that the decelerated depreciation would have to apply to all plant and equipment outlay that was not covered by the certificates that allow accelerated depreciation. Perhaps we could visualize a threefold division, and perhaps Mr. Harrod had that in mind, including a middle ground where investment is not given either accelerated or decelerated depreciation. One question to settle would be whether the disallowed depreciation was to be lost forever or whether it was simply to be postponed to a later year. The quantitative relations will require some careful study. If we denied half of depreciation, what would be the results when compared to denying all of it? Would there be a danger of going too far, as Mr. Harrod said, in raising interest rates? Essentially, this amounts to a tax on investment, in the form of a disallowance, partial or complete, of depreciation charges. The thing that rather bothers me, as it is apt to bother any public finance man, is the problem of equity, which Mr. Goode noted. Let me illustrate.

Company A's plant was constructed in 1942. It wears out in 1952. Now, let me oversimplify this to make the point. To continue in business, this company must build a new plant. The plant of Concern B, a competitor, was constructed in 1947 and will not wear out until 1957, so this firm can continue in business without capital outlays in 1952.

If we have the excess profits tax in operation, the first firm may find that the more prudent course, under Mr. Harrod's proposal, is to shrink in size or actually quit business, although there can be no equitable reason for requiring it to do so. Moreover, such a disallowance would tend to work against the more safe or assured type of plant investment and in favor of the risk-taking kind. Let us suppose that a one-dollar investment in an asset with a ten-year life, depreciated one-tenth each year normally, is subject as to the income it produces to a marginal rate of 70 per cent. Suppose that after deducting that tax the net return on the investment is 27 per cent a year (plant and equipment investments often have to show on paper 25 per cent before they will be undertaken by a business concern, owing to a variety of factors, including such things as what the stock sells for on the market and what the risks are). If depreciation is completely disallowed, they would net 20 per cent, a decline of less than 30 per cent.

On the other hand, let us take a more conservative or safer type of investment which the concern is willing to make, even though it nets only 12 per cent on the dollar investment after the present tax structure. Then let us disallow depreciation, assuming still the 70 per cent marginal rate, and we get a return of 5 per cent. Now, it is the same absolute shrinkage, obviously, from 27 to 20, and from 12 to 5—that is the reflection of the 70 per cent rate—but the percentage reduction in investment is far greater in the 12 to 5 per cent drop than in the other.

Perhaps we ought to broaden the question and ask, if we believe investment would not be checked adequately by the checking of consumption through the personal income tax and by checking directly through further increases in corporate taxes, should we then levy a direct tax on investments? There might be a constitutional question involved.

Just one more remark in passing. Mr. Goode correctly pointed out that compulsory lending, sometimes called compulsory saving, presents some grave problems. One of the greatest problems in compulsory lending is that it postpones until after the war the settlement of the pattern of sacrifice among the populace. Mr. Goode is quite correct in saying that the actual shortage, the actual refraining from consumption or investment, must be done now. Whether it is you or I or the other fellow who bears the burden is something that depends on the tax system largely, and compulsory lending defers the decision on that until after the war or the defense program.

On the whole, I am inclined to think it is not a good thing to postpone those decisions. I particularly wish to emphasize that this is a misnomer in Item G. We should not say "compulsory saving." Compulsory saving would be extremely difficult to administer. It means the government would compel the individual either to save a stated amount—which would not mean much in some cases, where that much would be saved anyway —or to save more than he would otherwise, which is almost impossible to define. Then there are problems as to what the government would do to the individual if he failed to save the stipulated amount. Compulsory saving on a substantial scale would scarcely be practicable without something like general expenditure rationing.

There is one other point I might make to avoid breaking in on the discussion later, and that is the effect of the income tax on willingness to work. It seems to me to be much more complex a problem than is commonly recognized. I would like to refer this problem to my friends in the labor field who know much more about it. It seems to me every increase in the income tax works both ways at once. By taking money away from me, it enhances the marginal utility of money to me and makes me more eager to go out and seek an extra job and have less leisure. But by promising to take away from me some part of what I do get when I work more, it tends to deter me from doing so.

I cannot see how our present degree of knowledge allows us to say whether another five points on the personal income-tax brackets would, on balance, cause most of us to work more or less. My impression is that, as far as we do know, it looks somewhat like a standoff, at least until one gets to around 35 or 40 per cent on bracket incomes of $3,000–$5,000. Then I would suspect it would have an appreciable effect on overtime, absenteeism, etc.

CHAIRMAN BLUM: Professor Shoup addressed most of his remarks to Item II of the outline. Professor Goode likewise addressed most of his remarks to that question. Professor Goode started out, however, by calling attention to Item I, taking the position that he thought we would be doing well enough if we balanced the budget without striving for a budgetary surplus.

This morning, Professor Harrod took the other position under Item I, saying he thought that the goal of fiscal policy on this occasion might properly be an overbalanced budget, or a budget surplus. It might be appropriate for us to follow the questions as they appear on the outline, considering, first, Item I and then turning to Item II.

I might also point out that, in a sense, the questions or points listed under Item I, A, are reasons for balancing a budget or going further in getting a budgetary surplus, while the questions in Item I, B, might be viewed as reasons either for not balancing the budget or for not going further into getting a budgetary surplus. Does anyone wish to be heard?

MR. GAINSBRUGH: As I warned the chairman at luncheon, I would propose at least some discussion of the problem of the level of government expenditures before we move on to the next field, the mechanics of taxation. I want to dissent, too, from handcuffing ourselves to a quantity theory discussion and from considering taxation so narrowly as an adjunct on monetary and credit policy as our agenda suggests.

I think we, as a people, grow steadily more concerned over the fiscal position in which we now find ourselves currently. There is a ground swell of citizen, business, and even occasional labor reaction, too, to the levels of government expenditures to which we find ourselves committed. Total government expenditures rose from ten billion dollars in 1929, of which federal expenditures were only two and one-half billion, to eighteen billion dollars in 1939. At that time federal expenditures had reached nearly ten billion and exceeded state and local spending. In 1949, a year of semipeace, the sum of all public spending approached sixty billion, and the contemplated level of government expenditure in the fiscal year immediately ahead of us is about a hundred billion dollars. Federal expenditures alone in fiscal 1952 would fall between eighty and ninety billion dollars, assuming the current defense program continued.

REPRESENTATIVE CELLER: Does he mean to include such things as pensions, etc.?

MR. GAINSBRUGH: Yes, I do. I will refer to that subsequently.

This time trend also includes a growth in the influence of the state over our citizenry which traditionally accompanies a rise in government expenditures. Millions of people have been placed on government payrolls, so that becomes one immediate area of influence. The second area of influence is found in the market place. As the purchases of goods and services by the government are ever widened, business first seeks out government as a customer and then relies upon it more and more to provide an outlet for its products. The third area of influence is the increasing resort to the federal government as a source of purchasing power, particularly for payments for nonproductive services. In that area I include the transfer payments that millions of individuals are receiving from the government for past military service or as welfare payments. The final area of influence is the growing concentration of assets in the government. The latest wealth estimates show that, by 1948, government already had within its possession some two hundred billion dollars of assets (including military items), or fully 20 per cent of the nation's total wealth.

How far can or should we go with the government as the prime originator of income, the greatest customer for goods, the largest holder of assets? If this trend continues, can we avoid reaching a position in which we have vested in government economic controls for all time rather than just in periods of crises alone?

I think perhaps that opens up some of the lines of discussion that I referred to at luncheon with the chairman. One final comment. The program upon which we are now embarked is not short run. We are told increasingly that we will be exposed to these drains not for a year or two but possibly over a decade or more. How much, as a people, should we, or are we prepared to, spend for defense and for related purposes? Senator O'Mahoney's committee has been concerned with that and has made some positive recommendations in that connection. I therefore suggest that in connection with our discussion of the role of fiscal policy, we ought not to turn immediately to the question of the mechanics but ought first to give serious consideration to the levels of public spending and their implications.

CHAIRMAN BLUM: If I may say so, the subject of the general level of government expenses will be considered at length in connection with the long-run consequences of the mobilization program, and that has been scheduled for the fourth session, so I will rule that out of order, and we will come back to it.

SENATOR O'MAHONEY: May I ask a question at this point, so as to get in the thinking of the group? Are you referring solely to federal government expenditures, or are you taking into consideration the very great increase of state and local expenditures at the same time?

MR. GAINSBRUGH: I am referring to both, but there can be no question about where the increase has been most pronounced in the past quarter of a century. It is definitely in the federal government section.

SENATOR O'MAHONEY: The extensive increases of federal expenditure have been on the war side much more emphatically than on the civilian side, whereas, so far as state government expenditure goes, it has been much more upon the civilian side.

CHAIRMAN BLUM: We will return to that topic.

MR. HAZLITT: Am I to understand that the chairman has ruled out the discussion of the level of expenditures while retaining the whole question of a balanced budget? The level is regarded as an irrelevancy?

CHAIRMAN BLUM: Not regarded as an irrelevancy; it is regarded as a topic to be discussed more properly in connection with another session.

MR. HAZLITT: Would it not make the rest of the discussion more real, and should not that question be raised now? If you try to separate the level of expenditures from the question of whether a balanced budget is desirable, and how it shall be financed, then you make the second part of the discussion unrealistic and academic.

CHAIRMAN BLUM: We felt not. We felt that the present level of expenditures would be maintained, or, for the purpose of this discussion, some other level could be assumed, and we could get to the question of which level is the more proper one at our subsequent session.

MR. HITCH: I was just going to make the point that I think you were making. I think it is extremely important, and I missed this in a great deal of the discussion this morning, that we have a pretty clear idea what level of expenditure we are talking about, and what we are assuming about the increase in the rate of defense expenditure in the future. I think that the controls, the efficacy of fiscal and monetary measures, will be very sensitive to our assumptions about this level, and about the rate of buildup.

It is not very clear just what the appropriate assumption should be. The plans which have been made public are not sufficiently definite. They cover a very wide range. We certainly cannot assume that the present level continues, because this is, as far as defense expenditure is concerned, not very much greater as yet than the level that we have had for the last three years. We are all thinking of something substantially greater than that, but I do not know how much greater.

CHAIRMAN BLUM: Mr. Hitch, to the extent of the discussions today hinging on the level of expenditures and of its increase that can be stated, and the discussion based on that assumption, I see no other way of separating the two elements and having an orderly discussion on both.

MR. HITCH: I agree. I am just asking for greater clarity of assumption about the level in our discussion of the fiscal and monetary measures.

CHAIRMAN BLUM: Mr. Harrod, did you have any comments you wanted to make in connection with Mr. Goode's opening remarks?

MR. HARROD: I made one or two notes for some brief points.

First, you say I have been wishing a budget surplus. I do not wish a budget surplus. I think very heavy taxation is harmful, and we should avoid it. All I was saying this morning is that a budget surplus is necessary unless we have also other methods of thinning out investment expenditure; it is not good enough to say that we will stop an inflation by "paying as you go," meaning by that an exactly balanced budget; unless we have other methods of thinning out expenditures in the civilian sector, we would have to have a budget surplus. I do not mean I desire that. I think it is necessary if we do not have other methods.

Second, the effect on investment of higher taxes—I am not sure that I do not somewhat disagree. It is said that the investment would be less because consumption would be less. But, after all, the government is going to spend the money we pay in taxes instead of our spending it, and that will equally give rise to certain investment requirements.

If the troops have to have uniforms made, etc., there will be investment requirements there. I do not see that the transfer of spending from the citizen to the government will affect the aggregate of investment requirements, and my contention was that, while we have to have new investment, and lots of it, for the defense effort, the rate of investment for civilian requirements should be thinned out as a contribution toward the release of resources.

Well, then, having said that, I ought to deal very briefly with the questions that were put to me. I would be inclined to put my plan for decelerating amortization in effect over the whole field where the capital expenditure was not deemed an important contribution to defense. I am sure there would be all sorts of administrative difficulties, but I think it is very important—and it is a thing we ought to stress—that the administration must be very vigilant to be sure that expenditures do not wrongly claim the credit of being defense expenditures when they are not truly so.

To the question as to whether the allowance on depreciation would be lost forever or postponed, my idea was that it should simply be postponed, not that it should be lost forever. You may say, "Well, then, it won't be a great deterrent," but I think it would be, for two reasons. One is the obvious reason. People are not so eager to do something if they do not see the money coming back to them for some time. They may be led to postpone it until they can have the bird in the hand. Also, there might be an actual permanent loss to the extent that we hope things will move into a better phase after two years and the rates of taxation may go lower then. In that case, by the post-ponement plan, the amount that the government would even-tually contribute to the investment would be less.

Third, about the plant to wear out in 1952—well, no doubt there is a certain amount of inequity there, but is there really a fixed year in which the plant wears out? Do not we want, rather, to say, "If this plant were installed in 1942, it can prob-ably be made to do until 1954 or 1955"? There may be a slight inequity there, but there is bound to be some inequity when a new big burden comes upon us, and we are all differently placed in regard to this burden—there cannot be exact equity. I sug-gest if it has the effect of making a man say, "I will defer my replacement from 1952 to 1954 and make do not quite so effi-ciently," that will be all to the good.

Finally, there is, no doubt, a very tricky point on the differ-ence between high-yielding and risky investment and safe and lower-yielding investment. Would not the burden be some-what commensurate there, since, the amortization being low, the allowance on the amortization would be correspondingly reduced?

I think that is all I have to say in reply to the points that have been made.

CHAIRMAN BLUM: Turning then to our outline, does anyone want to speak to the point which is made under Item I, A, 1, namely, budget surplus, because it would permit adherence to the easy-money policy of low interest rates?

MR. HALEY: Mr. Chairman, if I may adopt the precedent of not speaking to the question. . . .

CHAIRMAN BLUM: Precedents, in the plural.

MR. HALEY: It seems to me that the subsidiary questions under Item I, A, have the disadvantage right down the line of suggesting that we are here faced with a choice between monetary policy and fiscal policy. This, it seems to me, is a mistake. I think we are all agreed, as was pointed out in the summary of this morning's discussion, that a monetary policy with more backbone to it than we have had is very desirable. I suggest, also, that it would not be difficult for us to agree that

that monetary policy will need to be supplemented with a fiscal policy. These are not alternatives.

Now, with reference to Item I, A, some groups favor a budget surplus. Is it on the basis that in some sense we have to choose between monetary policy and fiscal policy? I am now speaking to the question. I would say, "No; this is not the basis." The argument which possibly would favor a budget surplus, it seems to me, is the view that some of us hold, as was evidenced this morning. As a practical matter, there are some of us who feel that monetary policy cannot be expected to carry the whole burden under present circumstances of defeating the inflationary effect of these large liquid balances, which we have inherited from the last war. These large liquid balances, these holdings of government securities in the hands of consumers and in the hands of business firms that can use these funds for quick investment if they want to, make it extremely difficult effectively to apply monetary policy.

Now, if monetary policy cannot be expected under these special circumstances to do as much as it otherwise might, and if we really are going to have something other than inflation— if we are going to have stable prices—then it seems logical that we might have to have something more than just a balanced budget. That, it seems to me, is the argument for something more than a balanced budget, although I would immediately agree with Mr. Goode that, as a practical matter, we would do well to shoot at a balanced budget; and if we got that, at the present contemplated level of federal, state, and local expenditures, which I am assuming, we would be doing pretty well.

Mr. MULLENDORE: For fear that silence might be taken as agreeing here to something on which I do not agree, I should like to state that I do not agree with the whole basis of this conference thus far in that it would seem to rule out reliance upon the free market and the penalties and rewards of a free market as the best controls available. I am particularly impressed, as I hear the discussion of the difficulties arising out of the proposed artificial controls, with the fact that in each case the difficulties thus arising would be solved by a resort to the time-tried and proved free market, which we are here apparently ruling out. I think that, in all our discussion, at least we should have in mind that we are comparing basically the desirability of a managed economy and controls with the controls of a free market and not assuming that the controls of a free market are not effective.

REPRESENTATIVE CELLER: May I ask you what generation you are speaking about?

MR. MULLENDORE: This generation.

MR. GOODE: Do I understand you to say that taxes are inconsistent with a free market?

MR. MULLENDORE: The question Mr. Gainsbrugh raises is directly involved, if we are talking about a free market. Let the question of the level of government expenditures be determined upon what can be taxed out of the people without the interjection of artificial purchasing power and borrowing. The use of taxation as a means of social reform and as a means of implementing fiscal policy, rather than taxation for revenue, is but another example of substituting controls for a free market. Of course, we must have taxes in a free market as well as in a managed economy.

MR. DIRECTOR: The only observation I want to make is directed to getting Mr. Haley to say more than he has said. As I understand his point, it is contained under Item I, A, 3. Expenditures may increase because of the large volume of liquid assets. In this event is it better to meet the consequences by a budget surplus or by a contraction in the supply of money? I hope Mr. Haley will indicate more fully why he prefers a budget surplus to a contraction in the supply of money. Is his conclusion only that we are not likely to use monetary policy, and therefore we ought also make use of a budget surplus?

MR. VINER: Would not a budgetary surplus be one of the means of contracting the supply of money?

MR. DIRECTOR: It may be used as a means of contracting the supply of money. Even so, what are the advantages of using tax collections rather than open-market operations?

MR. HALEY: I would undertake to answer Mr. Viner's question with a "Yes." I think it would have that effect. That is one reason that I am not sure that the questions are put here as all of us would like to see them. The suggestion somehow is borne out here in question after question that anybody who resorts to a strong fiscal policy must be doing so because the alternative of a strong monetary policy has been rejected, which, I think, is a mistaken premise on which to proceed. That is really my point. It seems to me that, in view of existing balances, we will need a strong monetary policy, and we will need as strong a fiscal policy as we can obtain if we are going to check inflation. They are not alternatives in my mind. Even Section 3, although it comes close to the point, it seems to me, in part misses the point, as Mr. Viner implies.

MR. KESTNBAUM: I would like to support what Mr. Haley has said and go just a little further. It seems to me that checking inflation will require the use of monetary measures, fiscal measures, a very strong savings program, real leadership on the part of the administration in the line of self-discipline, and a great many other things, because the basis for inflation is very great. I agree that to assume that we have our choice of remedies undercuts this whole discussion. It seems to me that what we ought to be thinking about is to what degree each of these measures can be used and whether the aggregate of all these measures really can keep us from incurring further inflation. The real question is: How far can each of these be effectively used, and what do they all add up to?

MR. FELLER: What I wanted to say has been said now twice, and I think I might suggest to the chairman that we discussed the head side of the coin this morning, and now we are discussing the tail side. We are going to keep talking about monetary policy until we forget about putting questions in terms of all other controls. The discussion will remain a discussion of monetary controls from the beginning to the end. I suggest that all the questions under Item I, A, are questions which are really of that nature and that the progress of the conference would be accelerated if we would get to the problem of assuming that something must be done other than monetary control and ask ourselves what must be done and how it should be done.

MR. FRIEDMAN: I just wanted to say that, unless we discuss the issue of how much we do, there is nothing to discuss. If we are going to say that we must do as much as we can on the monetary and on the fiscal side and as much as we can on every other side, then there is no problem.

MR. BLOUGH: Is that so?

MR. FELLER: If we assume that you were right this morning and that we can solve the problem with monetary controls, then it is true there is no point in discussing anything more. The whole purpose of the further discussions must be on the necessary assumption that we cannot do the whole job with monetary policy.

MR. FRIEDMAN: I believe you are misstating the discussion this morning. You will recall the discussion included some assumption about fiscal policy. The statement was repeatedly made that, given a reasonably adequate fiscal policy, it would be possible to supplement it by a monetary policy. We are coming to the fiscal policy side, and once again fiscal policy cannot do it alone. I think we would agree that there is no fiscal policy that can do it alone.

The fundamental issue before us is: What are the effects of these two? Ought we to rely on a fiscal policy completely? If we are going to keep within the framework of preventing inflation, then we do have, to some extent, an alternative. It is only as we take inflation as an alternative that these questions become pointless.

MR. ACKLEY: I think I would like to have the right-hand side of it.

MR. BRUBAKER: What about the area of direct controls?

CHAIRMAN BLUM: That is the third session.

MR. BRUBAKER: Do you not think you are putting us in the position, the way the discussion is now going, that everybody is going to feel he has to make a statement on the question to protect some reasonable position? Maybe the time has been reached in this democratic process for the taking of a hand vote to see how many people think we need a lot of fiscal policy, and how many think we need a lot of monetary policy, and how many think we need a lot of both, and how many think that both of those things together are not enough.

I happen to agree with my good friend Dr. Haley and several others in the formulations they have just made, but I see no point in each of us getting up and saying that. If we do not do something, we leave the impression that there is still a very substantial body of opinion here that thinks we have an alternative to direct controls. I do not think we do.

MR. ROSTOW: Mr. Chairman, can we add an unpleasant note of reality to this discussion? We have been talking so far about how desirable it would be to have a balanced budget. Of course no one would doubt, from the point of view of stabilization policy, that it would be very desirable to have a balanced budget, and I think we have been somewhat misled by the fact that so far, since the outbreak of the war in Korea, by a variety of accidents, mainly the inherent difficulty of spending large sums of money, we have had a balanced budget. But I, for one, do not think we are going to have a balanced budget very long, and I doubt very much whether any conceivable rate of taxation will be imposed that will match the level of military expenditure that seems to be coming. I think, therefore, that we might discuss this problem not on the premise that fiscal policy will attain a balance or more than a balance, a surplus, but on the premise that we are going to be running a fairly consistent cash deficit in about six months and from there on for some time.

MR. HAZLITT: I think it would also add a note of reality to the discussion if we remembered that, in spite of the fact that we have had a budget surplus, we have, nonetheless, had inflation, and at a minimum that proves that a balanced budget or a budget surplus is not of itself sufficient to halt inflation.

MR. BRUBAKER: Amen.

MR. FELLER: Mr. Chairman, I suggest then, in the limited time available to us, we all recognize that it will be a problem to balance the budget. Whether it can be done or not in the future—there is a real subject of discussion not in the question of desirability of doing it, or to what extent, but to get down to the topics listed here which talk about the ways of doing it, and that is beginning with Item II, which are the real questions. Whatever the view as to the relative merits of the thing, there is a problem of raising additional revenue now and the impact on the economy of such measures.

CHAIRMAN BLUM: Our commentator and interim summary expert for this afternoon's session will be Mr. Stein. Before we move off Item I to Item II, we might hear from Mr. Stein.

MR. STEIN: One thing revealed by the discussion so far is a desire by a great many participants to discuss questions that are not on the agenda for this afternoon, especially the level of government expenditures and the possibility of cutting the budget.

On the question which was on the agenda—namely, the balance between receipts and expenditures—there seemed to be general agreement. The desirability of at least balancing the budget was accepted by those who spoke. No one urged deliberate creation of a deficit in the kind of situation we now face. Reference was made to the desirability of a surplus but somewhat wistfully, as if that was too much to expect. There seems to be recognition of some kind of limit to taxation which prevents the achievement of a surplus when the budget is very large. But the nature of this limit has not been analyzed. Do considerations of incentive and equity set a limit to taxation short of what would be desirable from the standpoint of stabilization policy? Or is it accepted as a fact of political life that legislators just never do enact enough taxes when the budget is large? I think it would be important to be more explicit about the location and nature of the limit to taxation. Acceptance by economists of vaguely placed and ill-defined limits to taxation encourages legislators in their natural reluctance to raise taxes.

MR. THOMSON: I think there is a positive statement on the agenda that deals with almost every question that is coming up here.

CHAIRMAN BLUM: Before passing on to Item II, I would like to suggest that, if any formulations, statements, or propositions as to what we discussed in connection with the items that we thought we discussed under Item I will be submitted to us, we will try to fit them in at one of the later sessions. With that, we can move on to Item II to get the framework and background set forth.

REPRESENTATIVE CELLER: You have offered a challenge to members of Congress present here today. Congress is more apprehensive to the dangers of inflation. I do not think the members of the Congress should let this challenge go by without saying that members of Congress are no more or less apprehensive of the dangers of inflation than the Treasury and the Reserve System. We mean by inflation high prices and ever increasingly higher prices. I would say, and I am sure the members of the upper chamber who are here this afternoon will agree with me, that practically all our waking hours are involved with importunities from constituents from far and near and with bitter complaints about the high cost of living and their inability to meet with the take-home pay the family budget requirements. And, in addition thereto, these same constituents who complain in that direction also importune and bring every kind of pressure to bear upon us to widen benefits under social security, to provide for defense housing, and to provide for more and better pensions and for more and more government spending.

This being a democratic government, we naturally must respond. It is very difficult and takes a great deal of courage to say "No." You can theorize all you wish around this table, you can write all the books you want on the theory of fiscal policy, monetary policy, price control, but it will all be upset by the Congress, not because Congress wishes to upset your theories, but because we are a representative government and the members must be responsible and responsive, reasonably, to the public will.

With this increase of the level of spending which has been alluded to, it is difficult to balance the budget for long, and therefore it is difficult to respond to these theories. I listened attentively to all the discussions this morning, but I failed to see or hear a note of practicality. You have not been pragmatic, and I hope the discussion which will ensue will be a bit so.

I have a great respect for our friend Mr. Burgess here, and he says, "Yes, there should be voluntary controls by way of fiscal policy, controls by way of controlling prices." There is some measure of control in monetary policy, but I think he takes the position that bankers are somewhat sacrosanct and that they should not be controlled as labor is controlled, as merchants are controlled in their sale of commodities, that is, by regulation or law.

I cannot see that, Mr. Burgess. That is like plugging the holes in the barrel but leaving the big hole, the bung hole, unplugged. I cannot for the life of me see how you control the price of a commodity; you control the price of human endeavor that goes into the fabrication of that commodity or the sale of it, but you do not control the price for the money used by the manufacturer or that the fabricator borrows to enable him to make that commodity. You leave that end open.

If we leave any end open in the matter of control, whether it is fiscal or monetary or physical, we have the hole in the dike, and we are bound to have an inflationary influence which is finally damaging. There again, while that is not in line with my first premise about pragmatism in economics, I could not let the occasion go by without challenging your statements this morning with reference to considering bankers as a separate class, as being, shall we say, sacred cows, and that the public should rely upon their voluntary agreements.

I happen to be a tiny banker myself, strange as it may seem, Mr. Burgess. I am a director of a small bank. I am general counsel for that bank. But I know that our money gravitates to where it will give us the greatest amount of interest, and all voluntary agreements be damned. We just do not abide by them. That is the sum and substance of it. Maybe your bank is different because, the larger it gets, the more morality it gets; I don't know.

MR. BLOUGH: Before you leave the question of the balanced budget, I would be very happy to know whether I am to understand that, of the fifty or seventy people or thereabouts in the room, there is not a single one who believes that it would be better to have a deficit than to have either a balanced budget or a surplus. I hope that is correct, but I would like to put the question to see whether there will be an answer in the negative.

MR. FRIEDMAN: I will be the sacrificial sheep. I do not think you ought to have a completely balanced budget, because I believe, contrary to Mr. Haley and some of the others, that the range of feasible maneuver in the area of monetary policy is even greater than it is in the area of fiscal policy so far as its effects on incentives and so far as the equity distribution of the burden is concerned. So that, while I very strongly urge that we ought to avoid inflation, I would feel that the proper formula for this is a minor budget deficit. I do not want to argue that we could have a very major one, but, just in order not to let Mr. Blough get his unanimity, it seems to me that a minor budget deficit associated with a tight enough monetary policy to offset its influence on the level of prices would be my answer.

MR. BRUBAKER: How much would you suggest?

MR. FRIEDMAN: All I mean to say is that a deficit of a few billion dollars is one that can be managed easily enough by monetary policy and that it has certain advantages.

MR. GOODE: Mr. Friedman, do we understand that you feel there are certain circumstances under which you would regard it as not gravely wrong to have a deficit? Would you actually favor it for the present?

MR. FRIEDMAN: I am sure I would favor it under some circumstances. It depends on how much we have to push taxation. As of the very moment today, I do not think there is a necessity for it, but, as we push taxation a little more, I would see some positive advantage in such policy.

MR. HITCH: I would like to ask Mr. Friedman whether he is talking about a military budget of the order of about thirty-five billion dollars or a military budget of the order of eighty billions. I quite agree that, if it is thirty-five billions, there is a good deal of room here for maneuver and for choice. I would be very much inclined to doubt it, looking at the political practicalities of the situation, if we have a military budget of eighty billions.

MR. FRIEDMAN: I am not sure what Mr. Hitch means by "political practicalities." I very much doubt the political practicality of preventing inflation with a budget of eighty billions. But if we were to assume that inflation can be prevented. . . .

MR. HITCH: That is my point.

MR. FRIEDMAN: That may well be, but in so far as there is a question of choice, it seems to me this is at least as practicable as the other.

MR. HITCH: But our choice is at the lower levels.

MR. FRIEDMAN: That may well be.

Senator O'Mahoney: I am glad that Mr. Hitch raised this point. There is no sense in talking about budgets or deficits unless you have some idea what the cost of the mobilization program is going to be.

Any discussion to be fruitful has to be based on a stipulated set of facts or assumptions. May I suggest that we take those presented to us by the government rather than some fifty or sixty possibly equally plausible sets of alternative assumptions. The important question is: Can the government achieve what it states it proposes to do? Mr. Wilson, director of the Office of Defense Mobilization, has suggested that it can, provided something like, though not in excess of, 20 per cent of the national income is diverted to military production. For a noninflationary mobilization program which will demand not to exceed 20 per cent of the national income, a balanced budget would seem to me to be a reasonable requirement. Of course if we were launched on a military program comparable to that of World War II, our program and assumptions would have to be utterly different.

Before there can be any reason or logic to any conclusions drawn from this discussion, those who participate must make up their minds about what degree of government spending they are talking about. Since inflation is a general question affecting the cost of living as well as the cost of armament, we must make up our minds, for example, concerning the extent to which the cities, counties, and states of the United States should continue to engage in spending for welfare purposes.

The state of New York and the state of California, to cite but two instances, have state budgets now that are far beyond anything in their history. Yet we hear no talk about state spending; we hear talk only about federal spending. An examination of the budget will show that most of the federal spending—indeed as much as 85 per cent of total federal expenditures—is directly war-connected and has nothing to do with social programs against which most of the critics of federal spending are really directing their fight.

Mr. Viner: Do you include the pork in the veterans' program in that category?

SENATOR O'MAHONEY: Let me ask you, sir, to come to Congress and get some of the critics of federal spending to point out the pork in the veterans' program. When the Veterans Administration was established, and again when legislation for the payment of pensions and medical benefits to veterans was enacted, the bill as introduced in the Senate bore the name, as I recall it, of every member of the Senate.

My files are full to the bursting point with letters from leading financiers and taxpayers demanding, first, that the budget be balanced and all this terrible spending be stopped and demanding, second, that war plants be established in their communities.

MR. VINER: Nobody has ever claimed that the path of the statesman is an easy one.

MR. MINTS: Would you not really like, however, to have some guiding theoretical principles that would more or less aid you?

SENATOR O'MAHONEY: I spend most of my time trying to get guiding theoretical principles.

MR. FELLER: Restating a proposition which I have stated, it seems fairly reasonable to assume that our total program will be different, depending on the assumptions of different levels of military spending. But, whatever the level of military spending that is now reasonably to be anticipated, we will have a problem of raising considerable additional revenues by additional taxation; and this is so whether we desire a small deficit or a small surplus or a balanced budget. Therefore, we get down to the real problems involved in imposing that taxation so as to exert the type of effect we want to have on the economy. We can talk about the free market, as one gentlemen did, but obviously every tax has some effect on business and economic decisions, and every time we put on a tax we impede what we would call a really free market. Since we have taxes and we are going to have taxes, we have to talk about which way we want to impede the free market.

CHAIRMAN BLUM: With that as a springboard we will turn to Item II, A, "What tax increases would be most appropriate for a noninflationary mobilization program? The personal income tax." Does anyone wish to speak to Part A of Item II?

MR. HENDERSON: I would like to raise the question of definitions here. I have in mind particularly rewards for services which today can be translated into capital gains. First, we have the development and sale of a business, sale of a single invention, sale of a single book, stock options for executives, and those rewards are taxed on one basis. Rewards for services that cannot be tied up with a capital gain or capital increment are taxed on another basis. What is the economic effect of this situation, first on incentive and war mobilization, and, if we are talking about increases in personal income tax, do we include both or do we consider that we are going to redefine the subject?

MR. GOODE: At the risk of raising a very controversial point, I would just answer that in the short way. As far as I am concerned, all of those things you mentioned are personal income and ought to be taxed like other personal income. That is a categorical and dogmatic answer. I do not know how important they are quantitatively in the whole picture as far as our economic problem of controlling inflation is concerned. I think they have considerable importance in so far as the equities of the distribution of the tax load among individuals is concerned.

MR. SHOUP: I would like to add that there seems to be an inclination in some quarters to say that this is not the time to plug the loopholes in the income tax; we are too busy raising revenue. To my mind, that is about the most fallacious reasoning that I have heard. If there is any time to plug the loopholes and to remedy the injustices, this is certainly it; and even though in some cases the measures involved may not mean much in terms of absolute amount of revenue, still the effect on taxpayer morale and on administrative efficiency may be powerful; and surely at a time like this that is important.

To be specific, we should increase greatly this absurd maximum rate of 25 per cent on capital gains to decrease the disparity between capital gains and so-called regular income. We should also, in my opinion, make other changes which would include elimination of the present ability of oil companies and others to deplete their properties 100 per cent and 100 per cent and 100 per cent ad infinitum with no stopping point.

We should impose federal taxation on the interest of all future municipal and state bond issues, and we should do a number of other things I will not stop to enumerate here. But I want to state the general principle that this is the time of all times to clean up all those things which have made our federal income tax such an ungainly structure from the point of view of equity and administration.

MR. FELLER: The specific proposals by and large as they are listed in Item II are written on the assumption that we have to have certain new taxes, to which I agree. But I think that one general item that should be included is the question of eliminating the loopholes, not only in the income tax, but in capital gains taxes, depletion allowances, tax-exempt securities, and such matters. I would say that there are other loopholes which also should be considered and seem to be excluded by the categorization here. With regard to the income tax, I should say that not only is an increase in rate necessary but that it is high time that we recognized the desirability of eliminating the split-income provision which was recently introduced into the act and which has the effect of providing a lesser net tax on very high-income brackets, when actually the brackets themselves are as high as they were during the maximum period of taxation during the war.

In addition to that, I think there are other items such as changing of co-ordination of estate and gift taxes so as to increase gift taxes and to avoid the possibilities of tax evasion involved in annual gifts free of gift tax. I think also that problems involved in the collection of taxes are important, particularly of the income tax, involving the withholding of dividends, a proposal which has recently been made and which did not, unfortunately, succeed.

CHAIRMAN BLUM: This is not a conference on improvements in the tax law. I think we ought to consider generally the question of raising more revenue by way of the income tax.

MR. TANNENWALD: May I suggest, in line with what you have said, that we bring this down to a realistic basis. Just as we tried to do on the question of level of expenditure, somebody here ought to state what is the maximum that can be raised by these various changes that we are talking about, either technical or otherwise. I mean that we can only deal with this thing realistically in terms that we have at least ten billion dollars to raise and probably sixteen billion five hundred million, and we can talk all day about these technical changes which are important; but they will not come anywhere near doing the job.

CHAIRMAN BLUM: Will you indicate in a general sort of way the volume of revenue involved in the technical changes and then go on to indicate the magnitude of rate changes, Mr. Goode?

MR. GOODE: I prefer to talk about the rate changes first, if I may. Roughly, we can say that, with something like the present level of national income and the present exemptions under the income tax, we should get about a billion dollars by raising individual income-tax rates one percentage point in every bracket. In other words, if we raise rates by four percentage points all along the line, we get close to four billion dollars. The Treasury estimated a little less than that in its February 5, 1951, statement, but incomes are now somewhat above the basis they assumed for their estimate. So every man can be his own statistician and figure out how much can be raised, depending on how high he thinks rates can go. In principle, it certainly is not out of the question to raise ten billion dollars from the individual income tax with the present personal exemptions. If we cut exemptions, we can raise a good deal more, and I do not think we ought to exclude the possibility of cutting the exemptions.

As regards the technical matters, I think the revenue is hard to estimate with a degree of accuracy that would contribute much to the discussion. In any case, I agree with Mr. Shoup that the main reason for making the technical changes is to increase equity, not to raise revenue. I doubt that these revisions would result in much additional revenue.

MR. HAZLITT: Mr. Chairman, I am a little confused as to the course of this discussion. When Mr. Gainsbrugh raised the question of the level of expenditures, it was ruled out of order. Am I to understand that the level of expenditures is irrelevant?

MR. TANNENWALD: Except that we are faced with sixteen and a half billion dollars right now.

MR. HAZLITT: Then are we to take it for granted that what the administration proposes to do is proper and not criticize it and then merely say how to raise the money?

MR. GOODE: Mr. Chairman, is it improper to consider how we would raise a certain amount of revenue if we found that necessary and desirable?

CHAIRMAN BLUM: I think not.

MR. GOODE: I would hope that we could consider that at this time, and it certainly does not imply that there are no possibilities for altering the level of expenditures. But it seems not impossible to discuss how we would raise ten, twelve, or fifteen billion dollars if we found that advisable.

MR. HAZLITT: If we are going to discuss hypothetical revenues, we ought to discuss hypothetical expenditures. I think that, if one is going to be on a hypothetical basis, the other can be also. All I am asking here is for a little consistency. Mr. Gainsbrugh raised the question of expenditures, and the whole problem was ruled out of order. If one can be put on a hypothetical basis, so can the other. We can also discuss hypothetically how much the budget could be cut if we wanted to cut it.

MR. TANNENWALD: Do you think we could cut it sixteen and a half billion dollars?

MR. HAZLITT: I would not be surprised. If you think it is likely, that is another question.

CHAIRMAN BLUM: The assumption was necessary in order to discuss the problems before us. We later, in the fourth session, will consider in detail how proper or desirable the expenditure is. One can make necessary assumptions about revenue, revenue controls, and revenue needs in order to focus these issues sharply enough to discuss it.

MR. HAZLITT: My only point is that the two ought to be considered together, that they are both part of the same problem, and that it makes the whole problem unreal to rule out any discussion of expenditures.

CHAIRMAN BLUM: Mr. Arnold's suggestion was to have one side of the table discuss one thing, the other side another, and the middle to discuss both together.

MR. BLOUGH: It certainly is not unreal to ask the question,

if we have to raise any given amount—three billion, five billion, ten billion, fifteen billion, or more—whether we get a better anti-inflationary effect by taking it out of income taxes paid by persons with small incomes, or income taxes on persons with large incomes, or the corporate income tax, or the excess profits tax, or excise taxes, or payroll taxes. Surely we have plenty of material there for discussion. The question of the total amount of expenditures is important and is to come up later. It seems to me our problem here should be to consider which methods of taxation give the greatest anti-inflationary impact and why.

MR. GAINSBRUGH: If you look at the materials with which you have been supplied, you get a fairly good answer as to what we might expect from the personal income tax. How far are we currently from the level of taxation that was imposed under a total war? Here we are in a period of a quarter-war, and we are only two or three points below the rate that was effective in a total war.

If we are going to get higher taxes from this point on, we are going to get it in a way that hurts. In the main, we have tapped the easy sources of revenue thus far. We are reaching the point now at which equity considerations become extremely difficult to prevail, and that is particularly true in the case of the personal income tax. We are not far below the rates prevalent at the peak of a war effort, when we had psychological, polictical, and other factors that would lead in the direction of acceptance of an extremely high rate.

From this point on, if we want taxes to accomplish the purposes that we have in mind—to restrain consumption, to restrain investment, to expand production—the source from which more revenue must come increasingly is from the base rather than from the top of the income pyramid. I would be "agin" a balanced budget if it meant that in process of arriving at that balanced budget we would further continue the program of economic and social reform leading toward liquidation of the middle classes.

MR. JEWKES: I would like to say something about a special kind of tax which we have in Great Britain, some of the details of which may interest you. If you are looking for new forms of taxation, the best thing you can do is to look at the countries which have been most successful in putting the screw upon the taxpayers, and I grieve to say that Great Britain is one of those.

We have in Great Britain a purchase tax which I think ought to be looked at carefully if one is anxious to raise additional taxation with a minimum of hardship. Of course, we have long had very heavy taxes on individual commodities. We have very heavy taxes on tobacco and beer. Our commodity taxes do in fact yield us almost as much as our income tax. I am thinking now particularly of a purchase tax, what you call a sales tax, which was imposed during the war and which on the whole, I think, operated surprisingly successfully both during the war and since.

The purchase tax is a discriminating tax. It involves a differential rate on a very wide range of commodities, and it brings in a very substantial revenue. The merits of a purchase tax, as I see it—and for a moment I am putting the case rather more strongly than I think I myself believe it—are precisely those qualities which have already been referred to in one of the papers before us as the defects of the sales tax.

First of all, the purchase tax is regressive, that is to say, people, poor and rich alike, pay the same rate of tax per unit. I think that is a possible advantage at a time like this. There seems to me a virtue in some regressive taxes in systems which otherwise have highly progressive taxation.

Second, the taxation is discriminative. For example, in some cases it is as high as 100 per cent, and that seems to be an extremely useful device for using the taxation system in a period of rearmament when we want to divert resources from the consumers in general to the purposes of the state. So, for example, if we want to discourage the purchase of refrigerators or motorcars, we can put a much higher tax upon those commodities than we would put on the general range of goods. Discrimination can be exercised both as regards raw materials in short supply and in regard to labor; that is to say, we can put higher taxes upon those goods which use up the special kinds of labor which are in short supply in the early stages of rearmament. In fact, one of the most economical forms of taxation—it is a very topical matter I have gathered since I came to this country—is a tax on gambling. That, in our country, brings in substantial funds, easy to collect in the forms in which it has been imposed, and it is imposed at just the points where people are prepared to pay the taxes and where it does least harm to the economy as a whole.

The third advantage, as I see it, of a purchase tax is that it probably has a less serious effect on incentive, and that is a point that we clearly have to look at carefully in a period when we are asking people to put forth greater efforts. It probably has less serious effects upon incentive than the income tax, partly, of course, because the tax is hidden—one can be as cynical as that about it—and although the people are paying higher prices for the goods they have to buy, yet there is a psychological influence in encouraging people to work to get goods.

The fourth advantage of our purchase tax is that it is extremely flexible. I have always had my doubts as to whether it was really necessary to have a full budget only once a year. I think that in certain periods at any rate a quarterly or half-yearly budget may be practicable. But the essence of the purchase tax is that it can be changed almost at a day's notice.

As to the drawbacks of the purchase tax. If it is carried on in normal peacetime, it interferes with the consumer's choice. It puts into the hands of the state the machinery for dictating what people will buy and what they will not buy. There are certain administrative difficulties connected with the purchase tax, such as changes in the value of stocks in shops when the rate of tax is altered. But if you are looking for new taxes, then I suggest the experience in Great Britain in the use of the purchase tax is something that ought to be looked at quite carefully.

My only other point, while I am speaking, is perhaps an entirely frivolous one, but I do suggest that if you are thinking of another good tax, the best kind of tax is a high rate of interest.

REPRESENTATIVE CELLER: I take it that the program of accelerated amortization graded to corporate defense enterprise affects corporate taxes. Would I be in order therefore under Part F of Item II to say something with reference to it?

CHAIRMAN BLUM: Will you hold that until we have moved

off the income tax and general sales tax? I will recognize you then.

MR. HENDERSON: I think Dr. Jewkes may have overlooked something in the nature of direct controls that are available in connection with the prevention of high use of strategic materials. At the present time we have the National Production Authority, which is a rationing authority which has profited by the mechanisms developed in the second World War to an extent that overnight, if it wants to cut back the production of automobiles, it does not need to use the clumsy and highly discriminatory method of a higher purchase price. It just gets out an order, and the papers are full every day of cutbacks.

A perfect mechanism exists, and it is a direct one. By use of the higher rates, we immediately get into pocketbook rationing. A certain number of items are going to be made, and a large number of these on the selected groups are those which are in the family budgets. For example, 24 per cent of all the buyers of automobiles in the last recorded year, which was 1949, were people with incomes of $3,000 or less. A proposal to raise the price enormously would immediately make just a limited number of automobiles available to the higher-income groups, and that violates the very essence of equitable rationing. It immediately says that the fattest pocketbook gets goods which are in need.

MR. JEWKES: I would just like to mention the subject of physical controls which will come up tomorrow, which I am quite prepared to argue at length. Physical controls of the kind that Mr. Henderson is discussing are more discriminatory than the free market.

MR. HENDERSON: Not if we accompany it with a rationing system.

MR. JEWKES: On what basis?

MR. HENDERSON: On the basis of need.

MR. JEWKES: It cannot be done.

MR. HENDERSON: We did it.

CHAIRMAN BLUM: I will rule that discussion out of order.

MR. CORTNEY: I submit that there is very little room left for taxing personal incomes unless we go in the very low-income brackets. All of us are probably familiar with the following fact, that if we tax away 100 per cent of what is left after paying present taxes to those who earn $25,000 or more, we would get eight hundred million dollars.

Gentlemen, if any national emergency is going to be used for the leveling of incomes, I predict that we shall never get out of national emergencies, politics being what they are. Therefore, the only alternative to greater personal income taxes we have is the sales tax, or what Dr. Jewkes calls the purchase tax. I believe, whether we like it or not, that if we want to have something which labor likes to call equality of sacrifice, we shall have to impose the purchase tax.

Gentlemen, I draw to your attention that, since the outbreak of World War II, the low-income brackets are better off after paying taxes by about 27 per cent as compared with the prewar figure, while, if we take the so-called high-income brackets, we will discover that at least for those who used to earn $25,000 their real purchasing power is about one-half even when their income has been doubled since the war. I earnestly submit that there is very little margin left for taxing personal income, and I am afraid that, when we are talking about taxing personal income, we are always thinking of those who earn more than, let us say, $20,000 a year. The only alternative we have is the sales tax.

Mr. von Mises: In dealing with the problems we have been invited to discuss at this meeting, it is first of all necessary to realize that fiscal policies have reached a turning point. In the last decades all nations looked upon the income and the wealth of the more prosperous citizens as upon an inexhaustible reserve which could be freely tapped. Whenever there was need for additional funds, one tried to collect them by raising the taxes to be paid by the upper-income brackets. There seemed to be enough money for any suggested expenditure because there seemed to be no harm in soaking the rich a bit more. As the votes of these rich do not count much in elections, the members of the legislative bodies were always ready to increase public spending at their expense. There is a French dictum: *Les affaires, c'est l'argent des autres* ("Business is other peoples' money"). In these last sixty years political and fiscal affairs were virtually other peoples' money. "Let the rich pay," was the slogan.

Now this period of fiscal history has come to an end. With the exception of the United States and some of the British Dominions, what has been called the "ability to pay" of the wealthy citizens has been completely absorbed by taxes. No further funds of any significance can be collected from them. Henceforth all government spending will have to be financed by taxing the masses. The European nations concerned are not yet fully aware of this fact because they have found a substitute. They are getting Marshall Plan aid. The American taxpayer fills the gap.

In this country things have not yet gone as far as they have gone in other countries. It is still possible to raise an additional two or three or perhaps even four billion dollars by increasing corporation taxes, by excess profits taxes, and by rendering the personal income tax more progressive. But even four billion dollars is only a fraction of what the Treasury needs under present conditions. Thus, too, in this country we are at the end of a period of fiscal policies. In this country also, the whole philosophy of public finance must undergo a revision. In considering the pros and cons of a suggested expenditure, the members of Congress will no longer be able to think, "Anyway, the rich have enough; let them pay," for in the future the voters on whose ballot they depend will have to pay.

Inflation is certainly not a means to avoid or to postpone for more than a short time the necessity to resort to taxes to be levied also from other people than those belonging to the rich minority. If for the sake of argument we leave aside all the objections which are to be raised against any inflationary policy, we have to take into account the fact that inflation can never be more than a temporary makeshift. For inflation cannot be continued over a long period of time without defeating its fiscal purpose and ending in a complete debacle as was the case in this country with the Continental currency, in France with the *mandats territoriaux,* and in Germany with the mark in 1923.

What makes it possible for a government to increase its funds by inflation is the ignorance of the public. The people must ignore the fact that the government has chosen inflation as a fiscal system and plans to go on with inflation endlessly. It must ascribe the general rise in prices to other causes than to the policy of the government and must assume that prices will drop again in a not too distant future. If this opinion fades away, inflation comes to a catastrophic breakdown.

If the houswife who needs a new frying pan thinks: "Now prices are too high; I will postpone the purchase until they drop again," inflation can still fulfill its fiscal purpose. As long as people share this view, they increase their cash holdings and bank balances, and a part of the additional money is absorbed by this increase. But then comes—sooner or later—a turning point. The housewife discovers that the government will go on inflating and that consequently prices will always rise more and more. Then she thinks: "I do not need a new frying pan today; I shall need one only next year; but I had better buy it now because next year the price will be much higher." If this insight spreads, inflation is done for. Then all people rush to buy. Everybody is anxious to reduce his holding of cash because he does not want to be damaged by the drop in the monetary unit's purchasing power. The phenomenon appears which in Europe was called "flight into real values." The knell of the currency system involved sounds.

We have today in this country not yet reached this second and final stage of every protracted inflation. But if the authorities do not very soon abandon any further attempt to increase the amount of money in circulation and to expand credit, we shall one day come to the same unpleasant result.

We have not to choose between financing the increased government expenditure by collecting taxes and borrowing from the public, on the one hand, and financing it by inflation, on the other hand. Inflation can never be an instrument of a fiscal policy continued over a long period of time. Continued inflation inevitably leads to catastrophe.

Therefore, I think, we should not waste our time by discussing methods of price control. Price control cannot prevent the rise in prices if inflation is going on. Even capital punishment could not make price control work in the days of Emperor Diocletian and the French Revolution. Let us concentrate our efforts upon the problem of how to avoid inflation, not upon useless schemes of how to conceal its inexorable consequences.

MR. PORTER: I think the gentleman who preceded me touched upon the question that I wanted to raise with Professor Jewkes, and that is the issue of the noninflationary aspects of the sales or purchase tax. If I may, I would like to put it in the form of a question. Professor Jewkes, has the imposition of those levies resulted in any change in the wage level?

MR. JEWKES: No; if it did so, then, of course, the purpose of the tax would be completely defeated.

MR. PORTER: Therefore—and I would like to hear from some of our labor friends on this—where is the zone of tolerance at which an effective rate for revenue purposes could be developed without having a self-defeating effect and canceling out the noninflationary aspects?

MR. BRUBAKER: If you wish, I would be glad to make a very brief rejoinder on that point. I would like to say, first, though, that I must confess I am beginning to lose all perspective here. I thought that, if there ever was a champion of the use of a budget deficit in this country, it probably was labor and such groups back a few years ago. Now I come here today, and I find that one of the two voices raised in favor of a budget deficit is a champion of business.

On this specific question that you have raised as to the level of tolerance at which labor will accept higher taxes and still work, apparently the people who drew up the proposed discussion questions have suggested that perhaps we have almost reached that level or passed it. I think they are kidding themselves.

You must remember that the question is asked here not in terms of what labor would like. They are asking a question in terms of what labor would take. Well, labor will take an awful lot it does not like—if it feels it has to do so in the national interest. We will take levels of income tax which we do not like and which we do not think are fair or just. If we have to, we can go to the levels of income tax which we paid during the war. You are not going to find labor refusing to work or refusing to take new jobs or refusing to work longer hours or refusing to go to a new labor market if that is necessary.

I think you are talking a lot of nonsense when you suggest those as real alternatives. Just as a practical example, when you raise the income tax for labor, one of the first things labor wants to do in the plant is work more hours so it can earn some more to offset the income tax. Let us not kid ourselves—we will try to get more income if we can. The man in the mill is going to do that. It is not me; it is not President Murray; it is not Mr. Green; and it is not a lot of other people who are going to be campaigning for some way to defeat the nation's tax program. But our people are going to try to earn more, if they can, in order to meet higher taxes, just as a business is going to try to charge higher prices in order to meet higher corporate taxes.

But that is not quite the problem—if you raise it in terms of incentives. You can go to the tax rates you had on income during the war, and we will take it and work. But we will not like it. Particularly, we will not like it unless there are some real adjustments made in it.

We think the income-splitting provision which was incorporated in the tax a year ago was rankly unjust to us and to most of the American people, and before we see the income-tax rate pushed even to the level that is suggested by the Treasury under this new bill, we think the Treasury ought to go back and knock out the income-splitting provision.

Over in the area of the sales tax, I would like to suggest just very simply that we think it is a grossly regressive kind of taxation. I can put the thing a lot stronger than Mr. Henderson did a little while ago and be in full agreement with him. We are staunchly opposed to such a tax, and we will fight it with every weapon at our disposal.

I do not know what some of the people can mean here when they indulge in that gross perversion of simple semantics by suggesting that it brings equality of sacrifice to slap a sales tax or an excise tax on automobiles, for instance, to the level where no worker in the $3,000 bracket could ever buy an automobile, and yet a man who is paying an 85 per cent rate in the $100,000-plus bracket can go out and buy a half-dozen of them. If that is equality of sacrifice, I do not know what the term means.

If we are going to get down to something that makes a little sense to us, we must stick to some kind of a progressive tax system. I do not know that there is a more progressive tax arrangement available to us than the income tax. We have not bucked the income tax. We are in favor of it. We think it makes a hell of a lot more sense than most of the other kinds of taxes that can be suggested.

But in this particular time, when we are faced with raising ten or sixteen and a half billion dollars, depending on whose assumptions are taken, we are not too opposed to most of the program which has been suggested by the Treasury Department. We do think, however, there are certain areas that we have to plug up in order to bring back a little more equity in this tax system. One of those I mentioned is the split-income provision. Mr. Feller mentioned three or four others for you. Certainly, there is literally no excuse in a time like this for the level of profit which can be made from capital gains. How can anyone think it is equitable that if somebody goes out and gambles on the market and cleans up $100,000 he then has to pay only $25,000 as a tax, and yet if he goes out and earns that same amount as a salary, he must pay $75,000 of it as a tax.

Certainly, there are several loopholes that we have to plug. We have mentioned only three or four of them. Unless we do plug them, you are not going to find acceptance of the tax program on the part of our people.

I would like to add just one thing on the sales tax. I had thought that had gone out, in terms of rational justification at least, with the days when I was first reading simple economics. I did not suppose there was more than a handful of people left in the United States who would have the temerity today to stand up and attempt to justify the levying of a sales tax on our people. I will tell you frankly that is one tax we will not take.

Mr. Thomson: I would like to direct a few remarks to some of the questions that are raised here in Item II, as to the most appropriate way to raise taxes in a noninflationary mobilization program. The secretary of the treasury has said that he needs an additional ten billion dollars from tax revenue during fiscal 1952. That is a good figure to start with.

The federal government ought to economize more, but we may not get the economies. With the present inflationary trends, it would not do any harm to raise more revenue than necessary and have a surplus, so I would start with the ten-billion-dollar request by the secretary of the treasury. The Committee on Economic Development program called for a raise in individual income taxes, corporate taxes, as well as excise taxes.

I agree with the suggestion in Item II, A, 2, b. "The argument against such reliance is that an income tax is likely to be made very progressive, and the resulting high marginal rates will maximize the disincentives." The progressive income tax can be carried too far and has reduced incentives in this country. For that reason, CED has recommended that we have a 5 per cent rise in individual income-tax rates after present exemptions and taxes, with the direct intention that we will not maximize the progressive features in that tax.

As to the Item II, B, 1, a, the chief argument for a retail sales tax is that it is not hidden. It also has an advantage in that it can be kept out of cost-of-living figures, whereas a manufacturers' tax might not. Reduction of exemptions has been suggested. CED believes that it is much better to raise excise taxes, one reason being that it gives the individual the right to determine whether he wants to buy the taxed articles and pay the tax, or save his money, as indicated in Item II, B, 1, b.

As to Item II, B, 2, the chief argument against a general sales tax is that it is regressive and discriminatory because it cannot be made comprehensive. I think that is not correct. One of the principal arguments against putting in a general sales tax, either retail or manufacturers', is that we are adding another source of revenue for the federal government which experience shows would not replace other taxes. Another argument is that there are about twenty-eight states that now use a retail sales tax, and we would be duplicating in that field. I do not think that the statement that a general sales tax is regressive is a valid argument.

I would also like to comment on Mr. Brubaker's point about income-splitting. As I understand it, the largest proportion of the population, as well as of income, had or were about to have through state legislation the advantage of income-splitting. The Supreme Court of the United States had decided that the states had the right to do that.

MR. BRUBAKER: That is not true. Most of them did not.

MR. THOMSON: You were faced with a fact and not a theory. To say that the federal government can now arbitrarily wipe out income-splitting in the face of a Supreme Court decision protecting the states' rights to make such a provision does not seem a possibility.

I do not think anybody that recommends postponing the discussion of loopholes if necessary to expedite passage of an anti-inflationary tax bill has any thought of elimination of consideration of the loopholes. CED has said that we ought to enact a tax bill that will help to prevent the inflationary pressure as soon as possible and consider the loopholes later. I would think it was in the interest of every one of us, regardless of whether he is a labor representative or even a banker, to expedite passage of tax legislation that will help to stop inflation.

MR. BRUBAKER: We are in favor of such if you are asking the question.

CHAIRMAN BLUM: Congressman Celler, do you now wish to speak in connection with corporation taxes?

REPRESENTATIVE CELLER: I want to speak on the subject of the accelerated amortization certificate program of the Defense Mobilization Administration. Charles E. Wilson, in his first quarterly report, entitled *Building America's Might,* released April 1, 1951, stated that as of March 16, 1951, 660 certificates have been issued covering a total capital investment of nearly four billion dollars. I was informed subsequent to the release of that statement that applications to the extent of 2,000 more are pending and that the amounts involved are upward of eleven and a half billion dollars. The amounts that have been granted, already amounting to four billion, are about one-half of the total investment of seven billion three hundred million dollars certified in the period covering World War II, when 41,000 certificates were granted. Upon investigation, I find that many of the companies that have already been granted this accelerated amortization status had expansion plans in the mill, as it were, before the difficulties in Korea, and in quite a number of these amortization arrangements the benefits were made retroactive.

The experience of the last war clearly indicated that those thus favored were in the main used for peacetime efforts. They were only apparently used for civilian purposes and in the beginning may have only been used in a modified degree for defense.

I have this idea, and I would like to have it percolate through the mind of you men for advice: Should there not be some renegotiation as to these amortization privileges that are bestowed upon these companies? On paper it might look perfectly proper and feasible to grant these allowances. In actuality, in the future, the situation might seem different; and I wondered whether or not there should not be some method by which the government could recoup in the event that a major portion of these facilities were used or could be used in the future and were intended for peacetime efforts rather than for mobilization purposes.

MR. VINER: I should like to point out that whether or not speeding up depreciation allowances is a concession to the taxpayer depends on whether his income rises or falls in the future or on whether the tax rates rise or fall in the future; many of the speeded-up depreciations in World War II were bitterly regretted afterward by those who were allowed them, because the result was that they deducted depreciation from taxable income in years of low taxes and then had to pay higher taxes over all. To be sure that accelerated depreciation will involve loss to the Treasury, we must be certain that future tax rates will not be higher and that future incomes will not be greater. Neither of these seems to be a necessarily good prediction.

MR. VON MISES: I want to ask a question. What is a loophole? If the law does not punish a definite action or does not tax a definite thing, this is not a loophole. It is simply the law. Great Britain does not punish gambling. This is not a loophole; it is a British law. The income-tax exemptions in our income tax are not loopholes. The gentleman who complained about loopholes in our income tax—he did not refer to the exemptions—implicitly starts from the assumption that all income over fifteen or twenty thousand dollars ought to be confiscated and calls therefore a loophole the fact that his ideal is not yet attained. Let us be grateful for the fact that there are still such things as those the honorable gentleman calls loopholes. Thanks to these loopholes this country is still a free country and its workers are not yet reduced to the status and the distress of their Russian colleagues.

I do not want to assert that our laws are perfect and do not require any amendment. Let us discuss this problem in detail and let us examine every instance according to its merits. But do not confuse the issue involved by resorting to the meaningless slogan "elimination of loopholes."

MR. HENDERSON: I should like to speak to Congressman Celler's question along the line of what Dr. Viner has said.

I had quite a bit to do with the first of the amortization acts. In my opinion, one of the greatest contributions made, if any were made, by the Defense Commission was getting quick construction under way. If we had not been as expanded by the time of Pearl Harbor, we would have been severely crippled in the kind of war we could have carried.

The first question you ask is, "Do you need these expanded facilities?" It may come later—it seems most of the things I would like to talk about were either discussed this morning or are coming in the future—but it seems to me that one of the real questions on inflation is whether or not an expansion of capacity, and particularly at the bottlenecks, without which we cannot have an expanded economy, does not require great incentive.

Now, I would subscribe to the kind of examination that Congressman Celler wants to make as to the purposes. On the other hand, the question that he asked, whether a lot of these facilities will be used in peacetime, is important. That seems to suggest that we ought not to grant the rapid amortization. If they are not used, that justified the amortization. They were completely defense items for the government's own account.

In the second place, however, a real study of what the government's benefit has been from the fast amortization, along the lines of what Dr. Viner indicated, would show that the government has made a real profit, because, instead of the rates receding, they have been advanced, or are going to be advanced again to go with an excess profits tax. In that area the government does get revenue on what it has already granted as a quick amortization. The government is getting very substantial revenue on any facilities that are being used. I would like to say again that, to the extent that they can be used, the country is richer and better off. I think we get into a lot of confusion in this. This grant of rapid amortization is a gift in but a small percentage of the cases, and we can only guess on those when we are at a point as to whether we have to expand or not.

The limit to where we can go, if we had one measurement, is the amount of ore that can be brought into this country, and particularly brought down from the Mesabi Range. If we have a limitation on ore-carrying capacity either from the new sources or from there, then we have a limit on what we can do, and we have automatically added to our inflation potential.

REPRESENTATIVE CELLER: Of course, if the taxes are to be increased, that would be taken into consideration on the renegotiation.

MR. STEINKRAUS: I should like to comment on the question that Congressman Celler raised about this rapid amortization. I think we must not forget that, while we are studying an immediate problem of a defense program, we must also remember the long-range future of this country. If there is one thing that bothered me a great deal during the year when I was president of the United States Chamber, it was this job of job-making opportunities in this country.

There are coming into our economy every year somewhere between 600,000 and 800,000 young people looking for jobs. Those jobs have to be created. They have to be created partly, at least, by industry. The middle-sized and small industries are not too well financed, and if they come along at the time of a defense program and they get a good-sized contract, they are doing a bigger piece of business than they may expect to do after that defense program is over.

Therefore, if, while they have the income, they can rapidly amortize that plant, then they are making a contribution to creating jobs for the future, and I believe it would be a most interesting study to see what has happened to these plants. I think the most regrettable thing would be if the plants built for war purposes were not used later on.

I think it is a very well-established fact that the government does not lose the taxes on that. It simply defers the time when it gets them. Therefore, it helps the middle-sized and small company at a time when they can afford to amortize it at a more rapid rate and gives them first-class facilities when the emergency is over and permits them to take on more of these young people who need jobs. I think that is a true statement of the situation.

Mr. Cox: I have just one more footnote on Congressman Celler's question, and that is in this crisis the question is: Who bears the cost of the facility? In World War II, for example, in the basic commodities like steel, aluminum, and what-not, the government put up a hundred cents on the dollar to build the plant and then disposed of it on the average of thirty cents on the dollar. In this crisis so far, most of the expansion has taken place through this accelerated amortization. When we talk about the taxes, even though they are deferred, if the government is going to put up a hundred cents on the dollar, it has to get the taxes or the money from somebody.

Representative Celler: I would be inclined to agree with you, and I do agree with you on general principles, but the way the thing is working out we find some rather peculiar factors. I have a list of all the amortizations that have been granted, and there are mighty few small ones, Mr. Steinkraus, proportionately. One entity had seventeen applications for seventeen new facilities—not new, simply an extension of old facilities so called —and received accelerated amortizations of upward of 147 million dollars. I should like to question those amortizations and whether or not they were wholly for defense purposes.

Chairman Blum: We will hear from Senator Bennett, and then, owing to the lateness of the hour, we will turn to our summarizer, Mr. Stein.

SENATOR BENNETT: Will you forget that I am a senator and let me step back a time when I was the head of a small family-owned business, which is nearly seventy years old. One of the things that I learned in that position was that you can only completely amortize a given investment once. You cannot keep charging depreciation out indefinitely, and, when you have completely amortized it, you are through. I am not talking about the depletion allowances for mines or oil; that is on a different basis. But the building that our business occupied could only be amortized but once.

Now, I believe that in the end, the federal government would be money ahead if it permitted the owner of the property to set his own amortization rate and let him charge it out when he wanted to, because I believe it costs more for the Department of Internal Revenue to attempt to check tax returns and wrangle with the taxpayer as to whether this is 2¼ per cent or 2½ per cent than, of course, they could possibly recover. Besides, in the last twenty years, the income-tax rate has gone up continually; and every time a fellow hurried up his depreciation, or tried to claim a larger depreciation in order to save tax in a given year, it came up and caught up with him in a year or two.

So, Mr. Celler, these people are not going to cheat the government of any taxes. They may pay less taxes in 1951, but in 1956 they will pay the equivalent of more taxes; and I sincerely believe, as I said before, that if we just threw the whole depreciation matter out of the tax law and let the owner of the property write his own rates of depreciation the federal government. . . .

REPRESENTATIVE CELLER: Will you yield to a question? If what you say is true, why do two thousand, among them the largest corporations in the country, ask for these amortizations if they could amortize over a long period. Why do they ask for a short period?

SENATOR BENNETT: They are as shortsighted as the government.

MR. FORD: Accelerate civilian economy as well as defense—it does not contemplate merely defense plans being accelerated; it contemplates total acceleration.

REPRESENTATIVE CELLER: There is no accelerated amortization on the civilian end of it.

MR. LEVENTHAL: I think it helps them finance their cash requirements for their construction.

CHAIRMAN BLUM: Before turning to Mr. Stein for final summary this afternoon, I would like to announce that we have added a special meeting tonight at nine o'clock here on the subject of the level of government expenditures. The discussion will be led by Mr. Hazlitt, Mr. Brubaker, and Mr. Gainsbrugh.

MR. THOMSON: Are you dropping corporate taxes?

CHAIRMAN BLUM: Yes.

MR. STEIN: This has been a difficult discussion to summarize. A great many points have been made about the tax system by individual speakers, but few of these points have been explored sufficiently to indicate either a consensus or a difference of view.

The sales tax was discussed more than any other tax and mainly from the standpoint of its regressive character. The sales tax was defended by some precisely because of this regressive character—that is, because it would raise substantial additional revenue without the adverse incentive effects of more progressive income-tax rates. The sales tax was opposed by others because of its regressive character—that is, because it would place undue burdens upon the very poor. There was a tendency in the discussion to identify the choice between more and less progressive taxes with the choice between income taxes and sales taxes.

It seems to me that putting the choice in this way overlooks one important fact. There is a lot of room for raising additional revenue through the income tax at the lower and middle sectors of the income scale. Possibly tax rates on incomes above, say, $10,000 are already so high that any increases would have very serious incentive effects; in any case, the amount of revenue that could be obtained is probably not large. But the decision that most of the needed revenue must come from incomes below, say, $10,000 does not require a sales tax unless it has also been decided that the sales tax is a better means to reach such incomes than reducing exemptions and raising rates in the first four or five income-tax brackets.

Selective or discriminatory excise taxes were recommended by some as useful means by which the government could influence the flow of resources in directions favorable to the mobilization effort. There were some opposed to such excises on the ground that they lead to "rationing by the purse." This conference might well give some attention to the implied proposition that "rationing by the purse" is a bad thing. "Rationing by the purse" (i.e., distribution of goods to those willing and able to pay for them) is one of the basic principles on which our economy is organized. The question whether such "rationing" is good is one of the main aspects of the question about the desirability of government price control.

REPRESENTATIVE CELLER: I think my proposition was whether or not there should be renegotiation of the subject, and I did not express any disapproval of accelerated amortization.

IV

THIRD SESSION, FRIDAY EVENING
APRIL 6, 1951

THE LEVEL OF PUBLIC EXPENDITURES

CHAIRMAN DOUGLAS: Members of the conference, my being in the chair is perhaps the most serious misjudgment made by the host. I am not here nearly so much because I once worked in the Treasury, but because I now work for the Law School from time to time, and am a trustee of the University.

This meeting is being held, I think, because it is the feeling of the members of the conference that it was difficult to discuss taxation without more exact reference to the expenditure problem than our own assumptions or than the present budget statements. Tonight I am going to call on several members who have indicated their willingness to make statements on the expenditure problem, and whose views we will all be interested in, before throwing the meeting open to discussion.

Before calling on the first of them, to refresh the recollection of some of us, I will mention the bare revenue and expenditure figures, actual, for 1950, estimated budget message for 1951, and the estimates for 1952. For 1950, receipts as stated in the budget message in January amounted to 37 billion dollars; expenditures, 40 billion 100 million; estimates for current fiscal 1951, receipts, 44 billion 500 million; expenditures, 47 billion 200 million. For 1952, receipts, 55 billion 100 million dollars, without new taxes; expenditures, 71 billion 600 million, leaving a prospective deficit without new taxes of 16 billion 500 million. When I was in the Treasury, it was possible to talk about millions of dollars; you will have to be tolerant of any error on my part.

Mr. Gainsbrugh, would you like to make a statement?

MR. GAINSBRUGH: I would, Mr. Chairman, since I have been asked to do so. I do not know whether to regard this as a penalty for being out of order this afternoon, or whether to view it as encouragement to keep out of order for the rest of this session, since you are giving me a chance to talk on my favorite topic.

In laying out the roles Henry Hazlitt and I will try to fill tonight, I took over the problem of providing the longer-range perspective and some of the underlying problems that have arisen as a result of the long-term trend. That leaves to Mr. Hazlitt the more difficult problem of discussing the current position of government in a defense economy and proposals to deal with the cost of government.

In my comments this afternoon I sketched some of the time trends already apparent in state and private economy relationships. I should like to stress some additional aspects of the problems, now that I have a bit more time tonight.

Our studies at the National Industrial Conference Board, which span at least the last half-century, reveal that the race between government and private economy has steadily been won by government. Very frequently, we encounter the argument which might be labeled: Let's grow up to the size of our government. It is true, so runs the argument, that government is costing us more than it has in the past. But give us a wee bit more time, and we will then have the cost of government in reasonable balance with gross national product or total national income. Our studies for the last half-century reveal the same pattern decade after decade, whether the period be one of war or peace or whether it be boom or depression. When the federal government steps down its rate of spending, as in the twenties, then the state and local governments move in and accelerate their rate of spending. There is no evidence over the last half-century that we have as yet caught up with the demands of government by expanding national output.

That same pattern emerges when we look at the ratio of public debt and national income for the last five decades. I suspect it will also hold for the years ahead, keeping in mind the commitments we have already underwritten for the next quarter-century, not only in terms of social security and related provisions, but even more in terms of pensions and other compensation for past services of veterans and their families.

I turn next from this sequence of comments on past trends

to the question: Why is there foreboding about such a relationship? That question is frequently answered with another question: Is not that what the people want? Is not government thereby being responsive to the people's demand?

Put aside, for the moment, the influence upon the electorate and upon government itself of the political power that accrues as a result of the expansion of the state. My more immediate concern is with some of the broader social and economic problems entailed in this growing reliance upon government, first, as a source of employment, second, as a source of markets, and, third, as a source of income.

Let me give you in statistical form—but I hope quite readily grasped nevertheless—the relationships that emerge quite clearly from an appraisal of our social accounts over time. From 1929 to 1949 the government's contribution to the national income has risen from about 5 per cent in 1929 to 12 per cent in 1939 and to 19 per cent in 1944. I would put the figure at about 12.5 per cent for the year immediately ahead. The use of national income as a base, however, understates the influence of government. The national income concept takes cognizance of government only as an employer. The government's contribution to national income is confined solely to wages and salary paid by government.

Far more revealing is the trend in government as a source of market influence. The government's rising take of goods and services is clearly evident in the ratio of its purchases to total gross national product. This has moved up from 8 per cent in 1929 to 17 per cent in 1949. We estimate a further rise to 22.5 per cent of gross national product for 1951. Here, as throughout, I use "government" in its broadest sense to embrace federal, state, and local expenditure.

I come now to the most pronounced and disturbing trend of the three—government as a source of income to individuals. This may be paid for work performed for government, as interest on government securities, or as pensions and transfer payments. Only 8.4 per cent of all personal income stemmed from government in 1929; 20 per cent of all personal income stemmed from government in 1950.

The final question I would raise is: How far can or should we go in this process? An economy 5 per cent government-influenced and 95 per cent voluntary would, I suppose, qualify as a free economy; an economy of 95 per cent government and 5 per cent voluntary would conversely qualify as a totalitarian or government-controlled economy.

MR. HALE: Even if the employers were various different governments and had no collusion with one another?

MR. GAINSBRUGH: Even if the employers were various different governmental units and had no collusion with one another, so long as the basic source of income—95 per cent of it—was from government, I suggest we would have a government-controlled economy.

MR. HENDERSON: You mean there is compulsion in the thing—that they have to take this business?

MR. GAINSBRUGH: Can we have these questions after?

CHAIRMAN DOUGLAS: All right.

MR. GAINSBRUGH: Within the last ten years our social accounts reveal that we have certainly moved in the direction of a mixed economy, with the government influencing 20–25 per cent of total income. I would suggest further that, when we move up to 40 per cent or more of government influence upon the total structure of the economy, we are already close to, if not at, a controlled economy.

As the government's role in the national economy rises, it finds its financing more difficult. It is relatively easy to gain acceptance of a tax program, at least at the ballot boxes, when a small percentage of the population is asked to bear a heavy percentage of the total tax burden. But, as we move on in the growth of government, we reach a point at which it is no longer easy to pull taxes from a small percentage of the population. We must rely, increasingly, upon a larger and larger percentage of the population. At that point taxes begin to hurt. They hurt the politician in the sense that he can no longer promise high benefits without a growing degree of cost to the bulk of the population. They hurt other sectors of the population in just about the same way through their contribution toward higher prices. They steadily change the character of our way of life, too. An increasing number of individuals shift from one job to another, primarily because of tax consideration.

A popular topic of conversation increasingly is the minimization of taxes. I refer not to tax evasion but to tax minimization. There has been created a whole new fraternity whose primary job it is to educate taxpayers in this respect. There is a challenge to the professional within government to see how rapidly an area of minimization can be closed and to the professional outside government to see how quickly a new avenue can be found.

CHAIRMAN DOUGLAS: Mr. Gainsbrugh, might I suggest that you finish your remarks in three minutes, as we have four or five members in particular that we would like to hear from.

MR. GAINSBRUGH: I would be happy to do that.

In closing, I would like to stress what is now implied in a "pay-as-you-go" policy. Twenty per cent of the national output for defense purposes would mean, in terms of gross national product in 1951, about 60–65 billion dollars for defense purposes alone to be spent by the federal government. An additional 15–20 billion dollars for nonmilitary purposes yields about 80 billion dollars for all federal outlays, with the state and local units still to be counted.

We move, therefore, into the zone of 30–35 per cent of our national output used for governmental purposes. As I indicated earlier, that no longer lies in the voluntary zone, or even in the mixed economy zone, but close to the zone of controlled economy. This is a long-pull program to which we are asked to subscribe. We mobilize not for a year, not for two years, but conceivably for a decade or more. Should we not give serious consideration to how far we can go in terms of long-run commitments for defense and other government spending before we undermine the strength of the voluntary system we are fighting to preserve?

MR. PORTER: I take it you are making an economic and not a military judgment on this.

MR. GAINSBRUGH: I am simply accepting the figures which have been released by Wilson and a front-page story quoting Mr. Truman, I believe it was, three or four days ago, that we would be devoting at least 20 per cent of our total national output to defense purposes.

MR. PORTER: As a necessity or essentiality? Are you commenting on that? Your point is directed, I take it, solely to the economic aspects.

MR. GAINSBRUGH: The other I leave to the military.

CHAIRMAN DOUGLAS: If it is agreeable to the conference, I would like to proceed with several other statements. Before doing so, I should like to thank Mr. Gainsbrugh for what I think is an excellent introduction to the problem in dealing with the growth of big government and the hazards implicit in that growth.

I would like to call attention to the fact that, in connection with our problem of determining the policies to avoid inflation, Mr. Gainsbrugh has indicated that expenditures in the nature of 80 billion dollars may be expected in calendar 1952 rather than the budget figure. Am I wrong in saying that you expect the spending to exceed the budget figure?

MR. GAINSBRUGH: That would be implied.

CHAIRMAN DOUGLAS: That is what I thought. I think one function of this evening's discussion should be to express various views as to what our actual expenditure problem is in fiscal 1952, and remarks as to the following year are also certainly in order. But I believe the purpose of this discussion was largely to have a framework in which to proceed with the conference.

I would like to ask Senator O'Mahoney, if I may call on him, to express his views.

SENATOR O'MAHONEY: Thank you, Mr. Chairman. I am glad that Mr. Gainsbrugh has chosen to pitch the discussion upon this note. It is true that government is spending a larger and larger percentage of the national income. The growth in the power of the federal government has continued at a steady rate for over sixty years no matter what party has been in power, by vote of the majority and the leaders of each of them.

The best way to illustrate what has happened, I think, is to give two or three typical instances.

In 1887, for example, the Interstate Commerce Commission was created by a Congress, one branch of which was controlled by the Democrats and the other branch controlled by the Republicans. The law was passed practically without controversy, and, if I remember correctly, was signed by a Republican President.

Shortly after the Interstate Commerce Commission began operating, some of the railroads became a bit nervous about it. The president of the Chicago, Burlington and Quincy Railroad, a Mr. Perkins, wrote to his lawyer, Mr. Olney, and said, "I wish you would suggest to me a reasonable and practicable plan of repealing the Interstate Commerce Act." Mr. Olney, at that time a prominent attorney in Massachusetts, was later appointed secretary of state by a Democratic President, Grover Cleveland. Mr. Olney replied very wisely, "I would not recommend that you make any effort to repeal the Interstate Commerce Act. In the first place, you probably wouldn't succeed. The law is here to stay. The sum total of your efforts would probably be only to make the law a little bit more onerous from your point of view than it now is. Instead of trying to repeal the law, I suggest that you try to control the Commission."

Just a few years ago, before Senator Barkley from Kentucky became the Vice-President of the United States he introduced a bill to give the federal government the power to control stream pollution. The other sponsor was the senior senator from Ohio, Mr. Robert A. Taft. So the Barkley-Taft Bill was passed, imposing upon the federal government a new responsibility— to spend money to control stream pollution. Why? Primarily because business was growing, industry was growing, and new science and mass technologies were generating process wastes polluting the streams. The Izaak Walton League was complaining that one could not catch fish in the old fishing holes any more and demanded that the government do something about it.

It happened that the Barkley-Taft Bill came under my scrutiny as chairman of the Appropriations Committee subcommittee which has charge of the appropriations for the independent offices of the government. The Bureau of the Budget had sent up its estimate which contained a small appropriation for stream pollution, but there was no appropriation for a laboratory to determine the best means and methods of counteracting stream pollution. The senior senator from Kentucky, Mr. Barkley, now being Vice-President, appeared before my committee and asked for a special appropriation to conduct this Public Health Laboratory. It was purely coincidental, I am sure, that the laboratory was to be built in Cincinnati.

Many years ago I was the secretary to United States Senator Kendrick. He was a big cattleman, and, like all cattlemen throughout the West, he was complaining—I am sorry that Mr. Prince is not here—that the packers and the stockyard operators were taking too big a cut out of the profits of the livestock grower. So he began agitating with a Republican senator from Iowa by the name of Kenyon, and they introduced what was known as the Kendrick-Kenyon Bill to give the federal government the power to regulate the packers and the stockyards. That bill was passed by the Congress and signed by Warren G. Harding. It gave to the secretary of agriculture more power to regiment a particular kind of business than had ever been granted to any official of the federal government up to that time.

I could go down the entire gamut of legislation implementing the growth of federal governmental power, from the Interstate Commerce Commission to the Federal Communications Commission, and could spell out the manner in which these commissions were created under the Constitution of the United States because of the demand of the people for federal regulation to protect the public interest. It makes no difference whether the people are workers or businessmen, they never seem to hesitate to come to the Congress of the United States seeking more regulations (especially upon the other fellow) and more appropriations for themselves.

Such are the forces explaining the growth of government. There is not time to describe the process in detail, but I hope that enough evidence has been indicated to make clear that, no matter what party is in power, the pressure for the expansion of the government at Washington continues steadily. The major reason is simply this: that, as the means of transportation and communication improve, it is no longer possible for the states successfully to regulate big business in the interest of the people.

The budget for 1952 carries an item of 5 billion 900 million dollars to pay the interest on the national debt. The entire budget of the federal government in 1939 for defense, for military operations, for international obligations, for interest upon the national debt, and for all the other activities of the government was 10¼ billion dollars. Thus, today, twelve years later, we are paying as interest upon the national debt more than half of the entire cost of government for all purposes in 1939. Fortunately, the national income is likewise greater.

In discussing the budget, I prefer, Mr. Chairman, to use the cash, or expenditures and receipts, budget figures rather than the administrative or appropriations budget. It is the cash budget, that is, cash expenditures compared with receipts, that more nearly measures the real impact of government upon business and economic conditions.

In fiscal 1950, major national security expenditures amounted to 17 billion 500 million dollars; in fiscal 1951, they increased by nearly 9 billion dollars to 26 billion 400 million dollars. In fiscal 1952, the estimated expenditures will be about 49.7 billion dollars—an increase of 23 billion 300 million dollars. Every penny of that increase is for defense.

MR. BURGESS: Is that the calendar year?

SENATOR O'MAHONEY: No; that is the fiscal or budget year. I am talking about expenditures which will be made during the budget period July 1 to June 30.

MR. STEIN: Does that 49.7 billion include foreign aid?

SENATOR O'MAHONEY: Yes, and that item is a little over 7 billion dollars. It does not include interest on the national debt. It does not include veterans' benefits and payments. These amounted in 1950 to 9.26 billions, but are estimated for 1952 at 5.2 billion. That reduction, of course, is due to the fact that expenditures for training and educating veterans in the schools and colleges of the United States will not be anything like the burden that they were upon the Treasury in fiscal 1950.

Expenditures for all the civil functions of the federal government were 11 billion 8 million dollars in 1950, 11.3 billion in

1951, and are estimated at 11.4 billion for 1952, which figure, under the curious procedures whereby the budget is submitted to us in Congress, includes 1 billion 300 million dollars for the Atomic Energy Commission, which, during a period when we are manufacturing atom bombs and the like, can hardly be regarded as a nondefense expenditure.

Under the heading of defense production and economic stabilization, there comes, I am sorry to say, a request from Mr. DiSalle for about 304 million dollars. Only the other day Mr. Wilson, testifying before the Appropriations Committee in the Senate, was given quite an examination on the question how he happened to be before the committee to sponsor an appropriation request that is so much larger than the appropriation which was estimated at the time the Defense Production Act was passed.

Much more could be added. To those of you who are economic-minded, I want to point out the curious fact that last year there came out of the most conservative committee in Congress, the Senate Finance Committee, the revised Social Security Act which will bring in some ten million people who were never before covered by social security. I think the budget contains about 194 million dollars to cover the increased cost of administration. This is the surprising and interesting thing—two members of that committee, both Democrats, objected to the report of the committee because they said it did not go far enough. A third member, Senator Butler, Republican, of Nebraska, filed the only dissenting report. Neither Senator Taft nor Senator Byrd nor Senator George nor any of the conservative leaders opposed it. They voted for it.

MR. MEYER: How much was added?

SENATOR O'MAHONEY: The additional administrative expenses and the like will amount to 190 million dollars. What the additional payments will be from year to year thereafter I do not know, but in the budget for 1952 there is an estimate for a grant of 1 billion 300 million dollars to the states for public assistance. The same budget contains total grants to the states amounting to 2 billion 800 million dollars. Some of these expenditures are for items such as school lunches, which account for about 84 million dollars; vocational rehabilitation, 23 million dollars; public health, 31 million dollars; federal aid to highways, 500 million dollars.

When we were working this year on our *Joint Economic Committee Report*, I wrote a letter to every governor in the United States: "Please let me know what your suggestion is for the reduction of federal appropriation for federal aid to highways in your state." How many suggestions do you think I got? Without exception they emphatically denounced the suggestion that federal aid to highways could be reduced, at least in *their* state. To cut out that expenditure, they stated, would ruin business.

How, then, can federal spending be cut? Yet it has to be done. It is absolutely imperative if we are going to preserve what we call our free enterprise capitalistic system. What is this capitalism we talk about? In many countries it began as it did here as competitive capitalism. But in some of them it turned into monopoly or collectivistic capitalism, and in one or two areas into state capitalism. The trail is just as clear as this path between the two tables, but we sometimes insist on closing our eyes. We pay no attention.

If we want to cut down federal expenditures, let me emphasize that we cannot do it by crippling the national defense. We cannot do it by repealing present social welfare legislation. We will not be able to muster a corporal's guard at either convention in 1952 to urge the repeal of basic social security legislation, or the Federal Trade Commission Act, or the Communications Commission Act, or any of these laws.

The way to cut down the growth of regulatory agencies in the federal government is to make up our minds that we really want to keep business competitive, that we genuinely want free enterprise, that we want noncollectivistic forms of business to have a real chance. In my judgment, the only way to do that, and it is in the interest of big business that it should be done, is frankly to say: "Well, we will establish a clear line defining the powers of those great aggregations of capital which span the country from coast to coast and which are managed not by their owners but their employees. We the people will lay down in the realm of interstate commerce clear-cut national rules of the game for national business which will preserve a maximum of free competitive opportunity for private individuals to strive for individual honor and property rewards commensurate with that amount of individual ability and effort which each contributes toward building a stronger, more prosperous, cleaner and worthier America."

CHAIRMAN DOUGLAS: Might I suggest that it is getting late.

SENATOR O'MAHONEY: I have taken too much time, and I thank you for the opportunity.

CHAIRMAN DOUGLAS: With respect to the policy problems we are considering, do you think it is too pessimistic of this conference to accept the budget figure of 71 billion dollars for expenditures in 1952? Is it unlikely, in your opinion, that expenditures will be less than that?

SENATOR O'MAHONEY: I will say to you that, unless we stop inflation, the figures are likely to be much more than that, because not only is the cost of living going up but the cost of armament is going up. For example, the Air Force indicated that antiaircraft guns which before Korea cost $160,000 per unit are presently costing $250,000. That is what puts our defense expenditure up.

MR. ROSTOW: I am not clear from Mr. Gainsbrugh's speech how he answered Mr. Porter's question. I understand his comments on the trend of government expenditures, but is he suggesting that military expenditures be cut because of the social risks of a large government budget?

MR. GAINSBRUGH: I think I answered Mr. Porter that I left that to the military to tell us how much we did need. My emphasis would be upon the areas of expenditures that are open other than military.

MR. LAZARUS: May we ask Senator O'Mahoney as to what the total of his cash budget is for fiscal 1952?

SENATOR O'MAHONEY: The total of the estimated cash budget for 1952 is 74 billion 50 million dollars. To those who may be interested in this, you will find that all spelled out on page 32 of the *Joint Economic Committee Report* filed April 2, 1951.

CHAIRMAN DOUGLAS: I would like to suggest that, rather than calling on any other member now, it would be relevant to hear anyone who is of the opinion that the prospective deficit for 1952 may be overstated.

MR. PORTER: Mr. Chairman, a point of information before that. Was Mr. Hazlitt going to address himself to this question?

CHAIRMAN DOUGLAS: I would be happy to have Mr. Hazlitt address himself to it.

MR. PORTER: I understood from Mr. Gainsbrugh that they sort of divided the problem. Mr. Hazlitt may have felt that he was shut off this afternoon. I am sure we would all be very interested.

MR. HAZLITT: Thank you very much, Mr. Porter. In view of the lateness of the time, I will make my comments very brief. My concern this afternoon was to find nearly all the members discussing revenues and paying no attention to expenditures, and I thought that taking expenditures for granted was a very one-sided thing to do in considering a budget of this dimension or of any dimension.

I am not going to try to give any curbstone opinion about how many billions could be cut out of the present budget. Both the National City Bank and the Committee for Economic Development, I think, have already estimated that, if the nonmilitary expenditures were cut back to the level of the fiscal year 1948, it would save something in the neighborhood of 6 billion dollars. I think Senator Byrd has given estimates in the neighborhood of about 9 or even 10 billion dollars, and I certainly do not think that the military budget should be exempt from scrutiny.

There is a lot of meticulous attention being paid to what is going to be spent and collected in fiscal 1952. I do not myself know how seriously to take any of these figures. The President only a few days ago announced that the expected deficit of 2 billion 700 million dollars at the end of this June would be instead an expected surplus of 2 billion 900 million dollars. In other words, he was in error in estimates in the neighborhood of 5 billion 600 million dollars—an error made within a period of three months. I submit that that is rather a large error. If the Treasury is going to make errors of that dimension within a few months, I do not see why we should get ourselves too much upset about whether we are talking about 71 billion or 72 billion dollars.

SENATOR O'MAHONEY: Mr. Hazlitt, may I make a comment to you?

MR. HAZLITT: Yes.

SENATOR O'MAHONEY: The first estimate of which you speak was made before the Revenue Act of 1950 and the excess profits tax of 1950 were enacted.

MR. BURGESS: The President's budget message was in January, 1951.

SENATOR O'MAHONEY: I know, but how long does it take to make a budget?

MR. HAZLITT: You could come back another year from now and say the reason figures are different is because this and that and the other has happened in the meantime. The only point I am making is that we have made this error within three months.

SENATOR O'MAHONEY: I just contend it was not an error.

MR. HAZLITT: It was not an error, then; but, in any case, these figures are not reliable. They are not errors, but they are not reliable. You could put it that way if you want to.

The point I am making is that if we make a change, let us say, of that dimension in that period, then there is not much faith that we can put in the present estimates. That is all. If you go back, Senator, to the estimates that have been made by the Treasury—the predictions—and then look at the record, you will see that they have made errors that no private business could stand up against if it ever made such errors in its own estimates.

But I wanted to talk about something much different tonight, and that is this. I do not think it is very profitable to discuss what particular function of government we want to remove, what particular economy we want to make. I would rather like to suggest that we ought to re-examine our whole system of budget-making, and I would like to suggest that we ought to examine very carefully the British system of budget-making. Britain does have a responsible budget compared with which our own budget is merely an imitation. Congress is not supposed to do anything in particular about it and seldom does anything in particular about it. But a budget that is submitted by the British chancellor of the exchequer is adopted by the Parliament, and then it has to stick to it; and, when Parliament adopts a budget, the Parliament cannot raise any appropriations or make any expenditure beyond what the government calls for—beyond what the budget calls for—and that is a very sound and wholesome rule.

If we once establish such a rule, I think it would change the entire attitude toward our own budget. I would even be inclined to go a little further and say that maybe the Senate ought not to be allowed to raise any expenditure proposed by the House, just as the House ought not to be allowed to raise any expenditure proposed by the President. If this were done, it would take nine-tenths of the pressure groups off Senator O'Mahoney's back and off the congressman's back. All they would have to say would be: "Yes, we think you ought to get your new dam; yes, we think you ought to get your new post office—but I am sorry, I can't do anything about it. That is the President's budget, and we are not allowed to raise it." The whole change that that would bring about is that we would no longer have the President and the Senate and the House competing against one another in raising appropriations, increasing handouts. We would stop that whole system.

I do not think we are going to make any such change as that in the near future, but it is about time we considered it, because we are up against a very serious problem, and, from the tenor of Senator O'Mahoney's remarks, I do not think there is much substantial hope of cutting expenditures in this particular Congress or at this particular time very substantially unless we make some fundamental change of this nature. But I would like to suggest one thing that the present Congress could do as a matter of procedure apart from the whole question of having to change our constitutional system, and that is that there ought obviously to be a far more careful and expert scrutiny of the executive estimates than is made today. Now, I do not think that the Armed Services Committee of the two houses has more than four or five, at the outside, full-time research men.

I doubt whether they have that many. I am talking about the permanent staff. It seems to me that, at the very least, every member of the Armed Services Committee of either house of Congress ought to have a full-time research man who is able to examine the proposals of the armed services.

QUESTION: That would cost more money, would it not?

MR. HAZLITT: It would cost about a tenth or a hundredth of a cent for every dollar you would save.

I would like to finish on just this one point. I think that this body cannot afford to think of this as exclusively an economic problem. It has to consider the political setting of that problem, and I think that proposals of this sort ought to be very seriously considered when we approach the budget problem. Thank you.

CHAIRMAN DOUGLAS: Thank you, Mr. Hazlitt. It is twenty minutes of eleven. My suggestion is that some other member might have a suggestion as to procedural changes of the type mentioned by Mr. Hazlitt which might result in reducing expenditures.

MR. TANNENWALD: May I make one suggestion? I would like to hear from somebody who knows the government side of the picture and the expenditure side, somebody who has a little understanding of the history of this country and faith in the future and who is not a bookkeeper trying to balance the thing. Let us hear from somebody who will discuss the level of governmental expenditures in terms of what we face ahead, what we have to do, and how we are going to do it, and what it will cost, rather than how we can buy our security at a discount.

CHAIRMAN DOUGLAS: Is there a volunteer to meet that specification?

MR. PORTER: I have made a rough calculation here on the figures submitted in this mimeographed summary. It seems to me that as far as the 1952 estimates are concerned, if we could cut out such frivolity as military services, international security, atomic energy, etc., we could reduce this from 71 billion down to about 20 billion, and even that probably could be subjected to more reduction. So I would just like to add my voice to what Mr. Tannenwald has said. What procedure is there whereby we can scrutinize and make reductions in the important items of expenditures here which is 50-plus billion dollars in 1952 and devoted exclusively to security purposes? It seems to me that the whole discussion has been unrealistic because we have not focused on that problem.

REPRESENTATIVE CELLER: I think you have to ask Joe Stalin about that.

MR. PORTER: I am afraid that that is where the answer rests.

MR. TANNENWALD: Mr. Gainsbrugh raises the question of how far we can afford to go. How far does anybody go to defend his own home? I would like Mr. Gainsbrugh to answer that question.

CHAIRMAN DOUGLAS: There have been serious suggestions, which Mr. Hazlitt referred to, that if nonmilitary expenditures could be put back to the 1948 level, there would be substantial savings which might have a real effect on our tax problem for 1952. I think Senator O'Mahoney's remarks tended to be realistic to the effect that we are not likely to go backward in nonmilitary expenditures, but the purpose of this evening's discussion was to see whether there were reasons to discuss our policy problems in the light of any modifications of the budget estimates or to accept the budget estimates as the best expenditure figures that this conference could consider.

MR. HENDERSON: This is to confute those who think I might take a side in the thing, but I would like to suggest that there is very good reason to believe that the military chiefs in connection with next year's military budget were asking for 104 or 106 billion dollars, that the civilian chiefs had indicated something like 70 billion dollars, which means that some kind of revision was made. It is not at all improbable that some kind of a civilian commission on military expenditures might be considered. Maybe Senator O'Mahoney could tell us something about whether or not the military chiefs had wanted 104 billion dollars. Maybe the CED people who have kicked this thing around might say something as to the value of a citizens' committee.

CHAIRMAN DOUGLAS: Mr. Henderson, I take it your reference to 104 billion and 70 billion dollars refers to fiscal 1953, for which there is no general budget at this time.

MR. HENDERSON: To 1952. Senator O'Mahoney, I think, if he would speak, might be able to give us a little more official information on this.

SENATOR O'MAHONEY: Well, I am in the position of the young man who, having made a proposal to a girl, then fell silent, and she said, "Why don't you say something?"

"I think I said too much already," he said.

But the fact of the matter is that the Army chiefs did want a very much larger sum than was sent up to them. I might even go back to the tragic days of Secretary Forrestal. The Army chiefs came to him and requested a budget of something like 23 billion dollars. The President and the Bureau of the Budget had notified all the agencies of government that the budget would have to be very, very low. Secretary Forrestal said, "I can't possibly take that 23-billion-dollar request to the White House," and he tossed it back to his chiefs. They cut it to 18 billion dollars, and then he submitted that.

MR. HENDERSON: I think it was 29 billion that they wanted. He cut it to 23 and could not get it down further.

SENATOR O'MAHONEY: You may have the right figures. In any event, when it came out of the Bureau of the Budget it was about 12½ billion dollars.

I can say to this group, without revealing any confidential information at all, that Undersecretary Lovett has gathered around him a group of high-class experts, gathered from business, for the express purpose of scrutinizing every request that is to be sent to the Budget Bureau and to the Congress, and I know also that the Appropriations Committee of the Senate is asking the same sort of rigid economy; but economies of that kind are rather futile if we do not halt the continued inflationary spiral.

MR. PORTER: May I ask the Senator a question? What does your report show as to total figures in 1952 for civil requirements?

SENATOR O'MAHONEY: The figures, as I indicated when I was discussing them, are difficult to analyze upon the basis of the categories in which they come in the budget. Natural resources, for example, was estimated at 1.3 billlions. Well, that contains about 1.2 billions or 1.1 billions for atomic energy. Transportation and communications is about 1.6 billions. That includes some defense expenditures. But the truth of the matter is, unless. . . .

MR. PORTER: What is the total?

SENATOR O'MAHONEY: I do not have the total here, but it would not exceed 10 billion dollars. Marriner Eccles appeared before our committee to testify with respect to the Treasury–Federal Reserve controversy, and he discussed the budget. He gave it to us as his opinion that we would be very lucky if we cut 2 billion dollars out of the nondefense expenditure. I think it can go above that. I think it ought to go above that, and I think that this group ought to know that this budget which was sent down to Congress in January by the President had contained no appropriation, no budget estimate, for more than a hundred reclamation and rivers and harbors projects which Congress had authorized. It is a great error to assume that the executive has been trying to expand. The executive has been trying to hold down expenditures. I very well remember back in 1946, after Congress had passed a very substantial appropriation for rivers and harbors and flood-control improvement, as well as reclamation, the President impounded the money, whereupon a group of senators and congressmen called on him and said, "You can't do this to us." The money was not expended.

MR. ROSTOW: If, Senator, the total of the civilian side of the budget, as you estimated, is in the neighborhood of 10 or 11 billion dolalrs, as I get your statement. . . .

SENATOR O'MAHONEY: Let me say this. Out of 74 billion dollars, 49 billions are for defense and national security. That constitutes 68 per cent of the total budget. Now add 11 billion dollars to that for interest on the national debt and for veterans' benefits and payments—and, understand, we cannot cut veterans' payments or benefits unless we pass a law which will say that veterans shall not be entitled to certain treatment in the hospitals.

MR. PORTER: Unless you repudiate a previous contract.

SENATOR O'MAHONEY: That adds about another 15 per cent, and there we have, without atomic energy at all, 83 per cent of the entire budget which is war-connected, past, present, or future.

MR. ROSTOW: It is that figure that I had in mind in doubting very much the feasibility of cuts that would amount to 10 billion.

SENATOR O'MAHONEY: We cannot touch 10 billion.

MR. STEIN: I should like to say something about the possibility of holding the budget not 10 billion dollars below the estimate but, let us say, a figure of 6 billion below the estimate. In part this question hinges on what is military and what is nonmilitary in the budget.

As the Committee for Economic Development broke down the budget, we classified as defense a total of 51.9 billion dollars —which would correspond to the Senator's figure—which includes military services, the whole foreign-aid program, the atomic-energy program, stimulation of defense production, stabilization and production controls, civil defense, defense housing, and dispersal of government agencies. That seems to be a fairly comprehensive coverage of what might be considered defense. The remainder consists of 9.2 billion dollars of interest and trust funds and 3.8 billion dollars of veterans' pensions and readjustment benefits, and 9.1 billion dollars of other things. This 9.1 billions of other things is more than one-third higher than it was in 1948. I think the thing to remember is that. . . .

MR. PORTER: Have you adjusted that for the price level?

MR. STEIN: The 1948 price level is not very much below the present price level. We had a decline in 1948.

MR. COX: In veterans' pensions did you exclude other veterans' benefits? How do you get a figure of 3 billion? It is supposed to be 5 billion dollars, is it not?

MR. STEIN: The veterans' hospital benefits are covered in the 9.1 billions.

MR. COX: What other veterans' benefits are in the 9.1 billions?

MR. STEIN: That is all.

MR. KNIGHT: How much of the social security is part of the 9.1 billions?

MR. STEIN: It is not in there.

MR. BRUBAKER: What part of this 9.1 billions could be saved —what is that 3.8 billions composed of that could be saved?

MR. STEIN: A large part of it comes out of civil public works. Another large part comes out of aid to agriculture. Amounts for other items are smaller. Those are the biggest ones. The point I wanted to make about this is that it is not really appropriate to talk about whether we can arrest a long-term trend of rising government civil expenditures, which I doubt myself. The question is whether, if we have a two-year bulge here of a defense program, we can, for two years, hold back these nondefense expenditures. We did succeed in doing that during the war after 1941. We cut federal nondefense expenditures very sharply, especially federal nondefense public works expenditures, which were almost entirely eliminated. It seems to us if one looks at this in terms of postponing for two years what is not absolutely essential during those two years, there is an opportunity for considerable reduction.

With respect to the 3.8 billion dollars for veterans' pensions and readjustment benefits, I do not think there is much that can be done to cut that. I think it is reasonable to expect, however, that expenditure in that category will not be so large as the 3.8 billions included in the budget, since the fiscal 1951 expenditure in that category will be about a half-billion dollars below the estimate made last January. That is, the expenditures for readjustment and training have fallen off much more rapidly than was expected, because of the high employment opportunities.

Now, in the category of defense and related items, it seems to me that that cannot be accepted without question. In the defense program itself, the main question is one of efficiency in operating the program. I think it is the fairly general testimony of anyone who has had contact with the military establishment that, whenever it grows very rapidly, a great deal of waste enters into its operation which could be eliminated. Even relatively small percentage gains in efficiency would result in substantial economies. The Commission on the Hoover Report has estimated that by applying the recommendation that it had previously made, which has not yet been applied to the military establishment, 2 billion dollars could be cut out of that figure without affecting the strength of the armed forces.

Foreign military and economic assistance amounts to 7 billion 100 million dollars, the major part of which consists of a lump sum of 5.5 billion dollars just inserted in one line in the budget, without any justification as to its relation to any necessity, either military or economic. The expenditures under appropriations already made in the year 1951 in that category are also going to be about a half-billion dollars below the fiscal 1951 estimates, and I think it is generally conceded that the expenditure estimates and the appropriation requests put in for this purpose have a large element of bargaining in them and that the President really does not expect to get them all. And, then, what is gotten is never entirely spent.

There are 330 million dollars in this program for civil defense. The director of civil defense has already indicated that that will not be necessary, because they have abandoned the deep-shelter program. There is 100 millions here for defense housing, which the Congress already is looking at with a very jaundiced eye. Congress, I think, has already—or, at least, some committee of Congress—rejected several other things. There is 1 billion 100 millions in here for the expansion of defense production, which is to consist of direct construction and direct government loans. The private economy seems capable of maintaining a very high rate of private investment. With the assistance of accelerated amortization to satisfy the requirements of the defense program, it seems doubtful that that expenditure really would be necessary, especially if the consequence of reducing it were to leave some additional funds in the hands of private individuals for investment.

There are other points that might be made. Fanny May is expected to end fiscal 1952 holding 750 million dollars of government-guaranteed mortgages, which, in the kind of situation we apparently face, with a reduction in the volume of new mortgages coming into the market, ought to be salable, especially since they are, all of them, guaranteed either by the Veterans Administration or the Federal Housing Administration.

I am not intending to suggest that these particular items can all be cut in the amounts that I have mentioned or that there are no others that could not also be cut, but I think that there is great danger in looking at the long-term historical trend and looking at the big proportion of the total, which is military, and saying that nothing can be done about it.

SENATOR O'MAHONEY: I wanted to put in a plug for this economic report. Mr. Henderson suggested that I should have brought enough copies to distribute them free. I prefer to have you buy them at thirty cents per copy from the Superintendent of Documents. If you are especially interested, you will find, beginning on page 86, an appendix which contains the results of a survey which I had made of possible economies, if Congress would repeal certain laws which require expenditures, which the Bureau of the Budget and the President must make estimates for, lest they are to be accused of not carrying out the laws of Congress. That would probably, on this estimate, effect a saving of 1 billion 681 million dollars in 1952.

MR. MULLENDORE: May I express a point of view of a small group—maybe there are two or three other representatives here —which is so shocking, and which is so entirely out of line with general assumptions, that it at least will be interesting to this group. It is that the greatest danger to this country is not from without, and not that against which we are arming, but from within, and coming out of the breakdown of the economy of this country from inflation, from the unbalances which are developing and which have developed already far beyond the danger point.

This minority, usually referred to as pessimists, holds that this country is not prosperous, that it has not been prosperous in the past six years, that it is now in the worst condition that it ever was in in its history, and that all who have been misrepresenting us as prosperous have been misleading the people—and that includes the great majority of business leaders of the country as well as congressmen. Now, we do not expect the politician to give a correct assessment of economics. He is not an expert on economics. But the businessman has a responsibility to answer the question, "How is business?" correctly. Upon that score, he has been, as Senator O'Mahoney has said, representing to the people that this country is very prosperous and has been very prosperous for the past several years.

I say there is a minority, of which I happen to be a member, who have told their stockholders, and told their employees, and told their customers during this period that this is not so. These figures relied upon to prove the case for prosperity are entirely misleading. This so-called "prosperity" is on the same basis as would exist if a family had pooled all possible credit which they could get—all their resources—and borrowed all the money they could from the future and spent it in the present; and because they are presently enjoying an abundance of goods and services financed out of the expenditure of everything they hope to make during the rest of their lifetime, with all the credit they can get, they call themselves "prosperous." This country has, in fact, borrowed from its future to the full extent that it is capable of borrowing, and it is now "creating purchasing power" more and more each day by taking the savings of the country through the confiscation resulting from inflation. If this goes far enough, and it seems to be going further, each further step will add to the danger from which we suffer, which is infinitely greater than that arising from the strength of Russia—the danger of a great breakdown from within, upon which, in my judgment, Russia is relying much more than she is upon her own strength.

CHAIRMAN DOUGLAS: If the conference agrees, I would like to call on Mr. Haley for a summary of this evening's discussion and then look forward to an adjournment, as it is now ten minutes past eleven.

MR. HALEY: Mr. Chairman, as you yourself pointed out, the occasion for this particular session was to consider the question which was raised this afternoon: Whether or not it is right and proper to assume, in our discussions with respect to the next year or two, the figure for governmental expenditures contained in the budget estimates. It was also suggested, I think, that consideration should be given at this meeting to the question whether or not the steady growth in the governmental expenditures over the years does not represent a serious danger to our fundamental institutions.

On the one hand, the latter point has certainly been thoroughly aired here this evening, Mr. Chairman; and, with respect to the former point, I think the point has been made that it is right and proper to scrutinize very carefully the estimates for expenditures in the budget figures and that some possible reductions in those figures might be conceivable. Furthermore, certain specific recommendations were made as to steps by which such reductions might be actually brought about; namely, first, to re-examine the whole system of budget-making, to consider the British practice, and to see whether or not an improved budget-making procedure could be put into effect in this country. Second, whether or not some means could not be provided whereby the legislative branch of the government could scrutinize more efficiently, and with more expert aid, the executive estimates of expenditures required. Third, whether or not a special commission of civilians might not have some luck in finding some water in the military estimates which could be squeezed out without affecting the military establishment. I think that is about as far as we have reached.

CHAIRMAN DOUGLAS: Thank you very much.

V

THE ROLE OF DIRECT CONTROLS

OUTLINE FOR DISCUSSION

I. It has been said that price-wage controls deal with symptoms rather than causes of inflation. The chief causes of inflation are monetary—a total money demand for goods and services in excess of the available supply at existing prices.

A. If the excess money demand is not eliminated, can direct wage and price controls be enforced?

B. Do wage-price controls help to reduce the excess money demand:

    1. By inducing consumers to save more? Will the funds which cannot find an outlet in price-controlled goods be hoarded or will they be expended for "other" goods and services?

    2. By preventing the spread of wage increases? What then happens to the excess demand which would have caused the initial wage increases? Does not the excess demand raise the income of nonwage workers? Is the argument that nonwage workers will hoard a larger fraction of their increased income than wage workers?

    3. By increasing the availability of goods? The expectation that price control will be enforced may reduce speculative accumulation of inventories. What about the effect of the expectation that goods will be unavailable because of price control?

C. If the excess money demand is not eliminated will wage-price controls eliminate some of the inequities of inflation:

147

1. By keeping the prices of necessities within the means of fixed-income groups? But doing so (with excess money demand) means that the necessities will not be readily available at the controlled price, thus introducing new inequities.

II. It has been said that mobilization without price-wage controls may produce inflation even if government expenditures are covered by taxation and hence replace private expenditures. Mobilization increases the demand for particular goods and particular kinds of labor, thereby raising corresponding prices and wages.

A. Does a rise in the price of particular goods produce a general price rise? It is argued that people will interpret the rise of particular prices as a signal that prices in general will rise. This leads to anticipating purchases which raise prices in general. These purchases can be financed only if there is an increase in the stock of money or in the rate of use of money.

B. Does a wage rise in industries favored by mobilization produce a general rise in wages? It is argued that these industries will want more employees and will pay higher wages to get them. Other industries will give comparable increases in order to retain their workers, or to restore the structure of wages. The results will be a general wage rise that will be reflected in higher prices. This implies a larger money volume of transactions which in turn means an increase in the stock of money or its rate of use. If, as assumed, mobilization expenditures are financed out of taxation, will there not be a reduction in employment in other industries releasing workers for mobilization industries? Will wages rise in other industries when employment in them is declining?

C. If the price increases resulting from mobilization extend to cost-of-living goods, will this tend to produce a general rise in wages? It is argued that, as prices of necessities go up, labor will demand higher wages. These will have have to be granted in order to avoid disrupting production. The increases will be passed along in higher prices for goods.

This argument assumes that employers and consumers can get funds to finance the higher wage payments and the higher payments for goods.

III. It has been said that mobilization changes the relationship of prices. Relative prices change rapidly, as does the relative profitability of various businesses. Will such changes produce undesirable consequences which can be effectively dealt with by wage-price controls?

A. Are such controls a good means of preventing profiteering? It is argued that profits resulting from mobilization are wrong or bad and that it is better to prevent them by price control than to allow them to be made and then taxed away.

IV. It has been said that even if there is no inflation the government will have difficulty in procuring its supplies promptly through the usual market mechanism.

A. Will producer allocations assist the government in procuring its supplies for mobilization? The argument may take this form: allocation of resources is a better means of channeling needed supplies to the government than is the market. Since prices are not used to perform this function, there is no point to allowing them to rise.

B. Does not the preceding argument imply that entrepreneurs have no function to perform and that consequently all war goods should be directly produced by the government from the initial to the final stage?

Does this in turn imply that the government has more information about obtainable resources than private enterprises which possess specialized knowledge about the existence and location of the commodities and possible substitutes for them?

Do not direct controls limit the government to resources of which it possesses direct knowledge?

V. In the existing emergency, price control has not been accompanied by rationing of consumer goods. If such price control makes prices lower than they would otherwise be, it will mean that some buyers willing to pay legal prices will not be able to obtain the goods or services they seek.

    A. Which buyers will go unsatisfied will be determined by chance, favoritism, or bribery. Is this method of distribution obviously superior to the method of rationing by the purse?

    B. What happens to the money which the people wish to pay for price-controlled goods not available to them?

       1. Is it clear that they will hoard such money?

       2. Will it mean higher prices for goods not controlled or not controlled effectively?

    C. Will not the nonavailability of price-controlled goods stimulate demands for subsidies to expand output of such goods, thus adding to inflationary pressure and diverting resources *from* the mobilization program?

VI. Problems of distribution raised by price control without government rationing are likely to lead to governmental rationing of some essential goods.

    A. Is this type of rationing clearly better than rationing by the purse?

    B. Is the supposed advantage sufficient to compensate for the administrative costs involved?

    C. If rationing is used, is it necessary to have price control? Would not rationing alone, by limiting demand, keep prices down? Does the addition of price control stem from the assumption that it is easier to enforce the two together than rationing alone?

CHAIRMAN LEVI: There are some matters left over from the prior discussion which I may turn to before coming to "The Role of Direct Controls."

Mr. Burgess, you had a statement you wished to make.

MR. BURGESS: Mr. Chairman, I confess to having been a little disturbed when my good friend, Congressman Celler, suggested that I regarded the banks as sacrosanct from controls. It was not my intention to convey any such impression. It is not the way I feel. So I have been reviewing in my mind the discussion of yesterday to see where I failed to present the case adequately, for I am sure that must have been what happened.

Of course, it was a little surprising to me because, if there is one industry which is more controlled than any other business in the country, it is the banking business. We are examined twice a year by the government. Federal examiners go through us with a fine-tooth comb, forty or fifty people who stay there for several months. We cannot move without a lawyer's advising us over our elbow. The prices of our products and of what we pay are fixed by government agencies, not in emergencies, but all the time. The law gives the Federal Reserve the power to fix the maximum rate we shall pay on deposits, and the Reserve System and the Treasury together fix the range of rates that we can charge for our product. What we are talking about in direct controls is the prices at which people do business—we already have our business fixed in that way.

I think perhaps where I failed to say what was in my mind, and in the mind, I think, of other bankers, is with respect to this process of price-fixing which the Federal Reserve and the Treasury do through their monetary policies. Perhaps by suggesting some of the limitations on those powers, I gave the impression of being unsympathetic with a very vigorous use of Federal Reserve powers, and I want to say that my record is very clear on that point—that in season and out of season I have advocated a much more vigorous use of Federal Reserve powers than has actually taken place. So that, as far as the banks being sacrosanct, they are not and will not be and they cannot desire to be.

Now, this voluntary control business deals with quite a different field from fixing prices. It goes far beyond what we are talking about doing with prices and what Mr. DiSalle and his associates have to do with wages and with prices. It goes into the field of the allocation of one's product. If you want a comparison, it would be if the government were going to try to tell the General Motors Corporation to whom it should sell motorcars; and, when we begin to do that with regulatory agencies, we get into a very difficult field, as I am sure you would all agree.

Now, already in the field of bank credit we have had the Federal Reserve System given certain powers to lay down the rules under which loans can be made. That covers now something like half of the lending and perhaps the most inflationary areas on instalment credit, on real estate, and on security loans. If I had a personal position on that, it would be that the Reserve System was not tough enough and did not lay down rigorous enough rules when they adopted those regulations.

Now, when we come into another area, the general loans to business, there have been various suggestions for laying down rules in that area. It may be that somebody will think up ways of doing it, but in the meantime and as another method of approach, we have thought that we ought to go to work at it ourselves, "ourselves" being not the banks alone but the insurance companies and the houses of issue, to see if we could not cut back some of the marginal business that is least essential at this time. I agree with my fellow bank director, Congressman Celler, that this is an area that offers very great difficulties and that, if we simply make a speech and say, "Won't everybody please co-operate?" of course we do not get anywhere at all.

I do not call that a plan of voluntary control. It does not become a plan until we formulate definite rules, until we have an agency for carrying them through and require definite commitments from our institutions. That is the plan that is being worked on under a clause of the Defense Act that the Congress wisely put in. I may say that the group that is working on that is working with the representatives of the Federal Reserve System. We hold no meetings of our group which are not presided over and recorded by representatives of the Federal Reserve System. The various groups have all agreed to go ahead with it. Aside from a general committee which has met in Washington, there are local committees being appointed which are headed by some of the finest and best people we know of in the country, and what they are trying to do is to work out as far as they can some rules of procedure in making loans.

Now, I do not claim that this is going to cure the situation. I do think that in a democracy we do not just push people around. We try to give them ideas of what should be done, and I do not believe that in a time like this we can rely solely on people acting like the classical economic man. As American citizens, we have a responsibility for the whole picture, and I think that, by trying to educate our people at the same time that we push them around, perhaps we will get a lot further. There have been plenty of illustrations in our history of voluntary action where we appeal to something in people besides their immediate economic advantage.

We bankers all worked on the war-loan drives. We did it for nothing. It was not to our short-term economic advantage to do it because it took a lot of time, but it was a very successful move. We intend to do it again. I believe that in a democracy a great deal can be accomplished by trying to educate people in the line of conduct that they should follow, while at the same time I agree with Mr. Kestnbaum that we cannot deal with this situation except on many different fronts, making progress on all those fronts as rapidly as we can.

Mr. Lazarus: I was delighted that we had the meeting last evening. I thought that the presentation of the budget figures for 1951 and 1952 would give a good deal more meaning to the conference because it would take the discussions out of the academic field a little more and make them more realistic. The evening's discussion concerned itself largely with the size of the budget, and I think that there probably were some excellent suggestions made for its reduction. Beyond that, I do not think we accomplished what I had hoped would be the basic purpose of the meeting.

I think that, while Russia may call the turn as to when we are going to have all-out war, our Defense Department and the Department of Mobilization have called the turn as to the plan of defense that we are going to use against Russia's domination. I think, if I may take a few moments to read from Mr. Wilson's report to the President, it would set a basis or a framework in which the conference could practically and successfully proceed to discuss the issues that face us at the present time. Mr. Wilson says almost in summary the following: "What is the defense program? We must produce military equipment and supplies for our forces fighting in Korea; second, our expanding armed services in the United States and in Europe; third, assistance to the growing forces of other nations joined with us in resisting communism; fourth, reserve stocks intended in the case of key items to provide for the first year of full-scale war. While we do this we must build toward the productive power that would be needed and could be quickly put to use in case of all-out war.

"This has several aspects—stock-piling of scarce and critical materials, the addition of production lines for military goods, and the addition of basic industrial capacity that will support both high levels of military and civilian production during the defense period and which would be available to support the needs of all-out war."

Then comes, I think, the most important paragraph: "With the fullest degree of drive and unity we can do this job by 1953. By that date, our readiness to enter into a full mobilization should produce sufficient production which, in addition to meeting current military needs, should support a civilian economy at or about pre-Korean levels."

It seems to me that with the Defense Department having announced this policy and successfully followed it, I believe since the time Mr. Marshall and Mr. Lovett have come into the Defense Department, and then Mr. Wilson's division having announced this policy, we can accept it as basic for the emergency that is ahead. That means, as I read it, that in 1952 and, at the latest, 1953, the strains center on the economy. After that come much more normal operations than we have envisaged in our discussions here.

If that be true, then it would seem that the recommendations of a conference of this kind should take on the emergency characteristics that such a program should hold, the basis of imposing certain necessary restrictions and, at the same time of imposing them, guarantee that they can be quickly withdrawn so that the economy will not be fettered at a later time. As I understand it, the national program means the quick physical preparation to defend ourselves in a definite way and at the same time, as soon as that is done, to turn again to the kind of system which we in America believe has produced the sort of conditions under which men are happier than they are anywhere else in the world.

CHAIRMAN LEVI: May I suggest that now we turn to "The Role of Direct Controls." I will call first on Mr. DiSalle for a general statement.

Mr. DiSalle: Mr. Chairman and gentlemen of the conference: As you noted yesterday, I kept very quiet. The purpose of my attendance here was to pick the brains of the experts, a task at which I have become quite expert in the last four months.

I thought that here we could get the answers to some of our problems, but I found yesterday, in the three sessions that I attended, that the experts are much more effective talking to nonexperts than they are talking to one another. So I expect somewhat to play the role of an expert myself. Leon Henderson and Paul Porter have qualified because they were former price directors, and I suppose in a day or a week or a month or a year I will join that learned fraternity and also become an expert.

Today, coming into the auditorium, I had many of the members of the conference stop me with a sort of glee, saying, "This morning is your morning," and I thought possibly in self-defense I ought to make an opening statement.

First, on the role of direct controls, as we looked over the questions generally, we found that most of the questions were of the "Have you stopped beating your wife?" variety, directly related to the assumption that, if we had proper monetary controls, price controls—direct controls—would not be necessary. The first we do not subscribe to at all. We have the experience of World War II to draw upon, and also, since Korea, that lays a basis of justification for the role of direct controls in an emergency situation. We feel that, since Korea, the factors laying the basis for the need for direct controls were largely psychological —possibly more psychological than economic, in fact. People, remembering controls during World War II, on June 26 immediately started buying in anticipation of controls, in anticipation of scarcities, in anticipation of higher prices.

Although we had a period, possibly when the Korean situation was developing a little favorably, when we might have looked forward to a situation where direct controls might not have been necessary, where we might have been able to approach the problem with selective controls of some kind, the Chinese intervention immediately changed that picture and stimulated purchasing and anticipatory price increases. On December 19, 1950, we tried voluntary standards. Some people lived up to those standards and are now some of the most pressing customers in our office asking for relief. Those were the people who were caught in the squeeze.

We generally found that people fell into three classes. We found those people who leaned over backward and did the best they could do to abide by voluntary standards. We found a second class that would have liked to have lived by those voluntary standards but were forced into positions through no fault of their own where they had to make increases. Then we had a third class of people that just paid no attention to anything and felt it was a time when they ought to get theirs, and they did the best that they could. That third class, more than anybody else, sent us down the road to direct controls.

However, as we review the situation, we find that the rate of increase in the cost of living certainly was exceeded in other periods of history. From June 15, 1950, we had an increase of about 8 points in the index. We have had periods when increases have been much more than that. In fact, I think it was in July or August of 1946, in that one month, that we had an increase of 7.9; and in a five-month period in 1946, after the scrapping of OPA controls, we had an increase of 19 points in the cost of living. We also had the period from the beginning of the World War II controls—from the time that the National Defense Advisory Commission was founded until one year after the General Maximum Price Regulation was issued—between August, 1940, and May, 1944—when we had an increase of 25 points in the cost of living, or 25 per cent. And so we have had those increases in 1950. Certainly the factors were at work after June, 1950, that would have led us into a serious inflationary period if some action had not been taken.

The final part of the statement that I would like to make is to answer a good many people who say, "Well, we have had price controls, but nothing has happened." That just is not true. We have had a period in the last six or seven weeks where there has been a leveling-off. The wholesale index has been pretty level. I think there has been a net change of 0.3 of a point in that six- or seven-week period. We have had some declines in food prices. We have had some declines in other fields. The spot-market index of twenty-eight sensitive commodities shows a 4½-point decline from its high peak, which occurred on February 16, 1951. And so we feel that we are entering a period where we can achieve some price stability.

Of course, a good many people now will say that this is not the result of controls; that it is the result of just natural things that are occurring and will continue to occur. On the other hand, if prices had continued on up, then it would have been the fault of ineffective controls. We feel that the general freeze action that was taken January 26, 1951, was a psychological move directed to combat the psychological pressures that were driving us into the dangerous inflation that was certainly in the works after June, 1950.

In the process of discussion this morning, of course, we are going to be directed more and more to the question of what part monetary policies play in the eventual role of the government in control of inflation. We have some of our experts here this morning from the Office of Price Stabilization—Harold Leventhal, chief counsel, and Dr. Gardner Ackley, assistant director in charge of economic policy. Both of these gentlemen have had experience in OPA, and, of course, we do expect some support from Mr. Henderson and Mr. Porter, who, I have come to the conclusion, have certainly earned a reward because of the efforts that they expended during that time.

History shows us that King Edward applied price controls back in the thirteenth century sometime, and the Continental Congress tried it in 1776; and, although I have never paid too much attention to what success accompanied those programs, I have always wondered what happened to the price directors of those days. I certainly feel that they are engaged in some peaceful pursuit some place, a peace that they earned as a result of the efforts that they had to expend on earth.

Our program is one that is directed toward achieving checks and balances that would normally be present in the American economy without the outside interference caused by the defense effort or a dangerous international situation.

So, gentlemen, with that opening statement, we are ready to take you on.

CHAIRMAN LEVI: I will now ask Mr. Director if he will make a general statement.

MR. DIRECTOR: I will confine my remarks to the issue of price control, since Mr. Stein of the Committee for Economic Development will discuss the more difficult question of the proper role of allocation and priorities in facilitating the mobilization program. All I plan to do is to state the position that price control should not be used. I apologize for the dogmatic character of the statements I shall make. My excuse is that I find it very difficult to argue the position. This in turn may be due to the fact that the position is so much a part of the Chicago tradition that we have forgotten how to argue the issue. At Chicago the advantages of the market as a method of organizing economic affairs are valued too highly to be laid aside during so-called emergency periods.

I understand that recently this tradition has been spreading eastward. If that is so, it can perhaps be partly explained by the fact that one of the Chicago economists responsible for establishing this tradition has recently moved in that direction. I am told also, and this we shall be able to verify this morning, that many of the people who were responsible for administering price controls during the last war are very skeptical about its usefulness; and that only shows that there is a hard way of learning such things, by going to Washington, and an easy way of doing it, by staying at Chicago.

For some strange reason, it has become fashionable to believe that, while the market is a useful instrument in ordinary times, it is not a useful instrument when large and sudden changes have to be effected in the use of resources. This is like another fashionable view—that the market is a useful instrument for prosperous countries and not for poor countries. I contend that rich countries can afford the inefficiencies of other methods and that it is precisely in times when important shifts in economic activity have to be made that the advantages of price changes as signals for the relative importance of goods and services, and as incentives, become decisive.

If a general rise in prices is prevented, it would ordinarily be agreed that changes in relative prices have a useful function to perform. Higher prices for some goods provide a signal of the increased importance attached to these goods, and at the same time they provide an incentive to increase the supply of these goods and an incentive to economize on the use of these goods. A rise in the prices of particular goods leads to the economizing of such goods everywhere, and I submit that it is unlikely that everywhere, if I may use the phrase, is known to any group of experts.

A rise in prices leads to the discovery and use of substitutes, and again I would submit that it is unlikely that all possible substitutes can be known by any particular group of experts. As the relative cost of goods changes and relative price changes are prevented, I suggest that no one will know what the new importance of particular goods is, neither the enterprises that usually do nor the experts in Washington.

I want to say next that I make no assumptions about monetary and fiscal policies. While these are, within limits, alternative to each other in preventing inflation, price control is not an alternative to either. At best, price control will not be decisive in determining the magnitude of the monetary base of inflation. Hence its main contribution is to repress inflation while the control is operative, and even this only if price control is general and fully effective. If the ultimate amount of inflation is generally the same regardless of price control, then it seems to me that there is no advantage in postponing it. To the extent, as was argued by some yesterday, inflation has some incentive advantages, we might just as well obtain these advantages during the period of mobilization. In any event, I contend that open inflation is better than repressed inflation, and it is better precisely because it permits changes in relative prices, which price control, used to stop inflation, must prevent.

When not justified as a method of preventing inflation, price control is justified on the ground that the market is not an equitable method for distributing a reduced supply of consumers goods. But the distribution of income does not change adversely for the lower-income groups. Consequently, the defense of price control in emergency periods must be based on the assumption that consumers are not the best judges of what is good for them—an assumption which is as valid for ordinary as for emergency periods.

The real inequity of inflation falls on fixed-income recipients, and these will suffer the consequences of inflation whether it takes place during the emergency period or is put off to a more "suitable" time. No one contends that absence of a system of distributing goods and services—which is what takes place with price control—automatically assures equity. Consequently, advocates of price control must go on to argue for a system of rationing. But an effective system of rationing makes price control superfluous.

CHAIRMAN LEVI: Mr. Stein, do you have a general statement?

MR. STEIN: My assignment as I understand it is a quite limited one, and I shall try to dispose of it briefly. I shall address myself to the question, "Do we need direct controls of the priorities and allocations type to carry out a mobilization program, and if so why?"

The need for production and distribution controls is, I believe, very generally accepted, even by people who think that price-wage controls are unnecessary and undesirable. I believe this general opinion is correct. But asking why it is correct may be helpful in deciding how far we must go with such controls and under what conditions we can get rid of them.

Our economy is basically organized on the principle that anyone able and willing to pay the price can buy anything and will not have to use compulsion to do so. In general, this principle works. Then why cannot the government, if it wants ten million tons of steel badly next quarter, go out and buy it? Certainly the government has more money than anyone else. If the government and private purchasers want to buy more steel at the existing price than is available, the price will presumably rise, discouraging some of the purchasers. And since the government can afford to pay a higher price than anyone else, it will not be the government that is priced out of the market.

The trouble with this picture, as I see it, is that in some markets and in some circumstances prices do not rise fast enough and far enough to clear the market. Prices remain relatively stable despite an excess of demand, and a backlog of orders piles up. Of course, the available supply is parceled out somehow. But it is not parceled out on the basis of willingness to pay more than the quoted price, except for marginal amounts that flow through gray markets. It goes to the oldest or most valued customers or to the orders longest on the books, or it may be alloted on a proration basis. That is, there is a private rationing system. And the fact that the government and its contractors are standing there with the longest purse does not assure them of deliveries in this private rationing system. In fact, the munitions industry is likely to be an especially disfavored customer.

This kind of thing can happen whenever an industry is operating at capacity. It seems to have been true in the spring of 1950, before Korea, that defense expenditures were lagging because, as private demand increased, defense contractors had trouble getting deliveries. The occasional existence of such shortages in ordinary times does not necessarily require controls, even if they impinge to some extent on defense procurement. In ordinary times it is not a matter of crucial importance if tank deliveries lag three or four months behind schedule. But in an emergency, when schedules are for delivery as fast as possible and adherence to schedule is considered vital, the government must supplement its buying power by direct controls to obtain supplies in cases where willingness to pay the highest price is not sufficient assurance. Controls will be needed not only to satisfy government military requirements but also to satisfy certain privately financed or privately procured requirements that are essential parts of the defense program.

The fact of shortages, in the sense that prices do not rise sufficiently to eliminate an excess of demand, is, in my opinion, the basic reason why production controls are needed to carry out the defense program. The shortages would exist and the controls would be needed even if we had an ideal anti-inflationary monetary-fiscal program. Suppose that by taxes and general credit restraints we restricted private demand sufficiently to hold total demand constant while the military program rises.

Still there would be a shift in the pattern of demand and an increase of demand in those parts of the economy where the military demand is especially heavy. To avoid shortages in those areas, and to assure delivery to the government and everyone else willing to pay the price, the prices in those areas must rise. And where prices do not rise sufficiently, production and distribution controls will be needed.

Also, I think, the controls would be needed even if we did not have government price control. That is, even if there were no government limitations on price increases, the voluntary practices of private business would in some cases result in a sluggish response of price to an excess of demand. But of course inflationary pressure resulting from inadequate monetary-fiscal policy, combined with general price controls, will make the need for production controls more widespread and more persistent. The inflationary pressure will increase the number and size of the price increases needed to drive competing demands out of the market and permit the government to satisfy its military requirements. And the price controls will prevent those price increases from coming about, whether rapidly or slowly, as they would in an imperfect but free market.

Given an adequate general anti-inflationary policy, without price controls, we should expect the need for production and distribution controls to be limited and temporary. That is, even where prices are sluggish, they will tend to rise in the course of time to clear the market. In our present program, of course, the dominant factors in ending the need for controls will be the reduction of military requirements after a bulge in 1952 or 1953 and the increase in supplies of scarce materials. But there is no reason to think that we could or should increase supplies enough to satisfy all the demands that would exist for basic materials at present prices if we go on inflating money incomes at a rapid rate.

This point may be illustrated by a story that appeared recently in the *Wall Street Journal*. This story reported that the responsible people in government expected that it would be possible to dispense with production controls in 1955. According to their calculations, civilian supplies of basic materials would be back to pre-Korean levels by 1953. But civilian demand would have increased so much that shortages would persist into 1955. However, whether the shortages end in 1953 or 1955 or 1960 will depend in part upon how much we expand civilian money incomes and how much we hold down prices of the scarce materials.

I would like to raise two questions about this interpretation of controls as a means of supplementing the allocating function of price where prices do not rise enough to do the whole job. I am suggesting that we ought to have the controls and also ought to allow the prices to rise, if they will, to reduce or eliminate the need for the controls. It may be asked whether a distribution control system could work if prices were left free to rise. Would supplies leak out from under the control system, away from the rated orders, if nonessential users could be charged higher prices? The system might break down if suppliers could charge more on unrated orders than on rated orders. But I do not think the system would break down if suppliers were free to raise prices on rated orders and unrated orders alike. Some control might be needed to prevent discrimination but not to prevent nondiscriminatory price increases. Both in 1940–41 and in 1950 priorities controls operated without price controls.

A somewhat contrary question is whether prices would or could go up if we had allocation controls. For example, it is sometimes suggested in the case of meat that rationing would hold down the price without any direct price control. I believe that is probably correct. But I do not believe that the kinds of allocations systems we use for materials would prevent their prices from rising. The most likely and desirable allocations systems in a program of the new projected size would be open ended. That is, the supply would not be exhaustively allocated. Deliveries against rated or allocated orders would be compulsory, but after that there would be a scramble area where deliveries could be freely made. Demand in the scramble area will exceed the supply, so sellers will not have to fear that they will be unabe to sell their whole output if they raise the price.

Even if there is no scramble area and the supply is exhaustively allocated, I believe there will be a tendency for prices to rise, if it is the policy of the authorities to issue enough allocations to absorb the whole supply. If a price rise should curtail demand, allocations would be granted on requests that would have otherwise been rejected. As long as there is an unsatisfied margin of requests for allocations, the price can rise.

Although production and distribution controls are authorized and imposed to meet a real need of the defense program, once they are in existence there is very strong pressure to use them for a variety of other purposes. Thus we get production controls used to aid small business, to serve as a substitute for credit controls, to undo the mess caused by price conrtols, or just to direct production in a way that someone thinks is better—tin for soup cans but not for beer cans. All this is rationalized in the name of defense. And it is obviously difficult to find anything that does not have something to do with defense, broadly interpreted. If these incidental uses of controls do not go on beyond the time when direct defense needs require controls anyway, possibly no great harm is done. However, the danger is that a broad interpretation of the requirements of defense will serve as justification for controls long after the need for them to assist the strictly military program has passed. The more definite and extensive our notions about the particular pattern of resource use that is necessary for national defense, aside from the resource use the government itself pays for, the more necessity there will be for the controls to assure achievement of that pattern.

CHAIRMAN LEVI: I now direct the attention of the conference to Item I. I will ask Mr. Hansen if he will start the discussion on this point.

MR. HANSEN: Mr. Chairman, I will make just a very few comments. I thought when I read the report of the Committee on Stabilization in the *Economic Review,* September, 1950, that I detected some Harvard influence on Chicago, since one of the members was a distinguished member of the Chicago faculty, but now I learn that the unilateral trade is all flowing the other way.

I am a little bit confused on one point. I find that a good

many members of the conference seem, on the one hand, to be very much concerned about rigorous price stabilization, and, on the other hand, I learn today that they are quite prepared to go the whole way of any amount of inflation rather than pursue other than monetary policy supplemented by fiscal policy. Both of these positions seem to me to be very extreme indeed. I should say that it is quite easy to become too rigorous about price stabilization. I think there is very much in the little book that D. H. Robertson wrote in the middle twenties, *Banking Policy and the Price Level,* in which he called attention to, I think, a very important point, the difference between desirable price fluctuations and undesirable price fluctuations.

I do not know of any period in history in which there has been a substantial increase in output without some price increase. If we go back to World War II, we were then in an unusually favorable position to divert resources to the war effort because we had eight or nine million unemployed; but, even so, I do not believe we could have so successfully diverted resources quickly to war effort, as in fact we did, had we had rigorous price stabilization from 1940 to 1942.

We did not undertake fairly rigorous price stabilization until that transfer of resources had, in fact, taken place. Now, however, I should not wish to overstress that because I think that in the circumstances we are in now there is really no danger of excessive price stabilization. I merely call attention to it in view of what has been said by several members of the conference.

Directing my attention to Item I, I should like to say that I could not agree that we can determine the aggregate monetary demand from the monetary supply, the supply of money.

I am not going to talk a lot of theory but just call attention to the experience that we had from 1946 to 1948. The year 1948—and I think we are often inclined to overlook it—was a year of price stability. There was, to be sure, an upward flurry of prices, fairly strong, in the middle of the summer of 1948, but prices were lower—both wholesale and consumer prices—at the end of 1948 than in January, 1948.

Now, what were the causes of this price stability? If one considers simply the money supply and what has in the past been regarded as a normal velocity of money—if one were going to estimate on that basis—there is absolutely no reason in the world why prices should have ceased rising in January, 1948. We had virtually no increase in the money supply in this period. Demand deposits and currency stood at 106 billion dollars before price controls were removed in June, 1946, and they stood at 108 billion dollars as an average for 1948. There was a small increase in velocity, sufficient to care for payments that were necessary with the increase of money income that occurred. Estimating it on the income basis, the income velocity increased from 1.7 to 2.0. Now, there was, of course, no reason at all from a purely monetary standpoint why the income velocity might not have gone up to 3.3 where it has been over long decades in our history.

Why did prices stop rising? Well, I submit that it was fundamentally nonmonetary factors. When wires from all over the world began to bring in reports in January, 1948, that agricultural and food supplies were on the increase, we had a sharp break in those prices, and that was a very important factor. In the meantime, we had worked through very many of our shortages. The pipelines were being filled with inventories all around. The strategic shortages being overcome, the supply situation was enormously different. These bottlenecks and the food shortage, in my judgment, were fundamental factors in causing the increase in prices that occurred. There was indeed a monetary basis for such expansion as occurred, but the point that I am calling attention to is that there was a monetary basis for an enormously greater increase in prices than in fact occurred.

What is the relation of controls to the monetary situation, wage control, for example? I think it would be quite possible for us in this situation—I do not want to be dogmatic about it— to get by without price controls and wage controls provided we did certain other things vigorously; particularly provided we attacked vigorously the area of nondefensive investment.

We have now had for some years a perfectly enormous volume of capital outlays. Very much of it is quite unnecessary from the standpoint of the purpose presently urgent for this country. We could sharply reduce the nondefense investment by a number of measures, including some that are already in force but not being used very vigorously, such as the control of the real estate credit and the consumers credit. We have plenty of civilian automobiles in the country. We might very well cut out civilian motorcar production altogether, as we did in 1941–42. Mr. Burgess yesterday mentioned capital issues control, and Mr. Harrod mentioned a tax system which might curtail investment.

Now, if we rigorously controlled investment outlets, nondefense outlays, and backed it up in the next two years while we are building the capital facilities needed for military output, I think the situation will ease if we do not get into a general war. If, in addition to a drastic curtailment of investment, and nondefense investment, we could achieve a moderately overbalanced budget, then I think we might on that basis get by without wage and price controls. I say it is possible we might get by without wage and price controls. But so long as we have a situation in which investment considerably exceeds saving, or, putting it on a little broader basis, a situation in which private investment and governmental outlays exceed savings and taxes, prices will rise. And when they rise we can be sure there will be a very strong demand, and I think irresistible demands, for wage increases. Then we have the price-wage spiral going.

I say "price-wage" because I think regularly in these situations it is prices that go up first and then wages go up. To be sure, if we now introduced wage control in that situation and rigorously held wages down, the inflation would very quickly run out. Why? Because the excess of demand would raise prices, but consumption would not rise if we held wages down, and we would soon develop a sufficient volume of saving to balance the former excess of investment, and so our inflationary development would run out. But, of course, that is exactly what would not happen in the kind of society we live in. If prices were allowed to rise, then we would have the powerful demand for wage increases.

In view of the fact that we are not at all adequately attacking the investment field, and I doubt that we shall, it seems to me necessary to have wage control, and if we have wage control, we have to have price control. It is also true that we can go too far in the program of—going back to my original point of control of investment and an overbalanced budget—taxation, so that the very heavy taxes on the mass of people will lead to an irresistible demand for wage increases.

There is a nice balance there, and that is why I suggested it is one which we cannot be dogmatic about; but it does seem to me that, if we vigorously attacked the investment area and had a moderately overbalanced budget with a tolerable burden of taxation, then we perhaps could get by without wage and price control. I do not believe we are likely to reach that favorable situation, and for that reason I believe that in these circumstances we do need wage and price control.

Mr. Garrison: Mr. Chairman, I would like to make a general comment on wage controls which will run to the whole structure of the outline that we have before us. It seems to me that we are assuming this morning that wage controls can be legislated when we wish them and that the real questions are of the purely economic character which is set forth in the outline. In my opinion, however, the question that is most pressing is: What are the political, economic, and social conditions under which effective wage controls can be established? Because we had reasonably effective wage controls in the last war, we are a little too likely to take them for granted and to assume that we had them simply because we decided to have them.

The remarkable character of the achievement of wage stabilization in the last war can very easily be overlooked. It was, in fact, the first time in the history of any democratic government that a general program of wage controls by law was effectively carried on. Even in Great Britain during the last war, there was no wage control by law. It was entirely a voluntary system based on the pledge of the labor unions that, if industry would do so and so and if government would do so and so, the wage line would be held. So Great Britain got through the last war without any form of governmental wage controls, as distinguished from voluntary controls. We went through the war with governmental wage controls, and we managed to make on the whole a reasonably good go of it, but the circumstances which existed then were quite different from the circumstances which exist today, and so the question arises: Under what circumstances today can we make wage controls by government workable?

What were the differences which I have just mentioned? In the first place, we were at war, and the whole country was unified in a way that cannot be duplicated today. It was a time in which the foremost leaders of industry and labor and other people could be persuaded to go down to Washington and take top policy jobs, a time of pulling together and of tremendous determination to make the controls work. We are in a kind of twilight zone today, half in war and half in peace, and the difficulties are that much greater.

The second difference was that, partly due to the circumstances I have described, it was possible to obtain from the leaders of industry and of labor a national no-strike, no-lockout agreement, a common agreement by industry and labor that for the duration of the war these disputes would all be settled by resort to a board. Now, it is highly desirable—indeed, almost essential—if we are to have a successfully functioning wage-control policy (wage control by government) that we shall have a no-strike agreement, or at least a policy in fact of compliance with wage-bound decisions. We cannot have wage controls and large-scale strikes for increased wages at the same time if we are going to have an effective system, and so one of the questions, it seems to me, is: Under what political and economic and social circumstances can we get that kind of basic labor-industry understanding which is really the underpinning of the whole system?

A third difference was that in the last war we tackled the whole problem of inflation on a broader front and with more vigor all along the line than we are doing now. You remember that in the spring of 1942 the President issued a seven-point comprehensive program of inflation control in which it was recognized that everything was dependent upon everything else, that we could not have a successful attack on inflation by piecemeal measures. And then that was implemented in the Act of October, 1942, and we started off with a more comprehensive attack on all the inflationary factors than we now have.

To mention only one item, farm prices at that time were pegged like other prices. The situation was exactly turned around from what it is now. We started off in 1942 with a ceiling on farm prices. In the spring of 1943 a drive began in Congress to free farm prices and to make them flexible so as to conform to changes in the cost of living—the Pace Amendment to the Agricultural Act. That was considered by the Administration as so great a threat to the program that Mr. Byrnes, as economic stabilization director, issued an executive order freezing wages even more tightly than they had been frozen up to that point, as a *quid pro quo* for killing the Pace Amendment in the Congress and keeping farm prices stabilized.

Today we start off in just the opposite condition. We start off with the farm parity-price formula subject to an escalator provision under which, as the prices of the things the farmer buys increase, so does the parity price. That is written right into the definition of parity. In addition, we start off with escalator clauses in wage contracts to an extent that we did not have in the last war. We are starting off, then, with an economy that we have not dealt with nearly so effectively on all the inflationary fronts as we did before. Great difficulties ensue in singling out wage controls without comprehensively attacking these other problems.

I want to add two more points. I raise the question whether, if we cannot have an effective coming-to-grips with the problem of farm prices, an effective coming-to-grips with a serious tax program that will convince the laboring people, among others, that the government really means business all along the line of inflation, and more effective monetary and price controls—if we cannot do these things and do them quite speedily, I raise the question whether the attempt at present to lay down wage controls may not in fact be more inflationary than stabilizing. I know that under the 10 per cent formula many, many unions are seeking wage increases as a matter of right, which, if that 10 per cent formula were not in existence, would not give rise to the same pressures. If we were sure of stopping when the 10 per cent has been had all along the line, it might be one thing; but, with farm prices untied and with the general laxity in the whole program, the question is whether when we have reached the 10 per cent the pressures are not going to be such that we will again make exceptions and go on from there. Without attempting to argue that we should abolish the present controls—a proposal which seems to me under present conditions to be quite academic— I do want to raise very seriously the relationship between the inflationary possibilities latent in those controls if we do not tackle the comprehensive job of economic stabilization all along the line.

My last comment has to do with the long-range future. We have talked here about two years and about plateaus as though all we had to do was to bridge a period of some difficulty that lies immediately ahead and then somehow everything is going to be all right. My own conviction is that the situation is much more serious than that, that we are engaged in fact in an armaments race, we and the Western countries together, with Russia to which I can see no end short of either some kind of international settlement at some stage or an eruption into war—when, nobody knows. But to suppose that at the end of two years we shall reach some kind of plateau in which we will cease constantly going forward and increasing armaments and our preparations for defense, as the other fellows inevitably increase theirs, seems to me the greatest form of wishful thinking.

Therefore, looking at the situation as a whole, as we lay down controls, should we not say to ourselves: How are these controls going to fit a long-range program? We may be mistaken in that. We may be out of the woods before very long, but we cannot afford to bet on it. How is this program going to work, not for two years, but for five years, ten years, fifteen—who knows? I cannot answer that question, but I raise it because it seems to me basic to everything we are talking about. I should say that one principle that would come out of considering that kind of question would be this—that wherever possible we would try to work out our policies by joint agreement of industry, of labor, of farmers, as Great Britain did so successfully in the last war.

I agree with Mr. Burgess that it is possible to do a great many things by agreement and that that is part of the genius of the democratic system. We do not have to do everything by governmental controls, and the greater the area of workable agreement among the great groups that make up our democracy, the better off we are going to be for the long pull; and the principle ought to be to avoid complex controls and the building of a vast mass of regulations in so far as we possibly can find simpler measures for coping with the problem.

It is for that reason, it seems to me, among other things, that the kind of proposals for investment controls that Professor Harrod has made here, reinforced by Professor Hansen's discussion, bulk a good deal larger than if we were merely thinking of what we were going to do just for two years. We have a long, tough road to travel, more difficult, I think, than anything that is suggested by this outline.

CHAIRMAN LEVI: I direct the attention of the conference to Item I, as to which, as I understand it, Mr. Hansen has implied that the price-wage controls would have probable utility and as to which Mr. Garrison stated that all types of approaches for handling inflation should be used at once and has pointed out the difficulties of mandatory controls and has urged voluntary controls, having in mind the long period during which these may have to be effective.

I direct the attention of the conference again to the question as to whether price-wage controls deal with symptoms rather than causes of inflation, with the three related questions asked at this point. Does anyone wish to comment?

MR. MULLENDORE: Just one point. I am in complete agreement with the previous speaker, Mr. Garrison, upon the point of the length of time in which we are faced with an emergency. I think, however, that the assumption that inflation was controlled during the last war is something which needs to be questioned, because, if we proceed upon that assumption, then it would be a false one and would be quite misleading.

Inflation was not controlled during the last war. Inflation was more or less successfully postponed until the postwar period in the last war. We bottled up the purchasing power which we distributed during the war, making the purchasing power available in the postwar period through redeemable bonds and other transferable wealth, basing these not upon real wealth but upon wealth which was destroyed in the war. We stopped making automobiles and other things during the war so that the phony purchasing power could not then be spent; but we are now confronted with it, and we have been confronted with it for a number of years. At the point at which we now are, these high price levels and this excessive demand, and this false and phony prosperity we have had during the past several years, are the result of the inflation; and we are now talking about controlling inflation again when we are already suffering severely from the attempt to control inflation during the last war.

MR. HAZLITT: I want to suggest that it might be a very profitable use of our time, having Mr. DiSalle here, to use it to ask him some questions if he would be kind enough to answer them to clarify the position. I wanted to ask, first, whether such questions would be in order. If they would be, I have one or two that I would like to ask.

CHAIRMAN LEVI: I think it would really be better, although I understand the resistance to this, to go through with the outline first, to have as orderly a discussion on it as we can, so that we can clarify the disagreements among us. At the conclusion of that, if Mr. DiSalle is willing to answer questions, I am sure time can be provided during the day for that. But I think it would be better to have a discussion among us first so that the disagreements obviously within this group are clarified.

MR. HAZLITT: What I have in mind, Mr. Chairman, is that, if we knew the assumptions on which Mr. DiSalle was operating, the discussion would be clarified.

MR. ARNOLD: I rise to the question of voluntary agreements, a subject on which I look with considerable skepticism now as I did during the last war. Certainly we do not want to exclude them, but the type of voluntary agreement which we are likely to get was well illustrated by the oil companies in the Petroleum Administration for Defense which decided that they would save tetraethyl lead by lowering the octane content of all gasoline. That is nothing but a price rise and also a restriction on the ingenuity of great companies like the Sun Oil Company, which does not use much tetraethyl lead. It was due to a good fight on the part of the Sun Oil Company and my friend, Mr. Morison, that they took the tetraethyl lead, and the companies are free to make as good gasoline as they can.

The voluntary agreement method has great dangers, and it must be severely limited. I have no objection to Mr. Burgess' banking voluntary agreement, surrounded as he is with an enormous number of regulatory safeguards, but, when we talk about throwing the voluntary agreement into industries less controlled than Mr. Burgess' bank, I think we had better take a long look at it before we get it started.

MR. CORTNEY: It is rather painful to me to have to defend controls, but I shall have to do so. Your question is whether, if the excess money demand is not eliminated, direct controls should be enforced. I take the position that, even if the monetizing of debt by the government is stopped, we shall need some wage and price controls in the strategic points on account of the escalator clauses in the recent labor contracts and on account of agricultural prices and agricultural subsidies.

There is no doubt that because of the inflation we tolerated during the last war, and the huge expansion of credit after the last war, business has got accustomed to conditions of inflation, the labor bosses cannot exercise their power without inflation, and the farmers like inflation simply because the prices are rising. It has become the strategy of the labor unions to obtain wage rises in certain strategic industries where prices can be raised at the same time as the wages, and, once this is accomplished, wage rises spreading all over the economy cannot be avoided.

If we do not suppress the cost-of-living escalator and the productivity escalator, the following thing is bound to happen: Some wages have not yet risen and have not yet caught up with wage rises in strategic industries, and, as they rise and affect the costs of production or doing business, we are bound to have rises in prices. The sluggish wages are particularly those in industries which cannot increase prices as soon as wages are increased.

Second, we may have shortages as in wool and steel, which will rise in price simply because for a time there is not enough of these materials. Now, if labor, on account of the cost-of-living escalator is to exact increases in wages because of some scarcities, and not because of inflation pervading the entire economy, then I do not see why everybody else should not have a cost-of-living escalator. If there are to be escalators, then I believe everybody should have escalators and not only a privileged group of workers which, because they are in a privileged position, have been able to extort these kinds of contracts. Furthermore, if we try to put new excise taxes, we would get increases in wages due to the escalator clauses, because the cost-of-living index includes such taxes. Then we have a so-called productivity escalator. I doubt that we shall have increases in productivity in the present conditions so that prices will rise further.

So, gentlemen, all these considerations lead me to agree with Professor Hansen. I am, generally, in sympathy with what he has said, and I doubt that the policy of the labor unions, and the mere fact that the power of the labor-union bosses is based on inflation, will make it possible to avoid controls on wages and prices in strategic points of our economy.

I hear very often comparisons based on what our British friends are able to accomplish. I am often saying in international gatherings that British people are a peculiar nation, and what can happen in Great Britain is not going to happen here or elsewhere.

Mr. FRIEDMAN: I wanted to make one comment and ask Mr. Hansen one question. The comment bears on the question of whether wage and price control can, in fact, reduce the ultimate extent of the inflation. Much of the argument by Mr. Garrison, for example, and some of the others, rests on the assumption that wage and price controls can, in fact, do something about making the ultimate price rise less than it otherwise would be.

Mr. Mullendore's comment suggested doubt about that with respect to the last World War. I want to add a couple of figures that I think are extremely suggestive. This country has gone through three major wars, the Civil War, the first World War, and the second World War. It is extremely interesting that the ultimate price rise in all three wars is almost exactly the same.

In all three cases prices approximately doubled. There was one important significant difference among the wars that I think can be attributable to direct controls.

In the Civil War the peak of the price rise coincided with the end of the war, in the first quarter of 1865. In the first World War the peak of the price rise came fifteen months after the end of the war. In the second World War the peak of the price rise came approximately thirty-six months after the end of the war.

MR. VINER: It has not come yet.

MR. FRIEDMAN: I mean the initial postwar peak, because again, in these other cases, there were later peaks. The initial postwar peak came approximately three years after the end of World War II. Those figures suggest very strongly that the main advantage of direct wage and price controls is simply to postpone but not to reduce the ultimate price rise. In the light of this, I would like to ask Mr. Hansen the question whether, in saying that if we did not do the other things necessary to prevent inflation, he thought wage and price controls desirable—was he emphasizing the point he made that they were perhaps inevitable under those circumstances?—or whether he meant further to say that he preferred suppressed inflation to open inflation.

CHAIRMAN LEVI: The Chair will recognize the indirect control being exercised by Mr. Friedman and will call on Mr. Hansen.

MR. HANSEN: I would like to call attention to a point that, it seems to me, is being overlooked by several members of the conference. We still keep talking as though we had had ever since the war a strong inflationary development. That is simply not true. We had, from the beginning of January, 1948, until Korea, no price inflation. Prices were lower, substantially lower, just before Korea than they were in January, 1948. We had two and one-half years not only of price stability but of some price decline. Now, we are in another war. That is different. Somebody mentioned that prices have not stopped rising yet. But now we are in another war. I call attention to this point because I find people all the time talking as though we have been in a continuous price inflation all the time. That is not true.

Now let me refer to the historical cases that Mr. Friedman

mentioned. I think that they are very significant, though I draw somewhat different conclusions. After World War I, we had a very substantial price inflation after the war was over, as he intimated. We had first a short recession, and then we had a substantial price inflation, including a very substantial wage rise in a quite free market. We had a larger wage rise in a quite free market than we have had since World War II under collective bargaining. I think the collective bargaining has actually had the effect of slowing down the wage increase since 1945, and I cite the historical precedent of what happened after World War I, when, in a quite free market, we had a very rapid rise in wages in a competitive situation. Now, I submit that in both World War I and World War II the essential cause of the increase in prices that occurred was not this "suppressed inflation," which runs simply in terms of the money supply.

After World War I, we had—because we had been fighting a war, and all kinds of things could not be produced while we were fighting the war—tremendous shortages all around. Those shortages were the primary cause of the increase in prices that occurred. And similarly, after this last war, shortages dominated the market situation when the price controls were removed.

In my judgment, if we had been able—I doubt that we were able, because of the psychological situation in the country—to retain price control for another twelve months, we might have had very little price inflation. After twelve months the shortages would largely have been overcome, and supply and demand might well have been in balance. Such a balance was reached in fact in 1948. Prices stopped rising. But the monetary situation cannot explain the end of inflation in 1948. From the purely monetary standpoint, prices could easily have kept right on soaring.

It is a fact that after the price controls were removed under the impetus of the tremendous shortages that existed, we had a substantial increase in prices for nine months. After nine months, the price level rapidly stabilized. By January, 1948, it stopped rising. By then, aggregate demand and aggregate supply were in balance.

Now, the monetary situation—this alleged suppressed inflation

—would have justified an increase in prices three times what we got. I submit that the explanation is not "suppressed inflation." The main explanation is to be found in the shortages caused by the war. It is this that accounts mainly for the postwar inflation in World War I as well as World War II.

MR. VINER: Mr. Chairman, Mr. Hansen said that there was no simple explanation for any past event. I agree with him, and therefore I reject his explanation. I do think there is a tendency toward too simple explanations, and doctrine which explains the course of events in terms of the quantity of money alone, as if nothing else matters, is a grotesquely simplified explanation. I hope nobody believes in that kind of explanation, even though I occasionally hear talk that sounds that way.

I want to say a word about this suppressed inflation business. I do think that we had an extremely suppressed inflation in the war years and that we are not yet through with Leon Henderson, Paul Porter, etc.—that their consequences are still living with us. I do not think that Hansen's introduction of the word "continuous" is necessarily relevant. We were having a tendency toward an upward rise in prices before Korea. There can be lapses, changes in inventory situations, changes in business expectations, which bring temporary falls in prices; the ups and downs of human psychology can bring ups and downs in price levels, even though there is a basic trend in an inflationary direction.

There was, before Korea, in our methods, habits, and procedures of bank control, or in its absence, in our procedures for pegging interest rates, a factor permitting the accumulation of quantities of money and quantities of other liquid assets which, in time, it would be a reasonable forecast—although nobody could say it would certainly work out that way—would be steadily operating to produce a secular upward trend in the price level. We were not yet through, therefore, with the full expression, the full open expressions, of all the suppressed inflation that had been built up in World War II.

On the other hand, I would not for a moment say that we ought to scrap direct controls. I object myself to some of the course of the discussion by persons with whom otherwise I am in basic sympathy who separate fiscal control from monetary control and would rely only on the latter. I would rely mainly on the two combined. But I would for another reason want direct controls now. Rightly or wrongly, the American people believe that, if we do not have a fairly obvious system of direct controls, we are not serious in wanting to prevent inflation and that we do not really have in mind the building-up of the security of the country without recourse to inflation.

I am willing to make concessions to direct controls, even when I do not believe in them for economic reasons. If we cannot make the people believe that other devices are adequate, I am for direct controls, even though in general I think they will not work well economically and even though they may affect unfavorably the troop action in Korea. Beyond that, I do believe in marginal, carefully selected direct controls at strategic points of inflationary threat for a variety of economic reasons, which I do not have to go into, since many of them have been very ably expounded earlier in this session. There is one further point only that I want to make.

There are some enthusiasts here for monetary controls. There are more here who feel it urgent that there be other controls and who do not believe that monetary controls would be adequate to do the job. Let not the outcome of the discussion be, however, that the monetary controls are negligible or unimportant or will not help the direct controllers in doing what will look afterward like a very good job.

If I were a direct controller, I would not be preaching the need of direct controls. The American public are converted to them. I would preach the need of monetary control, so that their job shall be "do-able," and so that when they retire they will retire, not as price controllers have retired in the past, but with accolades and laurel wreaths.

CHAIRMAN LEVI: The Chair realizes that a precedent has been made in acknowledgment of the fact that Mr. Friedman directed a question to Mr. Hansen. The Chair has been told that this is unfair to Mr. Hansen, although I believe that that comment is undoubtedly unfair. In view of the precedent that has been created, the Chair naturally wishes to follow precedent and will permit questions to be asked of Mr. DiSalle, who has said that he is willing to answer them at this time.

MR. DISALLE: I said I was willing to try to answer them.

MR. HAZLITT: I understood Mr. DiSalle to say that, even if we had proper monetary controls, he thinks we would still need direct controls; and I was wondering whether that was his position—that he was not arguing that we did have proper monetary controls but that, even if we had them, he would still subscribe to direct controls. I was wondering whether he would be willing to give his reason why he thinks direct controls would still be necessary if proper monetary controls existed.

MR. DISALLE: I think that has been my position. I want to thank Professor Viner for his statements on the subject. My position has always been, from the beginning, that direct controls in and of themselves would not solve the problem. Direct price controls are only part of an integrated program that would be needed if we were to achieve stability.

Going back to Mr. Hazlitt's question, I certainly would think that we would need direct controls, even though we had a proper monetary system, because without direct controls forces would be set at work in a democracy that would create pressures, that would throw our economy out of balance in abnormal times, requiring the imposition of direct controls.

MR. BRUBAKER: First, I would like to say that I am grateful to Mr. Garrison for having given you a little bit of the background which made it possible for wage controls to function during the last war. There were a lot of lessons which we should have learned from that experience, which, apparently, we did not learn; and that is the reason for the great impasse that we have reached on the question of wage controls at the present moment.

I agree with Mr. Garrison that we certainly ought to try to reach all the voluntary agreements we can in this area, although I am inclined to agree with Mr. Arnold that the area of agreement we can reach is probably not so great as we would like. I am also grateful to Professor Hansen for having suggested to this group of economists, and others, that wage increases in our present economy follow upon price increases. For some strange reason, that seems to have been forgotten. We are customarily put in the position of being the goats for all the price increases that occur. Price increases presumably occur, we are told, because we insist on wage increases.

One of the speakers has just said that the power of labor leaders is based on inflation and on an inflationary economy. That, from our point of view, is plain and utter nonsense, and I would like to label it as such. If that were true—and let us assume for the moment that it were true—do you suppose that labor would have been pleading for direct controls and for an end to this inflation? We have, for months—long before the representatives in Congress seemed to think it was a smart political move last fall to pass a law which would permit direct controls —been asking for direct controls, because it appeared to us that the inflationary forces were already so far out of control that the only way of halting them and of trying to prevent another round of heavy inflation of prices and wages, and everything else, was some form of direct controls slapped on in a hurry.

Now, we are put in the position, as labor unions, of having to ask for wage increases for some very simple reasons, which I do not think I ought to have to go over, but apparently I do. We have to ask for wage increases because prices have already increased. Do I have to go back to what happened throughout the course of 1950 to make you realize how far we had dropped behind? Nearly every major labor union in the country had closed contracts during most of the year. We sat there while the price of everything around us was going up. Our cost of living was going up. The price of steel, believe it or not, even though there was not a general increase, was going up. The price of almost everything one could look at was going up, and yet we were sitting with wages frozen not by law but by our own contracts, by our own voluntary agreement to freeze such.

Now, we cannot be expected to sit on that lid forever. Higher prices forced us to go out and ask for wage increases. If we were to hope even to maintain anything like a reasonable equity as our share of the national wealth—and that is something which has been decreasing in the last several years—if we hoped to maintain even a reasonable share, we had to go out and ask for wage increases last summer and fall and this spring. Despite that, however, we have agreed—and I think you ought to give us a great deal of credit for this, whatever you may happen to think of labor privately—that direct controls of prices and wages are necessary in this time, and we are willing to be controlled—but at a price—and I do not think it is an unfair price.

We have stated our price very simply, and I think some of you ought to go back and take a look at this very brief little statement that the Wage Stabilization Board adopted unanimously—industry, public, and labor members—in which we agreed that we would take part in wage control if there was price control, if there was a reasonable tax program, if there was a sane and sensible and sound rent-control law. In other words, if the conditions were created which would permit some kind of equality of sharing in the price which we are forced to pay for the kind of program of mobilization on which we are embarking.

Now, I do not think that that is too much of a price for us to ask. We are not asking for special treatment. We are not asking that we be permitted to have wage rises while prices are frozen, while rents are frozen, while taxes are increased. We ask simply that you do all those things and that you do them together. But what has happened? We got caught out on the end of a limb by some clever political maneuvering here last fall, which finally forced the government into the position of slapping on some price controls and some wage controls far ahead of these other things which are an integral part of a fair-shares program.

We did not get, and we still do not have, any kind of rent control affecting most of the workers of the United States. I put it just that bluntly. We de not have it, and I do not think it is even in prospect at the moment. Now, how can you ask us to hold a wage line when an important item of our cost of living such as rent is uncontrolled and is rising, as any of you ought to know? If you go into any community where workers are coming in to go to work in a defense plant, you ought to take a look at some of the rents those people are being asked to pay. It is positively scandalous, and I do not think anybody has a right to stand up today and urge wage controls and a wage freeze unless he is willing to do something on the score of rents.

I do not think I have to remind you that one of the other major items of our cost of living is still free to rise, that is, the farm products which are not yet up to parity. It is a problem that Mr. DiSalle and others are struggling with at the moment and trying to make some sense out of, and which, I understand, they are going to ask Congress to try to make some sense out of. But do not sit back in your piety and say to us, "Take a wage freeze. Stand where you are. See your own cost of living rise. See your own real wages decrease, your own share in the national income decrease at the expense of corporate profits and at the expense of higher farm income. You just sit and take it."

Now, I tell you that you cannot, with honesty and integrity and fairness, force upon us that kind of arrangement. We have taken it, to date. I do not know how long we will take it. It is a crazy system, and it is an inequitable system, as it now works. And the worst thing that is wrong with it is not Mr. DiSalle and the people struggling with direct controls, even though we have been critical of some of the things they have done; the worst thing wrong with it is a lousy law. We certainly have one, and unless we are willing to sit down and change that law so that we bring back some equity and fairness in this system, we will have an arrangement that Mr. DiSalle cannot live with, that Mr. Johnston cannot live with, and that we cannot live with. I do not think that even the members of the National Association of Manufacturers and the Chamber of Commerce who sit with us on the Wage Stabilization Board are going to ask us long to live with such an inequitable arrangement. They cannot do so in good conscience. And I assure them we cannot live with it as it stands; and, if we cannot, obviously, we are going to have to breach the present wage-freeze line.

Now, we have not taken a no-strike pledge this time, and I think Mr. Garrison gave you some of the reasons why. I am not in a position to say whether we would or would not give such a pledge again. I think the answer ought to be fairly obvious to you, however, if you have followed at all closely the demands which have been made as a price for our participation in a Wage Stabilization Board.

We have asked, as one of our major prices, that there be an

arrangement for the settlement of disputes. Now, that can mean only one thing—that we are willing to take disputes to such a board to have them settled. That means we do not strike if there is a dispute. That means we go to a board and let the board settle it. It is just that simple. All I ask is that we try to get this problem of direct controls down onto a plane where we can make stabilization work.

We are critical of Mr. DiSalle, not because we do not like him, and not because we do not like price control. We realize that he has an impossible job at the moment, but, as price controls are now set, he himself says there is no question but what we are going to have a further rise in prices, even in the next few months. In the face of these facts one cannot step in and insist on a wage freeze—and that is what we have at the moment for the major group of organized workers in the United States. As long as we have not frozen prices, and as long as we have not done these other things to halt inflation, we cannot fix and hold wages where they are, and you might just as well realize it.

CHAIRMAN LEVI: The Chair will have to rule that from now on questions are asked of Mr. DiSalle, or we should move to Item II on the agenda, because of the lateness of the hour.

MR. HAZLITT: May I ask Mr. DiSalle whether it is not true that the Bureau of Labor Statistics figures show that, from about 1935 to 1939, weekly factory wages have gone up in the neighborhood of 180 per cent, whereas the cost of living has only gone up in the neighborhood of about 84 per cent, and rents have only gone up 34 per cent, or something of that nature. I wish to ask this question in relation to Mr. Brubaker's talk.

MR. BRUBAKER: How about including in your answer how much corporate profits have gone up in that period too?

MR. DiSALLE: That was not asked. The cost-of-living index, as of February 15, stood at about 183. I just could not give you the figure on what wages have increased since that time. I do not know whether Gardner has those figures.

MR. ACKLEY: I assume the figures are reasonably correct. I suggest that the question is not completely relevant, inasmuch as a period of fifteen years should have increased real income for all of us. I think the question is somewhat loaded.

Mr. Cortney: The increase in wages of labor after taxes has risen approximately 27 per cent as compared to prewar. The real income of the middle classes, and those were supposed to have gone up, has gone down, with insurance policies, pensions, and what-not. It is a great lie to say that the increase in the standard of living of one segment of our country has not been paid for by others. It has and is continuing to be paid.

Chairman Levi: Any other questions of Mr. DiSalle?

Representative Celler: Would this be a fair statement, Mr. DiSalle? That the existence of a farm parity is like asking you to fight inflation with one of your hands tied behind your back; and, if that is so, have you made any recommendations to Congress, or do you intend to, with reference to the change in the law concerning parity?

Mr. DiSalle: The question is before the President at the moment, and I would prefer to let the President make his recommendations to Congress without any undue pressure from me.

Representative Celler: I think it might be appropriate to make this following comment, Mr. Chairman. I do not think that you will get any change in parity and the parity law, and you will still have to fight inflation with your hand tied behind your back. Why do I say that? I say that because of the imbalance that exists in Congress concerning congressional apportionment of seats; because of outmoded, outdated reapportionment statutes in the various states, we have a great disparity between the number of seats allotted to the city districts as against the number of seats allotted to the rural areas. We have disparities of the following nature: In some districts, we have a representative representing 900,000 people. In another district, we have a representative representing 167,000 in population. As one cartoonist put it, it is like horse-and-rabbit stew—one horse, one rabbit.

We can readily see that if we have the imbalance obtaining, we will have a greater number of votes accorded to the rural congressmen representing the farmers as against the representation in Congress of the consumers, and parity militates—of course, we will all agree—against consumers. I cannot, for the life of me, see how, with the farm representation being as adamant as it is intransigent, and refusing to make any change in parity, we can adequately and successfully fight inflation.

CHAIRMAN LEVI: In view of the number of questions asked of Mr. DiSalle, I suggest that we move to Item II, realizing that, if the conference desires later to ask questions of Mr. DiSalle, this can be done.

MR. DISALLE: Mr. Chairman, I would think that, in view of the fact that both Mr. Henderson and Mr. Porter have been referred to in a somewhat difficult manner, they ought to be permitted to make a statement that Mr. Henderson has been dying to make since Professor Viner had the floor.

MR. HENDERSON: I should like to get into this argument that was started. If it means that the architects of price control can also take the glory for the false and phony prosperity of Mr. Mullendore, I will be glad to take the responsibility for post-ponements of purchasing power to a period in which it could be better expressed as a demand for goods under a competitive society. If Paul Porter wants to relinquish his share of that to me, I will be very glad to take that. But I think the record ought to show that there never was a time when the clumsy architects of price control ever thought, or argued, that it was a complete substitute for all other controls; monetary and fiscal policy was urged all the time.

In the hearings on the price-control bill there were constant references to the necessity for a heavy taxation policy. We seem to have been operating under something called a "deflationary gap" at that time, and in the program that was mentioned by Alvin Hansen there were seven points, as I recall, which were urged upon the President by the Office of Price Administration in the early part of 1942. The reason why the October, 1942, program had to be instituted was that only those under our con-trol—namely, the price, rent, further working-down of the agri-cultural prices, and certain amounts of rationing—had been con-cluded. That made it necessary for the September recommen-dation which became the October 2 legislation.

I rise to get a modest amount of association with the dis-tinguished import of thought from the Midwest to the East. There was never a time that the price administration group, as can be testified to by the large number of academicians we drew in, ever thought we could do other than keep a certain balance and direction and keep things from getting completely out of hand.

MR. VINER: I think I can satisfy Mr. Henderson. I do not know Mr. Porter as well, but I do know him well enough to know he has a keen sense of humor, and I do not think I need carry that any further. But, for many years, I had the opportunity of watching Mr. Henderson in action. I used to look at him the way a young girl looks at a movie hero. I used to see my idea of a civil servant, with unlimited courage and vigor, and almost always on the right side; and when I mentioned Mr. Henderson and Mr. Porter, I did not even mean their agencies, because their agencies were in a difficult setting over which they had limited control.

We just heard our new price controller say that on one matter that has to be settled elsewhere. I do say that he [Mr. Henderson] was fighting on these other battle lines. He never restricted his lines of battle, and I repeat that I was once young and could admire him. In this particular case, my admiration still remains. Mr. Henderson is my idea of a good civil servant.

MR. LEVENTHAL: I want to speak to a point raised by Mr. Director at the beginning that has not so far been adverted to in all the later comments. That is his assumption that a program of price regulation limits production and that price rises are necessary in order to obtain adequate production. Even Professor Viner in his aside remarks as to the necessity for price controls as a gesture to public opinion, and to convince the public that the administration is taking the stabilization program seriously, stated that he believed that price controls might be to the disadvantage of the troops in Korea, by which I assume he means that price controls limit production.

The fact is that there are certain reasons to believe that price controls increase production, or certainly do not effectively limit it. One of these points is made in Item I, B, 3, of the outline: "The expectation that price control will be enforced may reduce speculative accumulation of inventories."

It is also a fact that, under a system of price controls, we can set a price for the bulk of the commodity which is adequate to bring out the production of the majority of the producers, or the producers accounting for the overwhelming majority of the product, and set carefully selected prices for the margin of production. I submit that, not only does such a system permit maximum production, but it may even encourage more production than would be accomplished by a simple price rise, which would lead the producers to emphasize high cost deposits, in the case of mineral industries, for example.

Mr. Director was associated with the Army at a time when the services were co-operating with the Office of Price Administration under what has come to be known as the Henderson-Forrestal agreement. That agreement provided, in essence, that a wide variety of the goods purchased directly by the Army should be exempt from the formal price regulations. But the arguments made for such an exemption by the persons who had responsibility for procuring the goods were not so much that no price controls were needed as that the price controls would be those enforced by the contracting services and could not be effectively administered if there were a duplication of regulatory systems.

I submit that anyone who has experience in conducting negotiations realizes that there must be a conception of a price limit, or in effect of price control, in the effort to procure goods. If, on the other hand, the supplier of goods is encouraged to believe that, since his goods are urgently needed, the sky is the limit, that since his goods are so much in demand any price which he subjectively thinks is adequate for his supply is the price which will be written into the contract, then the amount of time and resources used in the procurement process would be greatly increased. Prices will be higher, and no more production will ensue.

There were various times during the OPA in which it was asserted in one context or another that the lack of price increases was holding down production. The assertion was made, for example, in the field of textiles and in the field of lumber. I think in each case careful analysis of the figures would show that there were physical limiting factors—in large part the limitations on the available labor supply—which were the reasons why production was not increased and that it was not the price-control program. On the contrary, the price-control program accompanied a maximum productive effort, and there is no basis in our history to believe that a price-control program is inconsistent with a maximum productive effort.

The question is raised whether excess money demand is not eliminated, whether direct wage and price controls can be enforced. The history of World War II proves that even though excess money demand was not eliminated, despite the efforts of Mr. Henderson and his staff, there was a reasonable enforcement of direct wage and price controls. There were gaps. Some of the reported figures may not be the figures of the true prices that were paid, but if we take a reasonable approach, a reasonable analysis of what was done at that time, we had an enforcement of these wage and price controls.

That brings me to another point with respect to total production, a point which can be related to the argument raised against direct controls that real direct wage and price controls merely suppress inflation and do not eliminate inflation. I do not have a firm opinion whether it would have been possible to avoid price increases if price controls had been maintained for an extra year, as Professor Hansen suggests, although I tend to think that that would have been the case. But I do not think it is a small matter that the price increases were deferred. On the contrary, I think that the fact that they were deferred enabled a stable wage and price position to be maintained during the critical years of 1943–45 under the "hold the line" order, and under the successful conditions under which the War Labor Board was operating at that time, with the co-operation of labor.

I submit that if, as Mr. Garrison has stated, it was a necessary condition for the operation of that disputes control board that there was a stable wage-price structure, it was of tremendous importance to the country that that increase was deferred, because it enabled those critical years to be years of maximum productive effort. But if there had been the complete mobility of prices and wage rates, which Mr. Director argues for, on the

ground that at any given point they tend to divert resources into
the area where they are more needed or more sought, we would
have had a general pattern in this country of disunity, conflict,
and disputes—disputes which could not have been easily
handled. That would have very much impeded and curtailed
the war effort, the productive effort, and the general backing
of the people of this country for the war effort that was being
made.

To the extent that that is true, there is an argument for price
and wage controls during any short-run period where productive
efforts must be maximized. I am assuming that the price and
wage controls will be in an over-all setting where they will lead
to a stable price-wage structure. But, if that is true, it seems to
me that the advantage of promoting unity, avoiding dissensions,
and avoiding hardships is so great, and is so great precisely for
productive reasons, as well as for psychological reasons that are
important in a democratic society in any event, that consideration of production is an argument for and not against a system
of direct wage and price controls.

MR. JEWKES: I would like to make one point on this matter. It
may be completely misplaced, because, of course, I know
nothing about the American scene. When Professor Viner tells
us that controls must necessarily be waved in front of the people
in this country in order to persuade them that something is being done, that is a strange idea to me, because in my country,
when a control is taken off, people say, "Now at last there is a
chance of something being done."

But I would like to put the case very briefly against price control as it is sometimes put in our British setting. It seems to me
that the danger of price control, under the conditions in which
we have seen it work, is precisely that price control raises prices,
and it is very easy to see the conditions under which that might
happen. First of all, before the controls are imposed, a good deal
of speculative increases of prices occurs. Second, because in any
system of price control general magins must be applied which
tend to make a maximum figure a minimum, some people therefore actually raise their margins in consequence of the controls
imposed. Third, once margins are fixed, the whole process of

competition in the distributive area, which over the long period may reduce the margins through increasing efficiency, tends to be slowed down. That may not be happening here, but it has certainly happened in Great Britain, and I wondered if there was any danger of the same sort of thing occurring in the United States.

MR. SCHULTZ: I may start by correcting the impression that Mr. Director may have left when he perhaps inadvertently implied there was only one point of view in economics at the University of Chicago. I can identify several, of which the particular one that is emphasized here today would be only one. We might call it the emphasis on price, as Mr. Director put it, and decentralization of economic activities in society. Certainly, there is another—the approach which emphasizes income and which emphasizes somewhat less decentralization. It is not represented here today. There is still a third. I would call it the historical or empirical approach, where one does look at history, political experience, and statistics and tries to draw lessons from these and, in doing so, uses both micro- and macro-theories as tools.

To turn now to a remark made by Congressman Celler about agriculture. May I point out that the agrarians are not overrepresented here today? Mr. DiSalle knows, despite all the economic limitations of parity, that the existing parity legislation does not tie his hands in the case of meats. Beef is far above parity. Meat prices cannot be controlled without rationing, and this country is not prepared to ration consumers on meat. I hasten to say that I am not a protagonist of parity, as most of you know from my many efforts to expose this "economic strait jacket."

My major comment may be put as follows: Why do we assume that what we have experienced in production and prices since June is bad, that great harm has been done to the American economy in the way prices and incomes have rearranged themselves? I should argue the opposite thesis. Our economy is, in fact, in a very good state of economic health. In a large part, it has begun to make the resource transfers and changes in production that we want of it. The changes in prices have induced and facilitated this process. I would like to see the case made that these developments in prices and production have not given us the adjustments we want of the economy. It is my belief that the American economy is, in fact, turning in a fine performance in readjusting and in producing what we now want from it as we mobilize.

We might draw the conclusion that Professor Viner implied—that wage and price controls have some political value in specifying particular preferences out of that sphere—and I would contend that in economic operations at least thus far the particular price and wage controls which we have had have, in fact, done little or no harm. If this is true, this country has had the best of both worlds! Why then are we not satisfied? Is it because we assume that the economy is, in fact, performing badly and that this is caused by existing price and wage controls? Where is the proof for this position?

MR. HARROD: I should like to draw together one or two threads very briefly. First, may I say that I am in complete agreement with the two speeches of Professor Hansen. Really, I find nothing to criticize in those speeches. I am also in agreement with Mr. Director's view that price control is a very great evil so far as the efficiency of the productive system is concerned and something to be avoided at all costs. It does great harm. I also agree with my fellow-countryman.

Mr. Director asked me point-blank whether I definitely preferred suppressed to open inflation. I should say that a little open inflation was better than a good deal of suppressed inflation. Of course, suppressed inflation, with all its evils, held down by control, is better than really bad open inflation, with the value of the currency going down—the sort of open inflations that have taken place in Europe in connection with both wars.

But because I am so much in sympathy with Mr. Director's view that these price controls are a great evil, I remind you of Professor Hansen's position. He said, "If we can do enough in the way of a somewhat overbalanced budget and a reduction of investment expenditures, we do not need to have them." We do not need to have them. "But what we are likely to do in that way is not going to be as much as that, and, therefore, we will probably have to have them." We should all urge together, therefore, a more strenuous forward move on the two lines of the balanced budget and of the reduction of investment expenditures. Further, to clarify the issue in relation to what has been said, I have just invented two words, which came into my mind only this morning, to express two radically different kinds of inflation.

By "basic" inflation, I mean that the situation that arises of the total demand on your productive resources is greater than you can meet. Your governmental expenditures, your investment expenditures, and what consumers are spending on consumption, a certain part of their income—if you add all those up and you have got a demand greater than you can meet, greater than your productive resources can satisfy, then you have "basic" inflation. Now, entirely distinct from that is what I call "spiral" inflation, where, if you have a rise of prices which may be due to basic inflation, you then get a rise in wages, and that may bring on another rise in prices, etc.

Now, what I submit is that if you have basic inflation, to any marked degree, you are not likely to avoid spiral inflation; but if you have basic inflation and spiral inflation, open inflation in the full sense, and you get far beyond that moderate amount of open inflation which I think Mr. Director had in mind when he put the challenge to me, you get going right along toward the destruction of the currency, Therefore, I say, unless you can eliminate the basic inflation, or reduce it to a very little amount, you have to take special measures against the spiral inflation, and that is where our price administration comes in. The price control, the wage control—they have no effect on basic inflation, but they do play a vital part in stemming the spiral inflation. I have no doubt that certain legislation under which they are working now may hamper the full efficiency of the price control —the farm escalator, etc. But it does play a vital part in stopping the excess of open inflation to have this wage control. You cannot have a wage control, as Mr. Brubaker pointed out, without a price control too. Therefore, if you have basic inflation to a marked extent, then you must have this price and wage control to prevent the basic inflation causing spiral inflation.

I disagree with Mr. Friedman, who suggested that the price

and wage controls do nothing at all, that they really do not prevent spiral inflation. I disagree. They do something very definite. If you have basic inflation tending to push prices and wages up, and you can stop the spiral, you have not stopped the basic inflation. That is still there. Price and wage controls cannot stop basic inflation, but they can stop spiral inflation. Therefore, if you have basic inflation in existence to a marked extent, you have to bring them along to stop the spiral inflation; otherwise you get, in the long run, a destruction of the currency.

I disagree with the point made by several speakers that the controls only defer something, that they defer some purchasing power which will later be expended. They do much more than defer it. Supposing you let the thing rip and prices and wages come up step by step, as they have done in Continental countries of Europe. You cannot go back on that. If the controls prevent that happening, they have done something very real. They have not merely deferred something; they have prevented the destruction of the currency.

So I come back to the first point. Your first aim should be to prevent basic inflation, or, if you cannot do that, at least to reduce it to such a moderate extent that it is not in danger of giving rise to this spiral inflation. That you do through the balanced budget (and perhaps a somewhat overbalanced budget) and through somehow restricting investment expenditures.

In that picture I regard a Federal Reserve policy, reinforced by Mr. Burgess' voluntary policy, as a valuable contribution toward reducing investment expenditures and therefore reducing the amount of basic inflation. These two methods of reducing basic inflation are, first, getting a balanced or overbalanced budget, and, second, what the Federal Reserve can do, and what Mr. Burgess can do, and any other methods you can think of, for reducing investment demand.

If you can use these methods sufficiently so that the basic inflation is only small, then you can reduce Mr. DiSalle's work to nothing at all. His function ceases to be important, and then you can get all the efficiency which Mr. Director wants so much; namely, you can let the price system function fairly freely—but only if you reduce the basic inflation. If you do not reduce the basic inflation, then you have to have these price controls to prevent spiral inflation.

CHAIRMAN LEVI: I will ask Mr. Rostow if he wishes to add anything to the subject of the price spiral as suggested by Mr. Harrod.

MR. ROSTOW: I was asked to comment on Item II, and I hasten, like other speakers, to announce at once that I do not propose to discuss the question put. My reason for this choice is not based on the emphasis in all these questions put upon the fundamental place of the money supply and the rate at which it is used. I think that, on the whole, that is salutary; I quite agree with Professor Hansen that there has been a remarkable change since the war at the rate of which income has turned over, a fundamental change, which to my knowledge has not been satisfactorily explained and which has certainly reduced the degree of price increase we have had in the period since the war. The money supply is, after all, the fuel, the essential fuel, of inflation, whether it is used or not, and its existence is a significant element in analyzing the problems presented to us by inflation and especially in determining the possibilities and probabilities of inflation.

Although I think I am the only speaker here from Yale, I hasten to reassure Mr. Viner that we are not still worshiping at the shrine of Irving Fisher in New Haven and do not blindly follow his oversimplified version of industrial fluctuations. Nevertheless, the size of the money supply is very important, and it tends to be neglected these days.

I do not agree at all with Mr. Director in preferring open to suppressed inflation on a large scale. I think that if we have what Mr. Harrod has called a "considerable basic inflation," then we should certainly have to do what we did during the last war; namely, to suppress it, to control prices, and to postpone the excess purchasing power to some later period. We could then decide with considerably more ease the balance we wanted between full employment and price increases and even perhaps indulge in some radical devices for cutting the supply of funds, if we choose to—devices of the kind which have been used with moderate success in countries like Belgium and France.

Mr. Viner: And Russia.

Mr. Rostow: Yes, and the Soviet Union, too. I do not propose those as necessary, although I agree that the question of a suppressed inflation is a serious one; and, if it goes on over a long period of time, we may wish drastically to cut the supply of money directly in a post-mobilization period.

My quarrel with the question put is twofold. One is that I should assume from the way these questions were all drafted that they were drafted by economists in Chicago, and not by lawyers, because they do not conform to the usual standards of Socratic neutrality which prevail in our law schools, especially in the Chicago Law School, which is so adequately staffed with well-trained lawyers from the Yale Law School. These questions, I suppose, could properly be classified as leading questions.

My first difficulty with this one is not its leading character but exactly what it means. The statement is, "It has been said that mobilization without price-wage controls may produce inflation even if government expenditures are covered by taxation and hence replace private expenditures." As put, the question seems to refer only to the net cash position of the federal government. Therefore, I should prefer to interpret it to mean: "Would direct controls be necessary or desirable if, by fiscal and monetary means, we could make sure that the *ex ante* total of demand, including private consumption and investment expenditure, government purchases and the net foreign balance, would equal the value of output at existing or current prices?" As amended, it is a much broader question than merely the question of whether the federal budget will be kept in cash balance. It presents the question of whether the banking system will offset any balance of the national budget by creating additional purchasing power.

Now, that is a very interesting question. It may even become a relevant question under certain conditions, although I think the discussion so far has brought out the fact that those conditions are remote and are unlikely to be satisfied. The conditions I suggest under which this might be a really relevant question are, first, whether we can raise taxes enough to balance the federal budget at the level of expenditure which is anticipated. And here I should suggest to Professor Schultz that perhaps one of the reasons why the situation in the last six months has not been worse is that the federal government has not succeeded in spending the appropriations which have been made and that in the next six months of the year it will almost certainly succeed in spending not only the older appropriations which it has but much larger new ones, which should fundamentally transform the rate at which prices go up, unless something effective is done about it by way of taxes.

The second condition under which this might be a relevant question is whether we can successfully cut the process of creating bank loans, either by open-market action or, as I should suppose would be necessary in addition, by more direct and selective controls of bank-lending policy, whether administered by the banks or by the Federal Reserve System. I think we might go back to the point Mr. Arnold made an hour or so ago in warning against voluntary action, perhaps not within the framework of the banking system, but otherwise, because Mr. Arnold and Mr. Porter, as some of you may realize, have just persuaded the Supreme Court to find that under the antitrust laws voluntary action to hold prices down is a prima facie violation of the Sherman Act.

The third condition under which this might become a relevant question, I suggest, is whether we can, by a combination of fiscal balance, plus restraint in the volume of bank loans, induce expectations of stability among the population and thus further affect the rate of use of liquid balances. That would further decrease the velocity of circulation of the existing money and terminate our inventory spree.

I would suggest that the question would even be relevant if we could only come fairly close to that goal. I share the objections to open inflation which have been discussed here very strongly. After all, Lenin pointed out a long time ago that the best way to debauch and destroy a middle-class society was to run a big inflation in it. That remains especially true in the United States, and in all Western countries, so soon after the 100 per cent increase in prices achieved during the last war.

I certainly share also the general distaste for direct controls, especially of prices and wages, both on grounds of efficiency and on grounds of their long-term social effect. They alter the balance of power in society as between labor and private business and the state, and they certainly reduce the competitive character of markets, whose organization many of our colleagues here today spend most of their working time trying to make more competitive.

Furthermore, there is an even more fundamental difficulty here, namely, that direct controls like rationing and price controls can be effective at best for a relatively short time and that if, as Mr. Garrison suggests, and I fully agree, we face a long period of semimobilization which may rise toward full mobilization, it would be prudent not to use too soon a weapon which, while very powerful and very useful, seems to have its own rather short rate of amortization. So that I should certainly like to defer the full use of those powers until they really become necessary. Then Mr. DiSalle can, with the full backing of the country, emulate his very distinguished predecessors in postponing inflation.

Now, I should like to discuss the question put in Item II. While we should certainly make every effort to keep aggregate demand down by increasing taxes and indulging in new taxes, to discourage both consumption and investment, I would disagree somewhat with the emphasis that Mr. Harrod has put on private investment alone. It is certainly crucial, but surely we should have to undertake at a given point a definite cut in consumption expenditure as well, by reason of the nature of military expenditure, which has a high multiplier. We should consider some form of taxation, perhaps increased social security taxation, which could be justified on other grounds, in order to restrict not only private investment but private consumption.

I think, however, that we shall not be able to escape a degree of inflation; and here, I think, we should return to the question that Mr. Arnold asked at the beginning of the proceedings: Is there a difference between a little inflation and a big inflation? I think there certainly is a difference between a little inflation and a big inflation. I do not think inflation is like a social disease in which a mild case is just as bad as a severe one. Furthermore, I think we must never forget the international position of the United States and the desirability from the point of view of the world balance-of-payments problem in keeping the United States somewhat on the inflationary side; it certainly makes a very marked difference to dollar earnings all over the world.

Well, in terms of the premise then that we shall have, at best, a little inflation, even though we are only attempting to mobilize, let us say, to the point of devoting 20 per cent of the gross national product to war purposes, what should we do about price-wage controls in the next couple of years—direct controls? Here I should like to go back to a point made by Mr. Stein, which I think is a valuable one. We have been talking so far with some horror about direct controls as bad and indirect controls as good. I share the general preference for indirect controls, if they could be made to work. But among the indirect controls which are valuable, and useful, are controls by way of allocation procedure and priority procedure, I think, which, in our experience, are somewhat different in their social effect and in their effect on competition from rationing and direct consumers' price controls.

I think that perhaps in the next period we could devote a good deal more emphasis to that type of direct control, if you like, priority and allocation controls, rather than to price and wage controls as such, and rationing controls, and hope thereby to make our present rather weak system, if I might say so in Mr. DiSalle's presence, potentially effective. In other words, I think if we couple fiscal policy and banking policy in the next period with a vigorous utilization of allocation and priorities controls, we have a very good chance of getting away with the type of precatory general freeze we are now undertaking. If not, then I suppose we shall have to go further into much more drastic price controls and rationing controls and things of that kind, which really impinge on the details of business life and are inefficient in various ways, in order to prevent open inflation.

Now, some of the questions put here under Item II, A, B, and C, have to do with whether rises in the price of particular goods do or do not produce a general price rise, or, correlatively, whether wage rises in one industry produce a general rise in wages. Here, again, I should welcome the emphasis which has been put on monetary and banking policy by those who drafted these questions, because I think it is often forgotten that wage and price increases, after all, do not as such cause further wage or price increases; if the total flow of income remains constant, higher wages or prices in one area could not lead to higher wages or prices in another. It might well lead to unemployment. Indeed, the classical end of any period of boom is that interest rates, wages, and raw-material prices rise and outstrip the willingness of the banking system to create further funds. In other words, a wage-price spiral will become a spiral if, but only if, we choose by fiscal policy or banking policy to validate a generally higher price level.

In a semimobilization economy, even under some controls, and especially under priorities and allocations controls, we do depend on wage differentials and price differentials to produce shifts of resources. Salesmen and law professors become unemployed, and they must go to work somewhere else in order to survive. Workers must be induced to leave Maine and Vermont and go to the war-production areas of Bridgeport, Connecticut, and Akron, Ohio. In order to accomplish this shift, I suggest we probably need some wage differentials, but I think the answer to the questions put here (Item I, A, B, and C, whether those wage differentials and price differentials would spiral, would depend entirely on whether we are willing to undertake a strict monetary and fiscal policy. If the total of aggregate demand is controlled, they need have no such effect.

One suggestion that has been made is that we should confine controls selectively on certain prices and wages, especially in the concentrated industries where there is not much competition and where prices can be set easily by industry action. The difficulty with this kind of approach, I think, is that it leaves food and clothing, and other competitive prices which are crucial to the cost of living, to soar as increased demand hits the uncontrolled markets. And, unless consumption is cut, that increase in the prices of monopoly-controlled industries may very well break the entire structure of stabilization.

My answers to your questions, then, are these: If we keep the degree of inflation, that is, the degree of excess of aggregate demand over the total value of production at current prices, to some sort of a bearable level, and indulge in direct control over the quantity of bank loans and priorities and allocations controls, we should be able to continue for this next two-year period on the basis of the present rather illusory wage and price controls. If not, if the degree of inflation becomes serious, then I should certainly support an intensification of our present price and wage control system on the model of what was done during the last war.

VI

FIFTH SESSION, SATURDAY AFTERNOON
APRIL 7, 1951

THE ROLE OF DIRECT CONTROLS—*Continued*

CHAIRMAN LEVI: I will ask our official summarizer and critic, Mr. Stigler, to summarize the discussion of "The Role of Direct Controls" at this point.

MR. STIGLER: There has been some complaint at the adequacy of the summaries or at their accuracy, and this is perhaps a natural complaint. One is prone to find that other people have missed the basic significance of a message, to say nothing of its subtle nuances, although I think on the side it should be said that what a man says is a good deal less important than what other people hear. This view has certain corollaries such as that what you say in the first five minutes is more important than what you say in the last fifty, and what you say the first day of a conference is of considerably more importance than what you say just before lunch on the second day. However, I shall try to lean over backward in being fair in this summary. I intend to summarize all the views at my disposal, and they include my own, but I shall devote more than half the time to other people's views.

If I may go back a moment, it seems to me that this last session has differed from the previous ones in at least one respect. In the first two sessions on monetary policy and on tax and fiscal policy, there was a considerably higher degree of unanimity. While there was a good deal of argument over the ultimate object and role of monetary policy, no one had defended the adequacy of the monetary policies that we employed in the months after June of last year. Again, in the field of taxation, although there was a good deal of argument over what are essential expenditures and what are desirable kinds of taxes, there was a general agreement that taxes should cover a higher proportion of the expenditures which are about to be incurred than our existing tax structure will yield.

Although these are points of basic agreement, I think they lead to a conclusion which differs for perhaps every person in the group. For what is the likely surplus of monetary pressures toward inflation after we have taken what steps we should and perhaps will take in these areas of monetary and fiscal control? I suspect some people emerged from the first two sessions with the belief that there was no problem left, that there is no further pressure toward inflation; and there are some people who emerged with the belief that, if only monetary and fiscal policies were employed, some inflationary forces would still be at work and perhaps that a major inflation would still take place. Part of the differences in attitude toward general price controls follow from these differences in prediction of monetary and fiscal policies and of their effects.

Turning now to the morning session, it seems that three general arguments were presented for a general price freeze or a system of controls which might not be quite so rigid as a freeze denotes.

There was, first of all, the very short-run argument which Mr. DiSalle presented, which was to the effect that in the short run we may have such a psychology of panic and fear of inflation that we must move rapidly, perhaps more rapidly (although he did not discuss this) than we can possibly move by monetary and certainly by fiscal policies. I think that we still ought to raise the question: How fast can the techniques alternative to price control be instituted? I think also we ought to raise the question: Is it possible to have a successful temporary control if people know it is going to be temporary? If one threatens, for example, to freeze prices for a few months in order to cool heads, it seems to me this will usually accentuate rather than solve the problems with which it is designed to deal. Even if we are threatening temporary controls, perhaps we should emphasize their long duration if they are to have any effectiveness, and, once we have done that, it is a separate question whether we can get out of our threat.

For the longer period, the second position was that of Mr.

Hansen and Mr. Harrod—that cumulative forces may be established which cannot be dealt with effectively by monetary and fiscal policy alone or, if they can be, are not likely to be. I would like to defer this question and the related question of the price-wage spiral for a moment, since that is presumably the subject on which we will resume discussion when I am done.

Then there is the third view—that of Professor Viner—that the popular demand for direct controls is such that we have to give them to the public whether we like them or not. I may say that I personally believe there is a good deal of truth in this. But I do think there is still the question of what ways are the optimum ways to make the population uncomfortable, and that perhaps alternatively a monthly income-tax return would be more effective.

On the broad question of the comparative evils of an open inflation and a general price ceiling, we had heard two opposite views. Mr. Director has argued that there were basic gains from having an open inflation with free relative prices, and Mr. Leventhal argued, on the contrary, that this was a costly policy. Mr. Director was, of course, emphasizing the fact that we get greater incentive effects with free prices, that the composition of our output is more appropriate, and that there are more incentives to growth and technologcal progress; whereas Mr. Leventhal was emphasizing the social disunity that comes from inflation, the frequency of strikes, the difficulties of procurement, and the like.

I am impressed here, as I am at a good many other points, with how fundamentally little we know about the factual position which underlies these general arguments. Those who believe the general price controls are efficient and not adverse to output—and I do not refer now just to those at the conference—generally look at the price system as a rather ineffective instrument at best. I might say just in passing that I think that we use the language differently at times. There are some of us here for whom the price system may be defined as a series of levies exacted by monopolists, excluding or especially unions; for some of us the price system as a series of numbers published by the Bureau of Labor Statistics; and for some of us the price system is a smooth system of integrated, impersonal forces governed by competition, which is best illustrated by an electronic computer. These views reflect themselves in our policy decisions.

Now, the view of those on the side of price controls in general is, I think, not caricatured by saying that they point with some satisfaction at the behavior of the price indexes during the last war, to the fact that they did not rise as much as during comparable periods in World War I (although they would argue that the pressure for them to rise was greater) and that the Federal Reserve Board Index, on the other hand, showed a very rapid and unprecedented increase. On the other side, people like Mr. Director, if I might put thoughts in their heads which they could easily disavow, are impressed by the general economic theory that we use to explain the regular operations of the economy and the great emphasis that theory places upon the necessity for a sensible system of relative prices to make the economy work effectively. These latter people in turn say that the Federal Reserve Board is just a dream of Frank Garfield; the Bureau of Labor Statistics Index is a bit of whimsey which does not cost a great deal; etc.

In response, those in favor of the price controls say that the general theory forgets that all the functions are inelastic. This is an impasse. I suspect that these general ideological positions are never going to be reconciled except by a detailed kind of study which no one seems willing to make—the academicians because they already know the truth, and the price-control people because they have not time to find out whether it is conceivable that they are wrong.

Then there is the second question: If we do have price controls, waiving their desirability, are they effective? Here we have a series of answers. The first answer was, of course, that they are effective, and, for example, Mr. DiSalle points to the fact that prices have risen much less in the last two months than they did previously. That position, however, has not been argued in very much detail.

There is, second, the position which is taken by Mr. Mullendore and Mr. Friedman—that they merely postpone the effects of inflation; that, during the period of the controls, people are forced to save larger sums of money which, however, they splurge afterward, so that ultimately the price controls are ineffective. I, personally, think that that is the most probable view, but I would point out that I do not like the way this argument can be extrapolated. Mr. Friedman says that the peak of Civil War prices came during the Civil War, the peak of World War I prices came fifteen months after World War I, and the peak of World War II prices came thirty months after World War II. It is obvious that, if we want to postpone the peak indefinitely, all we have to do is freeze prices indefinitely.

Then there is a third group that says that price control was unquestionably successful in World War II and at other times and in other places but that now it is less likely to be successful because present conditions are not so favorable as they were during World War II. Mr. Garrison has emphasized this point in connection with wages; now we do not have certain favorable conditions such as strong patriotism, considerable unemployment, and things of that sort.

I shall not say much on the question of selective price controls, although personally I favor them a good deal more than general price controls, because the discussion has not yet veered to any appreciable extent to this subject. I think the selective controls are preferable in part because it is impossible to establish for general controls criteria of prices to be set and criteria of the policies to be employed and criteria of the length of time for which to employ them. In the field of general price control we are always a creature of broad political movements. On the other hand, there are fairly objective standards in the administration of selective price control. I will therefore skip over the general question of allocations, because Mr. Stein's very fine remarks have not yet been followed up, but I presume they will be this afternoon.

I would raise one point, however. Mr. Stein pointed out that a great many people use a war as a pretext for foisting off on the economy the reforms that they have always had in mind and that they boldly link these reforms to the success of the war effort. This is certainly true, and from a certain viewpoint we can argue that these people who are trying to use the war (perhaps at a sacrifice of military strength) to advance their own creed are not being very patriotic. On the other hand, I think we can probably argue that important reforms are always slipped over on the public under the pressure of war. So there may be a good deal to say, for example, if one is a fervent believer in anti-trust, as I happen to be, for not changing the rules at all during the war and saying indeed that only by strong antitrust action can we possibly defeat the enemy.

Turning now to this question of the spiral, I merely wish to plead ignorance so that a more or less intelligent layman will be at hand for the speakers who support the spiral views to explain in more detail what they have in mind. In part, I do not know why there is any talk at all of such a thing as a wage-price spiral. It seems to me some prices by their rises lead other prices to rise and sometimes other wages to rise, and sometimes wage rises lead other wages to rise. And it seems to me that the whole system of prices, wages included, is an integrated system and that this spiral talk is really an indirect way of saying we have cumulative movements in prices under certain monetary conditions.

Then I worry about what is the implicit monetary policy which underlies these spirals. Can a spiral take place if we have a limitation on the amount of credit available and are operating on a balanced budget? Can a spiral still emerge and be financed, let us say, by velocity increases? Or is it implicit in all spiral motions that they put pressure on the banks and on the government to spend more dollars and hence increase deficits and hence add to the cumulative movement? In other words, is a spiral anything but a monetary phenomenon? Does it have independent force of its own? Questions like these I would like to have someone tell me the answer to as we resume.

CHAIRMAN LEVI: Are there any comments on the summary? If not, we will go back to Item II. Mr. Harrod, I understand, desires to speak on this. Mr. Harrod is not here. If there are some other people who wish to speak on this, they may do so now. Is there anyone who wants to comment on the price spiral?

MR. CORTNEY: There is no doubt that we cannot have a prolonged wage-price spiral unless it is fed by monetary expansion or credit expansion. However, we may have credit expansion even if we avoid deficit spending unless we reach the conclusion that we should stop the banks from extending any credit. Then there are available for spending large liquid resources in the hands of corporations and individuals.

The classic argument that, if we increase wages abnormally in some segments of industry, they might induce decrease of wages in other industries, or even create unemployment, has lost validity in our times because it has become national policy not to tolerate unemployment. We have adopted, wrongly in my opinion, as a philosophy that the government should not tolerate any unemployment. We are living now under a system in which a few labor unions fight to obtain wage increases in strategic industries, namely, where prices can be increased *pari passu* with the wages and then the smaller union bosses exact increases, whether the employers can afford them or not.

Then we have the parity of agricultural prices, which in turn increases the cost of living, so we get, obviously, a spiral unless we assume that we will stop completely any kind of expansion of bank credit, leaving aside the monetizing of debt. It has happened in this country in the last four or five years, and it has become a systematic way of doing things. Do not forget that on top of that the labor-union bosses cannot make good with their workers a promise to have every time they open a contract a new rise in wages unless we have inflation. You know that as well as I do.

So here we are in a system in which the labor-union bosses, for their own power over the workers, need inflation. Business has become soft and mellow, and they have reached the conclusion that the only way to fight this evil is to indulge in inflation. If we tell them, "Now, you had better be careful about the consequences because there will be bitter consequences," they say, "This is a very powerful country with a huge productive capacity"—all these arguments which are repeated every day and which are irrelevant in respect to the danger confronting us today.

I wish to repeat again that I subscribe entirely to Mr. Mullendore's statement. We do not know how good business is but how unhealthy it is. This country is in debt up to its ears. It is not true that labor has won advantages in the last ten years without sacrifices from the rest of the community. The owners of buildings are not paid the proper rent. Insurance policies have been depreciated. Even the plant and equipment is not being amortized adequately. In my humble opinion, we were already near the end of the rope when the Korean affair started. I believe Joe Stalin has become an accomplice of capitalism of the worst sort, because we cannot save capitalism by armaments.

CHAIRMAN LEVI: Mr. Stigler, do you wish to respond to the question put to you?

MR. STIGLER: Underlying my comment was this question of whether the spiral is an independent phenomenon in which there are, let us say, independent forces among the labor unions of the country or among the price-setting industries which can generate cumulative movement by themselves, or whether this is merely a translation of the ordinary classical argument that, as long as we keep injecting new funds into a society, we will have a cumulative rise of the price levels. In effect, you see, this amounts to a question: Can we have a spiral without a monetary basis, and, second, if we do have the monetary basis, are the unions really going to make it move faster than it would have otherwise? My own feeling is that the unions really slow down the rate of the cumulative process by their penchant for long-term contracts and the like.

CHAIRMAN LEVI: Are there any other observations on Item II?

MR. HENDERSON: We are still speaking to Dr. Stigler's excellent summary, is that it?

CHAIRMAN LEVI: That can be done, or to Item II, either one.

MR. HENDERSON: This question of the impact of price control at certain levels of the economy is not something which can be statistically determined, but I do suggest that in the postwar analysis a number of the controlled commodities have been analyzed, perhaps not in economic terms; but certainly a good basis is provided for those who are studying the question as to whether or not the price control was repressive of expansion. As far as World War II was concerned, moving with selective controls into such industries as steel and in constant association with members of the industry, it was possible to determine whether or not there was a repression.

Leventhal spoke this morning of the textile industry, which was one of the very earliest subjected to control in World War II. It had been under a really great depression, particularly in the wool textiles since the middle twenties, even before the break in 1929. Now came an opportunity for taking advantage of this sudden and emergent demand which was created by government or at least came as a result of government action on mobilization. In terms of the control of the spiral at that particular time, it seems to me that it was eminently justified. In terms of the expansion of the textile industry, the report shows that there was no restraint; there was no possibility that there had been any great check to allocation of resources which would have gone to them in the free market. Those who take the position, as has been taken, that there is a very, very destructive influence by means of control on what would be the expansion under a free-market system should look at some of those reports.

The price in steel, which is admittedly one of the basic products, was frozen in April, 1941, without benefit of clergy and legislation, as your remember. The plain understanding at the time of the freeze was that there would be constant review with the industry as to whether or not relief would be given for any variation in price, either in the extra book or in any of the import or export prices on commodities that they were using. I remember pointing out four principal places at which I thought prices did not represent true market prices. One of them was a low price set to meet Belgian competition.

The contention at the time the price was frozen was that we were going to have great demands on the steel industry for expansion, and, if we allowed a free-market price, we could make the choices as to where the new plants would be built, while under the freeze system the industry would lose fifty million dollars. Well, it just happened I had a University of Chicago economist and statistician at the time. We felt that the industry would make about ninety-five million dollars instead of losing fifty, and, as I recall the results, it was plus or minus correct of within 4 per cent of this estimate.

There was a time when the industry—and we were in constant contact with it—came in with a suggestion that the price control itself had been the interference with any expansion they would have done under the market. On the other hand, I submit that in that short-run period the government is the best judge as to the allocation of the steel that is being produced and knows more than the market does as to what the emergent situation requires.

As a matter of fact, under the considerations we are meeting here today, there has been damned little discussion of the facts. Most of it has been in the field of theory as to what might happen in a free market, instead of comparing what did happen, segment by segment; and there is a wealth of economic material for anybody who wants to review it. I happen to have reviewed some of it, and I know there were some restraints. In the main, considering the determinations that were made under the circumstances of price control, they were not, I would say, tremendously defeating of what the free market would have done as far as expansion is concerned.

MR. ROSTOW: At first, as I listened to Mr. Stigler's very elegant and articulate summary, I thought that he was retreating into the technique of asking supposedly naïve questions. But the last sentence of his summary persuaded me he was not going to accept that procedure, for he indicated that the question of wage or price increases becoming a spiral depends ultimately on whether we want to make them a spiral by providing enough new money to permit the spiral to become a spiral. I think perhaps it is worth adding that during a period of mobilization, or semimobilization, it is much more difficult for the monetary and fiscal policies of the government to remain neutral and to permit increases in some prices and wages to result in anything like considerable unemployment.

The main job is, of course, to divert resources from one part of the economy to another, and, in doing that, any general price decrease or general unemployment might reduce the pace of production. This is a reason, I think, as Mr. Stigler suggests, for considering certain types of controls which might facilitate such transfers of resources. Perhaps the most important of these techniques, as I said this morning, are priorities and allocations and perhaps even the direct licensing of certain kinds of construction.

If we want to facilitate certain forms of activity and to prohibit others, the direct licensing of construction and the granting of priority ratings and direct allocation of materials are practical tools for facilitating such transfers quickly and without great price changes. This, I think, is especially true in the controversial area of private investment. Control procedures of this kind would permit us to discriminate among those forms of private investment which we want to cut back quickly and those forms of private investment which we do not wish to cut back quickly. I have in mind the distinction between permitting business establishments to build new store fronts and more and more new and beautiful retail displays (or the kind of hotel decorations that we see around us here) and the construction of essential housing and other things. Perhaps if we take Mr. Stigler's oblique reproaches more seriously, we can get down to the discussion of the types of controls, direct and indirect, which could facilitate the transfer of resources that we need and those kinds which could not do that job.

MR. HAYEK: I was just a little disturbed, because, while there was a lot of discussion about using relative prices to bring about the redistribution of resources, the term "price decline" seems to have been carefully avoided, and the idea that we might have to bring about the fall of some prices, if we wanted to avoid (*a*) inflation and (*b*) have a change in relative prices did not seem to be mentioned. Now, I think, we ought to pursue this question a little further. Is it really assumed in this circle that any hope that any price might be reduced under the circumstances is entirely utopian? Then I think we will have to go a step further and say that any hope of avoiding not only minor inflation but major inflation is utopian.

If we are not willing to admit this, I think that we have to face a problem. What kind of policy will also bring about the compensation price declines which are required to offset the increases in prices elsewhere? Now, that, of course, forces us to face a doctrine to which Mr. Cortney has already alluded—that it is now believed that no price or no wage must ever be allowed to decline; and, if that is so, of course, we are again up against the problem that any change in relative prices must mean so much extra inflation.

But is it really true that, under the mobilization circumstances, the friction which a price decline inevitably meets and causes is an undesirable thing? Is it even necessarily true that, under these conditions, a bringing-about of some local and temporary unemployment is a loss of efficiency; or is it not, on the contrary, perhaps, an inevitable part of the process of speeding up the transfers?

I noted with great interest this morning that Professor Hansen rather unexpectedly used the phrase "in mobilization in 1940 we were in the fortunate position of having eight or nine million unemployed who could easily be guided into war-production channels." Now, we are not in that position, which I would not necessarily describe as a fortunate one, but I think it may be necessary to bring about these transfers to make sure not only that there is a pull from the new needs but that there is also a push which drives the people out of the less needed employments and production. What I really want to drive at is that I believe that the main reliance on direct controls not only does nothing in assisting this task but makes it very much less likely that any prices will be reduced.

Any system of price-fixing not only sanctions the existing price structure and gives a sort of moral approval for continuing with the prices which exist but generally recognizes the principle that in wartime, when efficiency should be the main consideration, the main criterion for price changes should not be economic but moral. In another respect, direct price controls are probably likely to prevent or make unlikely these necessary price reductions which would offset the price increase elsewhere. In so far as the direct control of prices prevents the rising of some prices, it must do so by preventing people from spending as much on those commodities as they would like with the result of leaving money over to be spent on the commodities, the production of which and the price of which ought to decline. So that, in a way, the whole system of price control tends to perpetuate the state of distribution of resources in which we find ourselves at the beginning.

If I may anticipate a point in the outline to which we have not yet come, it is mentioned that mobilization changes the relationship of prices, and this seems to be considered as something bad. I should have thought that the main argument against price controls and in favor of using the market system is essentially that these changes in the relationship of prices are highly desirable to bring about the necessary changes at every point where the government cannot bring them about without itself possessing all the knowledge which the individual entrepreneur has to use when it is a question of economizing on this material.

MR. HANSEN: Mr. Chairman, it seems to me that we have to distinguish, when we speak of relative prices, between the short-run and the long-run adjustment. In the short run, I do not believe we can have a fall in prices without running into the difficulty that it brings about a program of wage reduction and unemployment. I would not favor the creating of unemployment to facilitate adjustment of resources.

It was a fact that in 1940 we had unemployment. This I do not regard as desirable per se; but it *was* favorable for the process of diverting resources to the war effort. Now, in the long run, relative prices tend to adjust themselves to changes in technology. Backward industries cannot reduce prices. It is the industry that makes the most progress that reduces prices. Consequently, we do not have the kind of adjustment that creates unemployment. But in the short run, if we have a decline in prices, that decline can only take place by creating unemployment. I think there is a vast difference between adjustment of relative prices to technological changes, over the long run, and forcibly bringing about, in the short run, a decline in prices in which the cost structure does not permit price reductions.

Indeed, in 1946 we had a tremendous world-wide shortage of food. We had strategic shortages in many important areas. The minute we removed price control, we were bound to experience a sharp rise in commodities in short supply in relation to other commodities. If we had had at that time a rigorous price stabilization program, we would have forced in the short run a drastic decline of a whole lot of prices below current costs. This would have created unemployment. Readjustment of relative prices in accordance with the changes of technological progress is a different matter. In these circumstances it is the technologically advancing industries that reduce prices, not the industries that are faced with high costs. These latter could only reduce prices as a result of drastic reductions in wages.

MR. HAYEK: May I say a word more. I am very glad to have elicited an elucidation of doctrine. What it amounts to is that changes of relative prices should only occur subsequent to a previous change in cost and should not be brought about in response to a change in demand.

Now, what we are here concerned with is, of course, a large-scale shift in demand which undoubtedly makes it desirable that in many industries production should be curtailed or at least the use of certain materials should be stopped or discontinued. I cannot see that there should be any doubt that in the nonessential industries, the industries from which demand turns away, prices should fall actually below cost, that production should be discouraged, and so that, whatever stores there are, the available amount should be spread over a long period during the war. This would be a more effective means of bringing about a rapid transfer of resources from the nonessential industry than any other means conceivable.

MR. HENDERSON: As I gather it, what Dr. Hayek is saying is, if we curtail production in the less essential industries, which is one phrase I expect to use, that there ought to be a fall in prices. Certainly, under the free market those prices tend to go up. One of the reasons why, when we have a diversion from the industries, particularly consumer durables, which are competing with war products, we go into price control is because a relative scarcity forces the price up, and we want to maintain those prices. I should like to ask Mr. Hayek whether that would mean that the way to discourage it would be to use the price control to fix a drastically nonprofit level of prices in the industries from which we have diverted the material.

MR. HAYEK: Forgive me, Mr. Henderson, but you can hardly assume at the same time that the demand for the nonessential products does go up.

MR. HENDERSON: The demand for the things we are talking about is a reciprocal of income, and, in a period like this, there is rising income.

MR. HAYEK: Why, is not that what we want to prevent?

MR. HENDERSON: You want to prevent more hours being worked? Is that it? The income rises from various sources, one of which is that more hours are worked, because the demand on the economy is greater. It also rises from the increase in wage rates. Now, we cannot prevent the increase in the wage rates, but we are certainly not going to have, in a period of demand for labor, a use of the governmental power to cut the wage back to compensate for the increase in the number of hours and therefore to get a stabilized wage per week.

MR. HAYEK: I assumed it was the purpose of taxation to cut down consumers' demand to what was available for consumption.

MR. HENDERSON: That is one of the purposes, certainly; but I do not see how we can use our taxation directly in a short run particularly to reduce the price which a refrigerator, or a vacuum cleaner, or a sewing machine, or something like that will bear, particularly as there is still a very vigorous demand. One of the places in which we had the most vigorous pressure upward on retail prices was on the commodities being curtailed. That is what is happening in this period.

CHAIRMAN LEVI: Mr. Hitch, do you have a statement on Item III? That is on the relative price changes.

MR. HITCH: I should like to consider Items III and IV together, both of which are concerned with the problem of the shifts in relative demands that occur in a mobilized economy and with the shifts in relative prices that these shifts in demand would occasion if we had a free market. The question is: What direct controls, if any, either price-wage controls or allocation and priority controls, are required because of these shifts in relative demands? I had some experience during the war with direct controls, and I emerged with a considerable skepticism and dislike of them. I would say that my general preferences and prejudices are in favor of indirect fiscal and monetary controls. However, it was quite clear to me from the very interesting and provocative remarks with which Mr. Director opened this session that I have not moved all the way to Chicago.

I am sure that there are circumstances, given the institutions, political and economic, of the United States, in which we can do better with direct controls and need direct controls. It all depends, as I tried to emphasize in a remark that I made yesterday, upon the speed with which we mobilize and the scale on which we mobilize—two things which, I think, continue to drop out of our minds in this discussion. I believe that it has vitiated a good deal of the worth of the discussion of the inflationary spiral. I think that Mr. Director's remarks may be very shrewd and apt as far as our immediate problems are concerned. If we are talking about a rate of military expenditure of forty billion or fifty billion dollars per annum, that is one thing. If we are talking about a mobilization which will require 50 per cent of national resources for direct defense purposes, something of the same order as the mobilization that we had in World War II, that is an entirely different thing.

My own view is that the need for direct controls arises in two circumstances. The first is when we are mobilizing very rapidly and time is of the essence. This is the situation in which we find ourselves this year and next. The second is when the mobilization is very large. I am going to talk mainly about the first of those two circumstances, not about the second.

In the second, to dispose of that first, I think the reasons that apply in the first case also apply; but, in addition, with military expenditures of this magnitude, we cannot hope to close, or nearly close, the inflationary gap resulting from those expenditures by fiscal and monetary measures. We will find ourselves in the sort of spiraling inflation that Mr. Harrod has described unless we have some effective means of dragging our feet, and I think the function of wage and price controls in World War II was as simple as that. I think there are other possible ways of dragging our feet which might be more effective and which we might explore later, but I believe we did learn last time that we can, to some extent, slow down the spiral by price and wage controls, and that is very important. It means, I am sure, that in the end we will have less inflation. In answer to Mr. Stigler's question, I am making the realistic assumption that the monetary supply is "elastic."

Now, let me come back to the first of the circumstances which I mentioned. I want to talk primarily about the need for priority and allocation control in the mobilizing case, where it is important to mobilize very quickly. I am not going to say much about price and wage controls in this case, because they seem to me to be of much less significance.

The general economic theory to which Mr. Stigler referred, which is the basis for the preference which many of us have for free markets and the price system, is a theory of "comparative statics." It shows that in a quite technical sense we can get an "efficient" allocation of resources by using free markets—in certain circumstances. But the method of analysis used is comparative statics. I know of no satisfactory theory which shows either that the path which the economy takes from one position of equilibrium to another is an optimal one or that, when time is important, we traverse that path at the optimal rate of speed.

Let us consider the shape of the pattern of output in three quite different economies, all more or less fully employed. There will be at any time in a peacetime economy a certain production pattern, if you like, in the mobilizing period, with a shift of emphasis in production to the construction industry, to capital goods industries like machine tools, to certain materials, particularly certain metals and chemicals, and to certain specialized fabricating facilities. The production of each of these categories will have its own peculiar pattern during mobilization. Most of the "humps" in the outputs of investment goods come fairly early, we have learned, in the mobilizing process. For example, in World War II our construction of capital equipment probably reached its peak sometime during 1942. Then we will have, following the mobilizing period, when the period of capital expansion comes to an end, a quite different pattern of output. There will again be a heavier emphasis upon the metal and chemical industries, for example, than we have in the peacetime economy, but the pattern will differ from that in the mobilizing case.

Now consider our present situation. We are at the beginning of a mobilization. Our rate of expenditure for military equipment has not increased as yet very much. The expansion which we have had is very largely, so far, an accumulation of inventories and the beginning of expansion in plant and equipment. If I were in a responsible position in controlling the economy during this mobilization period, I am confident that I would want to use priority and allocation controls to make sure that the materials and the equipment were delivered to war industries. I think this is true pretty much whether we have price control or not, so I am going to make no particular assumption about whether or not we have price control.

What happens—it happened before we had price control, and it is happening since we had price control—is that, in the industries toward which demand has shifted, delivery times lengthen. They lengthen very drastically. A machine tool that we could get delivery on previously in three months, let us say, or even off the shelf, we are now able to get delivery on in eighteen months, or two years, or three years. In this market, and in many producers' goods markets, we do not have the market cleared every day with the price going up to a point where we are in constant short-period equilibrium. It is the practice in these markets to lengthen delivery times, to make people come in at the bottom of a delivery schedule.

It is, I am assuming, not only important but vitally urgent that we get the materials and the equipment to our war-production industries. Is there any way in which this can be accomplished except by stepping in with a priority system which will enable the highest-priority war industries to get the deliveries that they need? I do not believe that we can do it in any other way. If we attempt to do it by fiscal or monetary controls, following such a drastic shift in relative demands, controls which are strong enough to give quick delivery times for war industries will have to be so drastic that they will unnecessarily reduce output in the rest of the economy. Therefore, I would say that, given the kinds of markets, the kinds of price policies, that we have in these industries, the method of direct control, of priority and allocation, is the efficient instrument, and monetary and fiscal control the clumsy and slow instrument. I do want to emphasize, however, that I think this applies only to the rapidly mobilizing economy.

I do not know if we are going to level off at a rate of forty or fifty billion dollars a year or not, but assuming that we do and have a standing army and air force fully equipped, with requirements for replacement which are more or less the same each year, even though they may be at a very high level as compared with the past, I think it is quite clear that we want to get away not only from wage and price controls but from all direct controls. I agree with Mr. Harrod very strongly that we must set a limit to these controls. It is most important that we let the price medicine work when it has time to work. I think that, as I have said, price control is not very important in these particular producers' markets, as far as effective allocation is concerned while we are mobilizing. The humps of demand in mobilizing are short lived. This is known, and we cannot expect the supply of capacity to be responsive to short-lived humps. Even if producers' prices were allowed to move upward freely, I do not believe that it would help very much. I do not believe, for rather different reasons, that it would help very much on the demand side either, because of the way in which the services contract with their suppliers and the way in which prices are fixed in those contracts, which really leave very little incentive for economizing in the use of materials which become more expensive. This is particularly true when time is of the essence, as in this case where we want to mobilize very rapidly.

Maybe, if we started from the other end as a long-period venture, we could change some of these institutional factors, both on the contracting side and on the market side, so that we would have markets which worked more as they are supposed to work in our academic models. All I am saying is that we do not have such markets, and we do not have such conditions on the contracting side.

Now let me look briefly at the specific questions asked—Items III and IV. I think I have nothing more to add to what I have said on Item III.

On Item IV, A ("Allocation of resources is a better means of channeling needed supplies to the government than is the market"), I agree in these particular circumstances; since prices are not used to perform this function, there is no point in allowing them to rise. Here I think it is very important to distinguish between the short-period mobilization and the longer run, in which there is certainly point in letting them rise. If we are going to have to remain in a state of preparedness over a long period, we are going to have to change the character of output in the economy over a long period. We are going to have to give the economy and our basic industries a "military bias," and I am sure that the best way to get this military bias in the long run is to let the market do it.

Turning to Item IV, B, the first question seems to me to be a very peculiar *non sequitur*. I had never conceived of the entrepreneur's chief function as that of deciding which people placing orders should have their orders filled. It seems to me that there is a very great deal that remains for the entrepreneur to do. Perhaps he has less of a function in the mobilizing period, less of a price-induced function, than he does later on, but he still retains most of his important functions.

The second question under Item IV, B, attempts to draw a sharp distinction between the information which is available to the government and the information which is available to industry, to private enterprises. I think I see what is implied here, but where, I might ask, does government get information about what is required to produce on war contracts except from industry? I know of no other source. Allocations are not made by government, relying on its own knowledge, deciding that so much steel should be allocated, let us say, to the production of tanks, and then telling tank producers, "You must make tanks out of that." The government, the contracting agency, approaches the prospective manufacturer of tanks and asks him how much steel he requires. This information comes originally from industry. There may be checks of some kind which the government attempts to make to insure that the information is more or less honestly given, but there is no real source of information except the industrial source. The allocation decisions which are made turn on the number of tanks, the number of ships, the kinds and quantities of facilities that the government wants, assuming the correctness of manufacturers' bills of material. Once these allocations are made, if we have a good allocation system, we will be able to bring some pressure on the producers to economize in the materials which are in particularly short supply; but that is another question and not one on which I am going to speak at this time.

CHAIRMAN LEVI: I will ask Mr. Jewkes to discuss Items V and VI, and ask you to save your comments on Items III, IV, V, and VI, which will be taken up together.

MR. JEWKES: The points I want to make are connected closely with Items III and IV, the points that Mr. Hitch has already been discussing. Is the price mechanism too slow to bring about the kind of results we want when we need rapid rearmament? Mr. Hitch certainly believes that, although the price mechanism can be relied upon in other cases, where we want rapid readjustment, it must be replaced, at least for a time, by physical controls. That I would challenge, for the following reasons.

If we look at the experience of highly dislocated economies which, in the last resort, have gone back to free markets, we find that very rapid resuscitation can take place. For example, within the last two years, the German economy, which was completely disrupted, was provided with a sound currency and some measure of free trading, and anyone who was in Germany at that time would agree that the results were almost magical. To believe that any system of controls could have operated as quickly as that in bringing the whole economy into more active operation (in one or two days goods were coming into the shops, and people started to work) is misinterpreting evidence. There are other cases. Anyone who cares to examine what happened in the period of the New Economic Policy in Russia must be convinced that, even under those most unfavorable conditions, the sudden restoration of normal market processes tended to pull the system into some sort of order. And we have to remember that in periods of rapid demobilization, such as that which took place in America after the last war, the whole process was going on through a price mechanism. That particular period was a most remarkable instance of rapid changes brought about in a relatively smooth way through the market itself.

I submit that any experience we have of these things suggests that the price mechanism is of greatest value when rapid changes are needed and dislocation is greatest. Conversely, I would suggest that a system of physical controls designed to bring about such big changes by allocations and the like works very slowly. We all know what happened in the last war, and I suspect we all know what would happen if another war broke out. New control departments are set up very rapidly. Each department sets up its own type of controls independently of other departments. The first six months are occupied in getting together staffs and learning the job. The next six months are occupied in clearing up the muddles that have been made by the controls themselves. Once the system has survived that period—which it may do through the native energy of the people, the judicious use of the black market, and what Professor Mises has called "loopholes"—the controls may shake down into some kind of an organization and produce a lot of material, most of which will probably be described by the fighting forces as obsolete. Now that, I think, is quite inevitable.

Mr. Churchill, who understands the productive dynamics of an economic system as well as anybody, has put it this way in one of his volumes: "From our economy in the first year, we will probably get nothing; the second year perhaps a trickle, and the third year twice as much as we want." I am not prepared to believe that, if we are thinking of a partial mobilization involving 20 per cent of the national income, a widespread system of physical controls will necessarily be any quicker than reliance upon the market, provided we have extracted, by taxation, and other devices, the resources that we needed for rearmament.

My only difficulty in suggesting that the price system might do the job is this. Businessmen, in a period of this kind, are confronted with a novel type of risk. They do not know how long the mobilization will continue. They do not know over what period they ought to amortize the new plants that they are setting up. They do not know how long the orders will continue that are being placed with them. There is, therefore, some conflict between their responsibilities to their shareholders and their instincts as good citizens to get on with the job of providing defense materials. It is sometimes argued, because of that, that it may be easier to conscript businessmen and tell them what they ought to do rather than leave them to be guided by price changes, changes in supply and demand, and the proper central financial policies.

It may be true that businessmen would prefer to be told what to do, because they want to avoid this clash between their two loyalties. I am not quite sure what the answer is. Clearly, the government can take on a certain part of the risk of new capital by shortening amortization periods or even by providing capital itself. My difficulty is as to just how it fits into what we regard as normal market operations. Perhaps the answer is that, after all, businessmen are as loyal as any other group of people and that they can be relied upon to allow major loyalties to put on one side minor loyalties in a period of emergency. But it seems to me that, if in a period of rearmament we rely upon the price mechanism, there is a real problem: How do we induce businessmen to take risks which are really quite different from the sort of risks they are accustomed to dealing with; and, if we have methods of doing that, how far are these methods consistent with the normal market system?

MR. HANSEN: For the record, I would like to call attention to a fact correcting, I think, one statement Mr. Jewkes made about the American economy after the war. I make no argument pro or con about it, but this is just a statement of fact. The reconversion to peace in America took place mainly in a twelve-month period of price control. We did not remove price control until twelve months after the war, and within that period the major job of reconversion to peace occurred.

MR. JEWKES: It still is true that during the period of demobilization the government was not allocating peacetime goods, and my impression is that, although technically price control was still operating, it was an extremely rickety system with many loopholes.

MR. HANSEN: Not a free-price market.

MR. ROSTOW: I should like to make just one comment on Mr. Jewkes's remarks. As I listened to them, it seemed to me that the premise on which they rested, as I understand him, assumed the problem away. He said, as I understood him, that if we had heavy enough taxes to cut down civilian purchasing power in proportion to the increase in government expenditures, we could rely largely, with perhaps some minor direction, on the price mechanism. I think that is fair enough, but the premise which I think is the more likely to correspond to the situation is that we are not going to have that much reduction of ordinary demand through taxation. If this is the case, it follows that the price mechanism will be subject to a very erratic and powerful pressure, namely, the fact that the distribution of purchasing power to consumers, through work on military projects, through military benefits, etc., will continue very strongly to attract resources toward the civilian side of the economy and away from the military side of the economy in an uneven and disruptive manner.

I think the fundamental point Mr. Jewkes makes is the real one we ought to put very strongly before our congressional colleagues. We are, after all, talking about mobilizing 20 per cent of the gross national product for war purposes. There is a big difference between mobilizing 20 per cent and mobilizing 50 per cent, as we did during the war. We have, after all, only two choices. We can do that mobilizing through higher taxes or through higher prices. It should not be very difficult—it should not be impossibly difficult—or beyond the reach of our resources to come close to that 20 per cent figure through taxation. The refrain which has run through all our conversation, it seems to me, is that if we came close to that figure of 20 per cent, or whatever the military and government budget turned out to be, through a combination of taxing and banking policy, then our problems of coping with this particular brand of inflation would be infinitely less today and less threatening in the long run.

The question is: Can Congress muster up the will and the discipline to lay taxes and support central banking restrictions on private consumption and investment on a big enough scale to permit a 20 per cent mobilization without a general increase in prices? If Congress does that, we shall be able to get along with Mr. DiSalle and colleagues as a standby facility and with our present precatory and ineffective price and wage controls in existing form.

Mr. Feller: I should like to comment briefly on what Mr. Jewkes and Mr. Hitch said. I think the latter part of Mr. Jewkes's statement fairly well refuted the earlier part of his statement. The examples which he gave were, by and large, examples of a return to a period of normal expectations. While it represented a change, it was a period in which we did not expect any further change. The identifying mark of the kind of crisis that we have here is not only that it is large and that it is fast, that speed is of the essence, but also that it is in some measure unanticipated and nonrecurring. We have a particular need to meet in terms of diversion of capital resources which must be done now and will not continue in the future. Presumably once we have made those large-scale fast diversions, we will have the productive capacity to divert the end product of our system to military expenditures without severe dislocations. In that case, we can rely on the price mechanism, because then we will have, presumably, stable anticipations and expectations.

Now, let me add a footnote to Mr. Hitch's remarks. I think Mr. Hitch is quite right that, to do this kind of rapid, nonrecurring diversion in a period of mobilization, we cannot rely upon the market. As a plain matter of fact, we know that a steel producer would rather give his goods to a man who will be here five years from now than give it to a tank manufacturer who will not be here five years from now.

If we do not use the price mechanism, then the question does recur as to what we do about prices, since we are allocating some of the product by direct controls. The price question then becomes very much not a question of economics but a social question—a question of division of income between various classes of society. Prices can be higher or lower than a given level, and we will achieve the same kind of diversion to military purposes. Then the question is: If we allow them to rise in this temporary period of dislocation to market levels, will we get a large diversion of income to the persons who happen to be in the possession of those facilities at that moment and diversion away from other sections of the community? We have a social question, also, in terms of allocation of the resources which are temporarily scarce: Because steel is scarce, shall we allow the market price of steel and the price of automobiles to rise very high, so that temporarily different classes of people will consume goods than consumed them before and in different proportions?

It seems to me that there we have to stop and recognize something which Harold Leventhal showed recognition of this morning, and that is that in our type of society the only criterion is not the criterion of efficiency. There are other criteria in terms of equity or social justice, and there are certain elements of doing things efficiently which our society will not tolerate, because they involve too many social injustices. Allowing the price of shacks to rise to $300 a month may induce building in an army town or camp. Our society will not tolerate that as a way of doing it, because we recognize it as unjust. Second, our society will not tolerate the circumstances economically, because, strangely enough, laboring men—and those are the people with whom I have some familiarity—do not operate in a simple economic situation. They will sit down and go on strike for six months if they have to because they are sore about the way things are done. So, actually, what may appear to be efficient and socially unjust becomes inefficient, because the people will not work at it. There are other things besides monetary incentives.

Mr. Friedman: I think our discussion is getting confused because the words "direct controls" are being used to refer to very different things, without distinguishing among them. Mr. Stein, this morning, and Mr. Hitch, this afternoon, argued for a certain kind of direct control because prices did not rise fast enough. This has, I believe, been interpreted by Mr. Feller and Mr.

Rostow as an argument in favor of preventing prices from rising. It is precisely the reverse. Mr. Stein was explicit this morning that the kind of direct controls he was urging would be required only until prices had risen to the point at which they could do the "allocating." Hence, the advocates of price and wage controls can draw little or no comfort from the arguments of either Mr. Stein or Mr. Hitch.

The controls they have recommended are controls designed primarily to give priorities with respect to certain parts of output. With respect to the part that is not given a priority rating, there is no argument, on their grounds, against its allocation by the market through prices. Yet, Mr. Feller argued if, for reasons cited by Stein and Hitch, we do not rely solely on prices for giving a priority to military production that justifies giving up the use of prices throughout the economy and holding them down by a full program of direct price-wage controls.

Mr. Rostow argued along somewhat different lines. He agreed that, if we had a decent fiscal and monetary policy, price and wage controls would be largely unnecessary. But he then went on to say that, if we did not have a decent fiscal and monetary policy, we would have to have effective price and wage controls. I think that this statement needs much further consideration. If we do not restrain inflation by monetary and fiscal means, effective wage and price controls will mean that goods are unavailable in the sense that the quantities people will want to buy will exceed the quantities that are available. There will, in consequence, have to be some method of allocation among producers and rationing among consumers to serve altogether different purposes than those of which Mr. Stein and Mr. Hitch spoke.

Mr. Rostow was willing to face that. He said, "Well, let's go on to do some of this rationing and allocation." I want to suggest two things in this connection. First, that he ought to go on and ask whether, if we do the rationing and allocation he proposes, the price control would be needed. In that case, the rationing and allocation would themselves keep prices down. Strictly speaking, the situation is that, if we do not have widespread and appropriate rationing and allocation, price controls will not work. They will be associated with chaos in distribution and production. On the other hand, if we do have the rationing and allocation, explicit price controls are unnecessary to keep prices down. Second, he should examine the kind of rationing and allocation he thinks it is feasible to engage in when we are speaking about distributing essentially the whole national output among the classes in the community.

Mr. Feller remarks in this connection, "We must do that under those circumstances, whatever the problem, and whatever the cost, and whatever the difficulties, because the alternative to this is inequity in distribution." I would go much further. There is inequity in distribution in either case, perhaps just as extreme inequity with explicit rationing and allocation as with inflation. The appropriate way to solve the problem of equitable distribution of the mobilization costs is by taxation. The way to distribute the cost is directly by deciding what taxes we want various groups in the community to bear. So that, I think, along this line we still have no argument for price and wage control. At best, it may be an argument for rationing and allocation. I think that, as we examine the argument for rationing and allocation, we will be very skeptical that there is one for that either.

In this connection, I want to say a word about our own wartime experience, which has been referred to. The widespread reaction against price controls which led to their ultimate disappearance in the spring of 1946 was not unrelated to the effects which the price controls had upon the distribution of goods and services. I think there was widespread feeling that they had led to a highly inefficient, inequitable distribution of goods and services. One more point is that I think we want to be careful, in interpreting the wartime experience, to distinguish between fact and appearance. In many cases in which prices appeared to be controlled, we all know that they were not effectively controlled; that there were many ways to skin the cat. As Mr. Jewkes said, a judicious use of some measure of black-market activity and evasion of price controls can permit the market to perform the function which it performs so effectively.

If I am right so far, the only argument that remains for price and wage control is still the argument that was considered earlier—that somehow it stops some kind of mysterious spiral, which I must say I do not understand. I do not think there is any difference whatsoever between what Mr. Harrod called a "basic" inflation and a "spiral" inflation. This argument has been made a little bit more precisely by Mr. Cortney and others in saying that price and wage controls are needed under these circumstances because, if we do not have them, wages would go up. This in turn, they say, would force prices to go up. If we tried to hold down the money supply, this would produce unemployment; but we are committed to full employment, and hence strong political pressure would be brought to bear on the monetary authorities to expand the money supply sufficiently to permit the higher prices to be consistent with full employment. I find this particular argument very difficult to understand. If the political strength of the labor and associated groups is sufficient to force the monetary authorities to inflate, why is it not sufficient to force the wage-control authorities to supply the same increases in income? This argument assumes that somehow direct wage and price control can be insulated from political influence from which monetary controls cannot be.

I want to make a final point, somewhat unrelated to the preceding. Those of us who have been concentrating on the monetary sources of inflation have implicitly or indirectly been accused, by some of the few and rare individuals here who are our critics, of adopting an oversimplified view of the monetary mechanism. It has been implied that we believe that if the quantity of money doubles, prices inevitably double; that prices cannot rise without an increase in the quantity of money; etc.

I want to deny that accusation explicitly. We are not so naïve as all that. Of course, we recognize that prices may rise for a variety of reasons which need not, in the first instance, be related to an increase in the quantity of money. The reason why we emphasize the monetary factor is that, whatever may be the factors initiating price changes, or whatever may be the reactions preventing a strict covariation of prices and the quantity of money, it is possible to *offset* them by operating on this particular variable which can be readily controlled.

A person who believes in establishing dams to control floods is not properly to be accused of supposing that dams produce floods. The situation is exactly the same here. The relationship between prices on the one side and the monetary circulation on the other is a complex one, and under ordinary circumstances, where we do not have this particular strong effect of a wartime program, it may be extremely difficult to manipulate. Indeed, I am arguing here very strongly for a policy under present circumstances that I do not believe would be a desirable policy in ordinary times. But under present circumstances, where the pressures are all in one direction, it is particularly easy to avoid making extreme mistakes. Our argument, I want to emphasize, is that here is a lever which can be pulled and which will enable us to offset whatever the factors may be that are producing the tendency for the rise in prices.

MR. JONES: I would like to ask Mr. Friedman one question. I was rather impressed with Mr. Hitch's statement about un-filled orders in the capital goods industry, machine tools, etc., backing up so that we did not get them for two or three years. What is your answer to that?

MR. FRIEDMAN: I do not know what the facts are there. If it is true, that must suggest that those industries are monopolistic industries of a kind that many of us would like to make competitive. If it is true, why, it seems to me that that would establish a case for temporary priorities along the lines that Mr. Stein suggested this morning, and what we ought to do under those circumstances is to seek means of making prices in those industries more flexible and get the adjustment as much as we can through prices, so that we rely to a minimum extent on these priority orders.

MR. HITCH: In other words, we first reform the economy.

MR. FRIEDMAN: What you suggest may be the correct thing to do, given that we cannot reform the economy immediately.

MR. MULLENDORE: For the purpose of relieving an inferiority complex which I have been developing during this meeting, and partly for the purpose of referring you to older authority on the subject, may I tell you that I was one of the first price controllers in the United States thirty-four years ago. One year out of college, bearing two degrees, one of which stamped me as an authority on economics and the other as a leading lawyer, I became an assistant counsel of the United States Food Administration, which was our first attempt in this country to control prices during the war.

I want to recommend to Mr. DiSalle a book written by me on the history of the United States Food Administration which will disclose some very interesting lessons which we learned in an attempt to mix voluntary and direct controls during World War I. If we had time I would be delighted to tell you some of the things I think we learned, and which, apparently, have been discarded, and are never referred to, because the language which I hear here today contains expressions and phrases which did not even exist in that day and which must have grown out of subsequent experience without relation to the prior experience and the first experience in price control. After that, I had a year in Germany witnessing the inflation there, and I think that I may therefore relieve my inferiority complex by qualifying both as a college-trained economist and an experienced American price controller.

But what I wanted particularly to call attention to here is that I have, since that time, fallen through a succession of missteps into the position of chief executive of a utility which today has a million customers and collects from customers $110,000,-000 gross per year. (And there is the interesting point: When we refer to particular prices, whether it is of steel or any other commodity or service, we may be mistaken in supposing that all prices have risen.) Now, this utility of which I am the chief executive—which simply means I am the fellow who is pushed around the most and kicked around the most—has a lower price today than at any time in its history, a lower price than it had in 1939 or 1940 or at any time before then. How could that possibly be, when we are paying wages which are twice as high, when our capital is costing us twice as much—for the reasons I mentioned yesterday—when our taxes, which happen to be twenty-five cents out of every gross dollar, have doubled since 1940, and when the cost of most materials and supplies has also doubled?

Well, there are just a few explanations which will show why we must know what prices we are talking about, and some of the hidden influences, and not generalize and oversimplify this situation too much. One is that we have taken it out of the stock-holder. We cut his wages in two, in half, while we were doubling the wages of the workmen. That was one way in which it was done. We have increased efficiency. We have increased volume, because we are offering this biggest bargain in the market, and many customers have disemployed labor and instituted labor-saving devices, and there has been a general indifference as to how much electricity was used, because it costs so very little anyway. We are now accumulating a badly hidden deficit by selling to our customers each day some part of the power-house, transformers, poles, wires, and substations and all the parts of a $600,000,000 investment—we are selling to the customers each day equipment for one dollar which it will take two dollars to replace and thereby showing as earnings a hidden deficit.

There is an example of a prevailing price drawn from direct experience, which is not exactly borne out by some of the general statements made here.

SENATOR O'MAHONEY: Mr. Chairman, I am not quite sure that I understood Mr. Jewkes. He seemed to me to be saying that price and wage controls are not essential and that we may allow this matter to be controlled by the market. And as proof of the effectiveness of the market to do the job which is to be done, he cited what is alleged to have been accomplished by the market in Germany and here in the United States after the shooting stopped in World War II.

Now, if that is a correct understanding of what Mr. Jewkes said, and if it is a correct understanding of what is implied in the statements of those who are arguing for inflation, rather than for control, it seems to me that we have overlooked the facts about what did happen in the United States after the shooting stopped in World War II. The Congress of the United States, in order to promote recovery, provided the largest subsidy that was ever given to business anywhere. We passed the Contract Settlement Act, the purpose of which was to make a speedy settlement of all war contracts, regardless of accuracy. I wish those who think that that was not a subsidy would consult Mr. Lindsay Warren, who is the head of the General Accounting Office and who has told Congress repeatedly that we gave away millions of the public's money to provide business with the funds with which it could reconvert.

We passed the Surplus Property Law, by which we undertook to dispose of plants built by the people of the United States, in order that business and industry might undertake speedily to produce the goods which we felt were necessary in the reconversion era and which at that time seemed necessary to prevent the unemployment that the Russians were expecting to develop here in the United States. And so plants that were built by the taxpayers' money were sold at sometimes as little as twenty cents on the dollar.

I could refer to the repeal of the Excess Profits Tax Law, which utterly and completely overlooked the huge war debt which we had and which was passed upon the theory that it was much better to lower the taxes upon business and industry in order to promote recovery. And then, if I mistake not—what was the period, Mr. Ruml, of the famous Ruml Plan?

MR. RUML: 1944.

SENATOR O'MAHONEY: Then I cannot bring you into this picture of the windfalls that were given to business.

In any event, reconversion in the United States was not due to the market. It was due to the action of government in a most extraordinary generous mood toward business and industry, and, while the Congress was giving away the property of the United States to promote reconversion through industry, I never heard a yip out of the businessmen against those acts of Congress.

Now, why is it that we need price and wage controls for this event? I think the answer to that is that war is bad and that preparation for war is only a little less bad, because both of these operations take people out of production, take them out of constructive activity, and put them into destructive activity.

War is bad, and if we do not have price and wage controls, and profit control through taxes, then the price of rearmament is bound to rise and rise more rapidly even than the cost of living is rising to the millions in the lower-income brackets who must do the work of rearming. If we permit the price of rearmament to rise, it will be a cost to all the people of the United States.

We cannot discuss the economics of mobilization upon the theory that we can mobilize in a way that is going to be easy for business and easy for industry. It is not going to be easy for anybody, because now we are dealing with total war; and, in order to prevent a huge deficit of perparedness to be piled on top of the deficits we now have, we must have the controls, which alone, in my judgment, will keep the cost to all the people down.

Mr. KESTNBAUM: I am going to try to express some general views on direct controls, but I should like to point out in passing that, as usual, we have achieved through the American way a very happy solution to this problem, one that should satisfy all parties.

We now have price and wage controls—this will satisfy those people in our economy who feel that price and wage controls are necessary. And we have a price and wage control formula which will permit wages and prices to rise and economic forces to operate, and that should satisfy those who foresee the evil effects of price controls. It seems to me therefore that, as Professor Schultz has said, the economy has handled this thing very satisfactorily, and this is not said in a spirit of levity. I am serious about it.

I think one is driven to the conclusion that price and wage controls work unevenly in different industries, that they work with reasonable effectiveness under some circumstances, but that there are certain areas where they simply do not work at all. One can argue either side of the case by selecting the right examples. There has been some reference to concealed price advances, and it is supposed that this is something quite evil. In my judgment this is not necessarily so. The fact that shirts got an inch shorter was a rather small price to pay for what was accomplished. It was not a serious imposition of hardship on the American people.

One of the weaknesses of the general argument lies in the fact that some of our very good and honest citizens who want to see justice done argue that it is necessary to hold the cost of living down so that increased wages can buy the things that are needed in larger amounts. This creates certain difficulties with respect to those goods that are in short supply and which, through no fault of anyone but simply through difficulties of nature, cannot be increased rapidly. I think a good example is meat. It is impossible suddenly to double the quantity of meat available in the country, and therefore it is impossible to make all the meat available that is wanted by all the people who have the incomes to buy it. In the circumstances, I think there is no answer to the argument that either the price of meat has to go up or we have to have a rationing system—which is difficult and may lead to a black market, which is even more difficult.

Now I should like to advance the proposition that what we are facing in this country is essentially a management problem. We are confronted quite suddenly with the need for converting our economy from a peace to a defense economy. We must use a very large portion of our productive capacity for that purpose, and we must hold down inflationary pressures while we are doing it. It must be obvious that, if all our people were angels, there would be no problem. Everybody would exercise a kind of self-discipline and would accept his proportionate share. Business people would forego higher profits. Wage-earners would forego increases. Other elements in the community would make proportionate sacrifices, and there would be no serious problem.

Because we now introduce questions of social justice, equitable distribution, and other factors, we raise very deep and difficult problems which are inherent in the character of our economy and of our people and the nature of our democracy. These things cannot be separated out. This is why I said yesterday that we must regard our problem as unique, that many of the things that might work elsewhere will not work in our own economy, and that, unless we can find ways to manage skilfully, we shall get ourselves into difficulty. Unless we recognize that the work of this country is done by millions of people who must adapt their actions and decisions to the needs of the circumstances quickly and who do not have time to wait for an order from Washington telling them what to do—unless we recognize these facts, we shall get into serious administrative difficulties with virtually every type of control and regulation.

Therefore, it seems logical in these problems with all the devices available to us. I am not proposing at all that we allow inflation to go on unchecked. On the other hand, I think that it does not do to advertise the inflation, as our administration did for months by announcing that it was coming and that we would probably have to use price and wage controls. In many cases, price increases were purely in anticipation of possible regulations, and this was true to a large degree of certain wage increases.

Since some guidance is necessary, the best policy is one which allows the economy to operate as naturally as possible. We must give certain power to intelligent administrators, and we must encourage them in using these powers to interfere as little as possible with the economy. Obviously, the more rapidly we expand our defense requirements, the more difficult these administrative problems become.

It will take a great deal of wisdom, character, and leadership to make clear to our people that what is called for at the present time is a contribution to a defense effort rather than a rearrangement of the economic and social values that exist in our economy. In this respect I am inclined to challenge Mr. Rostow's argument that we should make progress in times of crisis. I believe that he is historically accurate, but I think it is too bad that it has to work that way.

MR. ROSTOW: You have got the wrong horse.

MR. KESTNBAUM: I am sorry. It is Mr. Stigler's, I think.

On monetary and fiscal controls which were advocated by a great many business organizations, I invite your attention to the fact that this is the first time in history, so far as I know, when all business organizations recognized that increased taxes were necessary. This has never happened before, Senator. I believe that Congress was slow in doing the things that everybody agreed needed to be done and that we might have checked some of this earlier by moving somewhat more rapidly and thus avoiding this long period during which everyone got set for an inflationary movement.

Now that it is here there are some signs that it is leveling off, partly because these movements usually go too far, partly because the productive capacity of the country as usual was greater than was anticipated, partly because the defense program was slow in getting started, and partly because the existence of even a few surpluses tends to discourage the psychological effects of inflation. We ought to take advantage of this period—which is likely to continue for a few months—to minimize the pressures that will inevitably develop later on if we are going to devote some 20 per cent of our national income to a defense program.

I should like to refer to Senator O'Mahoney's observations because I have great regard for the Senator and because he said something about what government does for the economy. In my opinion there is a fundamental error here. The government does not support the economy; I think that the economy supports the government. The government can to some extent direct the distribution of the benefits produced by the economy, but the notion that there is some mysterious process by which the government *creates* benefits is to my mind at the bottom of a number of our difficulties.

Allow me also to say a word on the question of sacrifices. I am very much in agreement with what Professor Mises has said. We have now reached the point where sacrifices will have to be made by the great mass of our people, and that includes members of the labor unions. If we are going to devote a large portion of our production to the defense effort and if there are real sacrifices involved, there is no way in which we can maintain the standard of living of the large groups in our society. If we examine this critically, however, we find that we did raise the standard of living of our people throughout World War II and that we have raised it since World War II. I shall make the prediction that we shall maintain our standards during the defense period partly through the process of inflation and that we shall continue to raise our standards after the first impact of this particular period is over. Our industrial economy is the principal expression of the peculiar genius of our country. It has done surprisingly well because it seems to respond to our native talents. Our economy has been venturesome, dynamic, and forward-looking. Organized labor has made an important contribution, and I agree with the observation made here that labor has in general been a stabilizing factor.

And now, lest I seem to have wandered too far afield, I should like to repeat that there is nothing wrong in the light of the record of our economy in asking all groups including labor to make such temporary sacrifices as are necessary in order to minimize inflationary pressures at this time. If, on that basis, we can develop a well-rounded national program which is consistent within itself and which seems likely to be well managed, the fear of further inflation will decline. It is the fear of inflation more than any other factor which is responsible for such inflation as has occurred up to the present time. This calls for leadership and quality on the part of those to whom we intrust responsibility. Groups such as those assembled here can be helpful to those who are administrators. I hope that it will be possible to distil some wisdom from a summary of this conference, even though there are conflicting ideas. At least it is clear that there are no simple answers to complex problems.

To my mind the most useful lesson which can be learned from this conference is the recognition of the fact that there is no single device or set of devices or no simple formula by which we can manage this tremendously difficult problem. We can manage it only if we are intelligent enough to allow the economy to operate as freely as possible.

CHAIRMAN LEVI: Mr. Gainsbrugh!

MR. GAINSBRUGH: My comments are directed primarily to Item IV on the question of priorities and allocations and in part to some of the statements made by Mr. Hitch.

We find ourselves now coming to the close of the first year of defense. In the safe retrospect of mid-1951, perhaps this might be said—that we have had an experiment, involuntarily I believe, with the response of the free market to the desirable allocation of resources in a period of quarter-war. Perhaps we have actually blundered into a working process for an economy in the state of

quarter-war in which we find ourselves. I say "blundered" because this was not planned, nor was it premeditated. What actually happened, and this we have been told frequently—I can cite
General Harrison in connection with it—is that we lacked manpower tables, material tables, and all the other requirements for
a shift to a controlled economy. We still lack them as of this date.
That is one of the reasons why CMP has not yet been imposed;
we lack the basic supporting material.

In the interim we had to rely primarily upon voluntary adjustments, and where do we find ourselves in the second quarter of
1951? So far as the metropolitan area of New York is concerned,
we seem to be faced with a glut in many areas of production
1ather than with scarcity. I wonder, if we had had manpower
tables and material tables, for example, whether we would have
had the almost record-breaking level of automobile production
in the first quarter of 1951? What would the situation have been
in numerous other areas—refrigerators, television, and I could
go on and name a host of other areas in which we find ourselves
in a good position currently? I cite in connection with this same
position General Harrison's statement that, as of the present,
defense production has not been held back for lack of materials,
strategic or otherwise, because of this high level of civilian output. We simply were not ready as of the first or second quarter
for any greater flow of materials into defense industries than
that actually taking place.

I do not mean by that to sound too confident about our ability
to manage equally well in the months ahead. But certainly, in
retrospect, there is indication perhaps of a better rationing of
resources through the voluntary system than had we in existence
the materials and blueprints that would have been required for
a controlled economy. I might also cite in that connection that
since mid-1950 we have had about an 11 or 12 per cent increase
in industrial production; we have had a rising gross national
product, a rising volume of goods available for civilian purposes,
as well as a rising volume of goods available for defense purposes. I say this all, of course, in the calm serenity of April–May,
1951. It could not have been said in the panic of December,

1950, or January, 1951, when all-out war seemed imminent. But the international situation envisioned in December and January did not come into being.

I agree there is necessity that we do have in government the plans and blueprints which can be put to use, Mr. Hitch, in the event that we do move into a period of total mobilization. But we did not have such materials in the first year of defense, and as a result our primary reliance was upon the voluntary mechanism. I think the result of the first year of defense is favorable in terms of allocation of resources.

I am quite conscious of the fact that in the period ahead we face banked-up pressures to which Mr. Kestnbaum and others have referred. We are going to have to find additional ways of reducing those pressures in the second stage of defense. Higher taxes and tighter credit and monetary policies have been proposed. I would think that this conference would likewise place some degree of emphasis upon the encouragement of private saving if and when that becomes desirable.

Macy's ran an ad in January, 1951, saying to its customers, "Please don't buy so much; it is not good for you, and it is not good for us." But in March or April, 1951, Gimbel's in turn ran a full-page ad saying, "We are letting the cat out of the bag. Goods are in abundance. Please come in and buy, and we will give you real values." Now, those are market considerations which were met by market adjustment.

On the saving point, why is it that we as a group do seem to shy away from that particular area? Is it because we feel that there is an awfully tough road ahead of us in terms of encouragement of private saving in the inflationary environment in which we have existed for the last five or ten years and to which most of our populace is awakening? Is there a growing lack of confidence in our price structure, in the fiscal strength of our system, perhaps even in the solvency of our country? Is that why we are reluctant to test the market in terms of further increase in private holdings of federal bonds? We do know that that was an effective vehicle in World War II in neutralizing the impact of expanded consumer incomes upon short supply.

I have heard no discussion of the contribution savings might make to an anti-inflationary program. Ought not savings to be included in our kit of anti-inflationary weapons?

CHAIRMAN LEVI: Mr. Hazlitt, do you wish to speak?

MR. HAZLITT: No, I had just a remark to make with regard to the speakers who have been boasting about the achievements of price control immediately after World War II. All I was going to suggest is that, if they wish to boast of those achievements, they ought to have boasted about the meat famine, which was the chief achievement of that price control.

MR. PORTER: May I ask Mr. Hazlitt a question? Do you recall what the per capita consumption of meat was during the first six months of 1946?

MR. HAZLITT: No, I do not. I know it went up; but I do know this, Mr. Porter, that after the price control was taken off the meat famine disappeared.

MR. PORTER: I challenge that statement and make the observation that an analysis of the Bureau of Agricultural Economics figures will indicate, and I am basing this on recollection and reserve the right to correct the record more accurately, that meat consumption during the first half of 1946, based upon federally inspected slaughter, was the highest in the last four and a half years. So therefore the famine, it seems to me, was an illusion by those who said, "Let us decontrol," and was not based upon any accurate actuality.

MR. HAZLITT: That thing was wholly debated during the campaign of 1946.

MR. PORTER: It was a political issue and not a famine.

MR. HAZLITT: The outcome of the campaign proved what the public thought of the outcome of that debate. I think it is quite clear that the supply of meat was simply not coming forward. It was quite notorious that the bidders of the big packing companies went down to the meat markets and said: "We offer so-and-so much" and would not offer any more; and, of course, the lambs and steers simply did not turn up. That is all that happened. Nobody brought them in, because the price ceiling did not allow them to be brought in. As soon as the price ceilings were off, the meat came out. That was all there was to it. It is as simple as that.

MR. GOODE: Mr. Porter made an assertion of fact. I was just trying to determine whether you were disagreeing with the determination of facts.

MR. PORTER: Senator O'Mahoney points out that he was a staunch supporter of price control and was re-elected that year from a cattle state.

MR. FELLER: I should like to ask Mr. Hazlitt a question, and that is whether he would permit the accuracy of his statistics to be determined by the election returns in every case as well as in the case of the election of 1946.

MR. HAZLITT: I think that the whole point is that, if we are going to deny now that there was a meat famine during 1946—that the whole thing was an illusion—anybody who wishes to have that opinion can have it. Maybe the whole thing was a mistake, and history should omit any mention of the whole business.

MR. FRIEDMAN: I just want to make a minor comment which puts me in between the two of these. I think the real argument against price control is precisely that it produces this illusion of famine when there is none.

MR. PORTER: I would say, in response to that, that at that particular point the real argument I had against price control was the threat of decontrol.

MR. HAYEK: Does it mean that price control, once imposed, must go on forever?

MR. PORTER: It is a question of timing. I think it was decontrolled prematurely. That was my official position. I stated that under oath, and, even though the statute of limitation has probably run out, I will not incriminate myself by withdrawing from that position.

MR. BRUBAKER: I do not intend to make a long speech at this time. I think I have that out of my system for today. I would like to come back to one point that the Senator from Wyoming gave voice to a while ago. He committed what for him, in this gathering, must have been a grave theoretical heresy when he

suggested that there are times and places in our economy in recent times when the market has not functioned quite as it is supposed to function and when government or somebody else has
had to do things that this theoretical market is supposed to do.
With this heresy I concur.

I do not want to quarrel too long and publicly with one of the
statements that George Stigler made in his summary along this
same line. He suggested—and I noticed Mr. Kestnbaum also
gives us credit now—that we were responsible as labor unions
for having held down the level of wages in this country. I hope
we are not going to be killed by our friends in that fashion. I
know that this charge has been true to a certain degree, but
I hope to qualify it to the extent that it makes a little sense.
Yes, we do have collective bargaining contracts. They run until
December, 1951, in steel. We cannot get a wage increase between now and December, so between now and December we
are holding down wages for all we are worth, but do not accuse
us of anything more than that. If the prices go up another 10
per cent between now and December, we are not going to sit
and hold down wages some more just to satisfy this theory that
has been developed here that somehow unions now function
to hold down wages.

Apparently there is an immediate corollary of this theory that
wages have been held down by unions, which I acquired over
cocktails with some of the University of Chicago economists last
night, which has not been given quite such explicit statement
today, namely, that the function which labor unions play in the
setting of wages in this country is, to put it mildly, virtually nil.
I do not know for what unions get credit under this theory—but
I guess it is only for holding wages down. We certainly do not
get any credit for having raised them.

The assertion is made quite bluntly that wages follow immediately, except for this holding-down of wages by the unions,
upon rises of prices. If that is not the sheerest and utterest nonsense that I have ever heard mouthed in a long, long time, I do
not quite know what is. I only wish that some of you who are
sitting in that ivory tower, which I once sat in for some time,
could get out of it for a little while as I have done.

I have spent the last ten years of my life working very closely, outside the ivory tower, with the question of wage determination. I spent several years working with the War Labor Board during the war, helping to set levels of wages. This I did not as a union representative, for I was not associated with the union then. I worked as a public representative in that capacity. I think I know some of the problems and some of the areas in which it was possible to operate at that time, some of the things which Lloyd Garrison said so well this morning, some of the things which are not quite present in the atmosphere in which we are forced to operate today. But for the last five or six years of my life I have been working with a labor union, participating in negotiations in an effort to set levels of wages, not by the free flow and operation of the market somewhere way out there, but by the process of bargaining collectively with major employers in one of our major industries—steel.

If anybody here wants to stand up on this floor and say in all honesty that he thinks we have a free price set in the steel industry on the basis of the market and that we have had such any time within the last fifty years—well, I would just like to hear him get up and say so. How, in the light of these facts in steel— and that is not an isolated circumstance; I can go down a whole list of industries with you where we have that same kind of a situation of prices not set by any free market—can we pretend that wages are set equitably by some free and automatic market device? They just are not. I only wish that some of you could come with me into a collective bargaining conference with United States Steel, when the union's representatives are sitting down to bargain about a wage increase with United States Steel.

If you think that this is easy and that they come in to us and say, "Well, prices have gone up 10 per cent, boys, and here is your 10 per cent wage increase, just take it now"—that one flows right after the other—well, boys, it just ain't so. We fight for those wage increases, and we fight hard for them, and we fight for them despite the fact that the price increases have already occurred.

Let's not get all confused about the all-pervasive character of this market device for setting either prices or wages or for furnishing some kind of automatic control for them. It is because we do not have such a free device that we have to come here and say, much as we dislike controls, that we think we must have some of these direct wage and price controls.

SENATOR BENNETT: Mr. Arnold said that the words he likes best to hear are "and finally." I hope that my very brief remark is the "and finally" for the afternoon.

I enjoyed very much what Mr. Kestnbaum had to say, because much of what he said I would like to say in different words. But tonight I have two observations, one which is drawn out of a little passage at arms between Mr. Porter and Mr. Hazlitt. Where do we hope this economy will arrive after this particular mobilization period ends? I am sure there is no one in the room who expects it to end in the pattern of a completely controlled economy. If they do, then we might as well put on the controls as quickly as we can get them there and begin to operate them as successfully as we know how.

Since I firmly believe that none of us hopes for that end, but rather hopes that we can go back as close as possible to a free market for a free competitive enterprise economy—I have felt ever since this problem of direct controls came into the picture that it is not too soon now for us to begin to consider the method of taking them off.

Mr. Porter suggested they were taken off prematurely before. Mr. Hazlitt does not seem quite to agree with him. As a businessman, living under them, I was sure that we could not get rid of them fast enough. We were just fed up with them, anxious to be freed from that load as we were to be freed from all the other loads that were imposed by the war. That was an emotional decision perhaps. Maybe we would be much better off if those who have the responsibility for developing the pattern that takes us into controls should be working just as hard on the pattern that will bring us out where we want to be.

As this is the final session, this may be the proper session in which I should share with you what I think is the most potent capsule of wisdom on this question of direct controls, on prices, on wages, or on anything else. I stood in a little country store, in a little mining town off the railroad during last fall's campaign, and we talked about inflation during that campaign, and, apologizing in advance to the ladies, the proprietor of that little store said to me, "Well, remember, Mr. Bennett, you can't cure dysentry with adhesive tape."

CHAIRMAN LEVI: I am sure that the remark about "and finally" was in reference to the speaker who used it and not to the speaker who is to succeed him. I therefore call on Mr. DiSalle.

MR. DiSALLE: Not being equipped with adhesive tape, I suppose I might go right ahead and say something.

When this conference is over tomorrow, a good many of you gentlemen will be returning to your different pursuits, continuing to think about the problems. Three of us will have to go back and have to work on them, and, in working on the problems, we will have received some encouragement from this session. I suppose, if any conclusions have been arrived at, we find that it has been concluded that the government's monetary policies have not been effective, the government's fiscal policies have not been effective, and so we will come to the conclusion that, since we were definitely starting in a spiral in December and January and the only action that has been taken has been a price-wage freeze, that if the velocity of that spiral has been reduced, then the price-control action that was taken is largely responsible for it. That is a conclusion.

In this present price-control effort—and you must remember that it is just a baby about two months and ten days old but a very lusty baby at that—it has thus far taken action that has frozen prices generally and has taken specific tailored action which affects possibly sixty or seventy billion dollars of commodities at the retail level. Those are not the final actions that will be taken. We will have a good many regulations to write. We will have a job to do; but, as we do it, we are going to attempt to do it just as fairly and honestly as we think it is possible. We are going to try to make a real analysis of each particular situation, and the regulations to be issued will be issued on the basis of those studies. And I think that they will prove to be effective techniques if we are supported by the other controls that the people here generally have said are necessary.

Over and above that, we need a great deal of that philosophy that has been expressed by Meyer Kestnbaum today. We are going to have to stop kidding each other. We are going to have to start admitting that we have to have reasonable profits if we are going to operate. We are going to have to admit that fair wages are necessary. We are going to have to say that the government has to play a part of leadership in periods of this kind, and these are periods of emergency, and that the government cannot play this part of leadership without the support of both labor and management joining together and realizing that they have a mutuality in this undertaking.

Those are things that we are going to have to face. And then over and above all we are going to have to stop talking coldly about things like "rationing by purse." Although the American people accept price rationing in normal times, the human being is governed by certain natural aspirations, emotions, and impulses other than those that are ordinarily ascribed to the birds and the bees. People, just individual people who grow up in the United States, grow up with the idea that here they will have a chance to go into a business of their own; that here they will have a chance to educate their children; that here they will have a chance to improve their standards of living. When we talk about rationing by purse and just coldly admitting that we are going to let prices rise and let the necessities of life go to the highest bidder, we certainly are not being realistic in our approach to the problems that we have to face.

And so we are going to go back to work and continue to do the kind of a job that I think has been an effective job and a responsible job. And we are going to do it because we feel that it is a necessary implement in a time of dislocation, whether or not the University of Chicago experts think that price controls are necessary.

When I was in the Ohio legislature, we considered a bill that made the thrush a gamebird instead of a songbird. We used to have bills before us that would affect the economy of the state, establishing budgets of three or four hundred million dollars to operate the state for a two-year period. When we had those bills up, nobody ever came into the legislature to see what we were doing. But the minute that thrush bill came up, you just could not get a hotel room in the city of Columbus. You just took your life in your hands walking through the aisles, people buttonholing you on one side or the other in reference to that bit of legislation.

Finally, the debate had gotten to its height on this bill, which provided for certain lands where the thrush could fly and no one could shoot at it. One legislator said that by shooting at the thrush you would scatter it, you would avoid inbreeding, and consequently you would have stronger birds all the time. We had a little woman in the legislature from Trumbull County, and she was about this high, and she stood up to her full height and said, "I never knew that you could make more thrushes by shooting them." The same thing is true about price control. I never knew how you could keep prices down when all the elements were at work to drive prices up unless you took some positive direct action.

So, in spite of anything that people might say, and in spite of all the noble sentiments of some people, there are always going to be those people who are going to lead the drive and inspire pressures that are going to drive prices up when the conditions are ripe for it. And that is when the government steps in, not because government wants to step in, because certainly no one ever wants to make a career out of being price director. There are more noble careers that one would naturally aspire to.

Certainly we have things in a democracy that we do not have in the case of a dictatorship. On June 24 the President did not have a set of controls on his shelf that he could just reach for and say, "This is it." We had to have legislation. Congress did very well; it was only sixty days later, on September 8, that it passed a bill. It had to have hearings. That is the way we do things in a democracy. Then the President had to find someone who wanted to take the job of economic stabilization adminis- trator. It took him thirty days to do that. Then it took him sixty days to find anybody silly enough to take the job of price direc- tor. All those things happen in a democracy. We just have to operate that way.

Certainly we pay a price for that, but the freedoms and the guaranties of opportunity that exist in a democracy are well worth the price. And so, if we just realize that, and realize that there are some adjustments that have to be made back and forth, but we can make them in a democratic fashion, this country will meet this emergency just as it has every other emergency and will go on to an ever rising standard of living that will furnish the incentives that are needed to permit our people to become leaders in the nation and our nation to continue as the leader in a free world.

CHAIRMAN LEVI: I will ask Mr. Stigler to summarize the discussion.

MR. STIGLER: I think we have reached the hour where leisure is more valuable than wisdom, and so I will be brief.

I have had a feeling all afternoon that there are at least three different analogies that might be applied to our economy. One is that the economy is like a rather neurotic, high-strung racehorse which can do wonderful things if carefully led; another is that it is a rather powerful but very placid workhorse which sooner or later will always finish its task; and still a third is that it is a wooden horse full of Trojan union leaders. My own feeling is toward the second of those views, I should say.

Apropos of the effects of changes in relative prices on output and the use of price inducements to procure the kinds of output we want, there were two or three questions raised which might be mentioned very briefly.

The first is that relative price falls and perhaps absolute price falls in the industries which produce nonessential goods might lead to unemployment. Mr. Hayek, on the one hand, welcomed a small amount or perhaps a moderate amount of unemployment here to encourage efficiency and expedite the transfer, and Mr. Hansen feared that there would be a possibly severe loss of output because of the resulting unemployment. I have no omniscient adjudication to make on this issue. I would personally be surprised at any protracted and considerable unemployment under almost any monetary policy at the present time.

There is, second, the question of the effects of the price structure on the efficiency with which we produce things and on the nature of the things we produce. As Mr. Henderson points out, some studies have been made—which apparently only he has read—of the effects of price control in the last war on the composition of output. I have a feeling, perhaps morbid, that it will be very hard to prove to either party to this dispute that the price controls are or are not harmful without showing almost grotesque triumphs or grotesque deficiencies in performance. If ever you say, "Look, cotton textile prices rose only x per cent, whereas output rose $12x$ per cent," another can reply, "Actually, the output should not have risen that much; you set too high a relative price on that commodity." If I am right, the fundamental difference of opinion is likely to persist for a long time in this area.

When we come to the speed with which relative prices induce industries to make the goods we want, there was of course a wide difference of views. Some people said that the price system is too slow; and, on the other hand, some, like Mr. Jewkes, said that the control system is really very slow. In this connection, the mobilization analogy played a fairly big part. I thought Mr. Feller's point, that the expectations which we have concerning the future when we enter a demobilization are different and more comfortable than those which we have when we enter a mobilization, is a perfectly valid point, although, in my own case, my expectations showed no trend toward optimism. There is another point, however, that was not emphasized enough: mobilization is usually a much slower process in time than demobilization. A demobilization is frequently substantially completed in twelve months, whereas it is rare mobilization on a big scale that is completed so quickly. This tends to make demobilization more difficult than mobilization.

If we encounter industries in which prices will not perform their task, Mr. Stein and Mr. Hitch very persuasively argue for the use of priorities and allocations. I may say here that there appear to be two kinds of price situations in which this is especially likely to be true. One is the situation where the marketing structure of the industry interferes with acceptance of military orders, where there has been a piling-up of orders and only by violation of contracts could we insert our munitions demands ahead of other people's orders. The second situation arises in those industries where prices do not respond quickly to the quantity demanded. For example, steel prices are not changed rapidly without prior clearance from the Senator on this side of the room and the Congressman on the other side of the room. Whatever the causes, it is then argued that we should use priorities to divert a considerable share of limited outputs to the munitions industries.

I think that here is a real difference between Mr. Stein and Mr. Hitch on how we are going to get rid of these controls after we are over the bulge. Mr. Hitch apparently visualizes a deliberate decision that the fundamental production and procurement problem has been solved, and at that point the allocations are to be eliminated. Mr. Stein, by leaving the prices uncontrolled, looks forward to the time when, owing to adjustments in supply and demand, there is no longer any real pressure on the priority authorities, and people at the end of the queue, so to speak, are being adequately supplied.

I do think it is an important problem to devise methods which will permit removal of the controls in the long run. We really feel that it is essential to give considerable scope to the appearance of new concerns and to the appearance of new techniques, over the next few years. It is one objection to controls that they work best when they do not have to deal with a new set of people each week and when they do not have to change their bases of allocation through time.

Let me just make one point, which I will precede by the phrase "and finally."

I think that there is an easy temptation to exaggerate the differences which are so marked in the discussion this afternoon. There is a group that says, "Let us look primarily to monetary and fiscal policies. These are basic. They do not deal with symptoms. We do not have to engage in capricious and clumsy and continuous intervention with a price system which through history has shown itself to be extremely efficient and capable of stimulating an economy to enormous growth." That sounds all right.

On the other hand, there is a group that says, "Let us be realistic. We are in a hostile world environment, and we face an enormous problem. We are making vast expansions of munition output. We must change a lot of established habits of the public, and we are foolish if we do not use every tool that we have at our disposal. It is only a purist and academician who will insist on using one type of policy because it fits into a particular theoretical framework better than others." That makes some sense, too.

Yet it seems to me that if either of these views were pressed very far, the differences between them would diminish sharply. For example, those who believe in the basic use of monetary and fiscal tools, among whom I number myself, will say that in particular cases, such as those raised by Mr. Hitch and Mr. Stein, the price system is not too efficient; it should be supplemented by direct intervention of one sort or another. The question arises of how many cases there are of this type, and this has not been determined at all previously. On the other hand, those who say, "Let us use all the tools," must really be aware of the fact that it is not entirely a case of more or less. The various methods of controlling inflation are rivals with one another for power, for position in the administration, for popularity with the public, and the like. Indeed, I think one might make a rough hypothesis that there is a sort of conservation principle that there is a fixed amount of opposition to inflation in society and that whether that opposition is used up in one direction or in another will not change radically the aggregate effort we will put forward to combat inflation.

VII

THE IMPACT OF REARMAMENT ON
THE BRITISH ECONOMY

CHAIRMAN BELL: I salute the hardy members of this conference who are still with us. To me, this has been a most revealing experience. I do not know whether the persons here who are not connected with the University of Chicago realize that we have been under fire for many years because we were "radical" and because we were verging on the "subversive." I have wished again and again during the proceedings so far that either the representatives of La Salle Street in Chicago or the representatives of the various commissions in the state of Illinois could listen to the observations of the members of the University of Chicago faculty. I think that would end once and for all the idea that we were "dangerous."

There have been other things that have impressed me as a layman who knows only a few of the words and none of the music; there seems to be something short of complete agreement on these major questions. Someone called attention to the fact that all these gentlemen who have spoken are experts and that somebody hires these experts to tell them what to do, and, when the expert has spoken, the poor layman says, "This is gospel." If those persons could be here and see how many gospels we have a choice among, it would have been a real treat. Another thing that has impressed the layman has been the extent to which these discussions revolve around what may happen, what with more or less conviction is going to happen, and precious little—although there has been some—about what has happened.

It is our privilege this evening to hear from some gentlemen who know what has happened, what is in process of happening,

254

and do not have to deal quite so much in the hypothetical. It is a real privilege, therefore, to be able to have with us this evening these two gentlemen from that rather uncomfortable island who have watched all this in the making, and I shall call first on Mr. Jewkes, of Merton College, who is professor of economic organization—which God knows we need—at Oxford.

MR. JEWKES: I do not think that you will be particularly interested in any array of statistical material about the British war effort. Very briefly, Great Britain is trying in the next two or three years to raise the level of rearmament to about 20 per cent of the national income, about the same percentage as in this country. I thought perhaps in the time available it might be most useful to me to pick out one or two points which seem to represent peculiarities of the British system.

I have been trying to decide as I have sat here through these two very interesting days whether, if this discussion had taken place in England, the talk would have been any different from that which we have heard. I have come to the conclusion that on the whole it would not; that is to say, the same kind of issues would have been raised, the same differences would have been brought out, and, generally speaking, the whole tone of the argument would have been very similar.

But there is one difference of emphasis that I think we might have found if this conference had gone on in England. There would have been a much greater distrust of physical controls: of specific control and allocation of raw materials, distribution of labor, specific pricing of materials, etc. I have been speculating as to the causes of that possible difference because it is rather remarkable that it should exist.

The reasons, as I understand them, are these: First of all, I think we are much more conscious in Great Britain of the shortage of the kind of administrators needed to operate a rather complicated system of controls. It uses up large numbers of men with qualities which are, generally speaking, rare in any community. If we move large numbers of good administrators from other work to the task of control, then either we must argue that those people were doing no useful work before or we must admit that the transfer will tend to weaken the effort put into industry. In Great Britain we realize, I think, that if we try to rebuild the controls on the scale which existed during the war or on anything like that scale, then we will be drawing good men out of industries and away from other useful work.

The second reason, I suspect, is that in Great Britain we have a greater confidence in our power to control and eliminate inflationary pressures than I think is found here. The period of two years up to the outbreak of the war in Korea represents, on the whole, a very successful effort to eliminate inflationary influences. Sir Stafford Cripps must take a great deal of credit for that, both in understanding the problem and in being courageous enough to apply the measures which, painful as they were to the taxpayers, had these very important consequences. Apart from that, the British trade-unionists, and particularly the British trade-union leaders, showed in those two years a statesman-like quality, a sense of restraint, an understanding of what inflation meant, and, in consequence, were prepared to accept voluntarily a virtual standstill in wages which enabled the economy to be brought into something of a balance.

The third reason why it seems to me we in Great Britain are reluctant to apply controls on too wide a scale is, of course, the general recognition that in many ways our controls system has failed. The controlled economy has fallen into disrepute. That is due to matters on which I need not enlarge—a series of stupendous economic blunders, the losses on our colonial experiments, and, finally, the serious difficulties over our food supplies culminating in the very distressing shortage of meat at the moment. There is widespread belief, too, that the nationalization schemes have certainly not brought any great advantages and do not constitute a more efficient way or organization of industry than that which we had before or that which is found elsewhere in the world.

What I believe has become clear from the solid thinking that has gone on in Great Britain about the experiences of the last ten years is, first of all, that if individual prices go wrong or if the individual prices are directed wrongly, then all sorts of most serious upsets and dislocations can occur. The outstanding and the most recent case of that, of course, is the attempt on the part of the British government to buy abroad food at prices lower than existing world prices. The consequence has been, of course, that, though the British government thought they could fix prices, the foreign sellers have different ideas about that, with the consequence that the supplies of food tended to fall. The same sort of difficulty is being encountered, because of mistakes in the fixing of the relative prices of milk and meat, in the production of those two commodities. I think there is a growing knowledge, certainly among the better-informed section of the community, that it is very difficult to try to apply controls at one point or controls of one kind without finding one's self dragged into more general controls over the whole of the system.

There has been a good deal of talk today, for instance, in the conference, about the possibility of picking on strategic points, of having special sorts of controls for strategic materials, and leaving the rest of the economy to work freely. Now, I am not sure from our experience in Great Britain that there is any such thing as a strategic material, just as I am quite sure, for instance, that there is no such thing as the one strategic wheel on a locomotive. The essential thing about an economic system is that it is a system, that at any one moment any one article may become strategic, that no one can know beforehand what the strategic articles will be; and, in consequence, to attempt to simplify the control of the economy by picking on certain points is bound to fail. At the moment, for example, I am prepared to argue that the strategic material in Great Britain is meat—not iron or steel or sulphur but sufficient food to maintain the energy of the people in the tasks that they have set themselves.

Control one thing and inevitably you find, through the constant movement of the economic system seeking to adjust itself to changing circumstances, that you are dragged into a wider and wider range of control. My own guess is, from the speeches recently made by the chancellor of the exchequer, that there will be a determined attempt in the forthcoming budget to do as much as is possible, by higher taxes and other financial devices, to guide the system along the necessary channels without a very great enlargement of the physical controls.

Another interesting difference between your economy and

ours, which leads to some results which I fancy were not expected, is that our level of taxation in general is very much higher than yours. One consequence is that we now seem to have reached the point at which further taxation could probably only be imposed at the cost of reducing incentives. Another consequence of the high taxation is this. If you have very high rates of taxation such as are now found in Britain and if the taxes are highly progressive, then you have in a way embodied in your system some sort of ultimate safeguard against runaway inflation. The reason, of course, is that, if prices or general incomes rise, then automatically a larger section of the taxpayers pass into the higher income-tax grades and pay a very much larger proportion of their increased income in taxation. That is to say, it might be possible to finance the British rearmament by allowing prices to rise, which would automatically take money out of the pockets of the people in the form of taxation and hand it back to the government. What the consequence will be I do not know. Clearly it means that there is a greater temptation on the part of any chancellor of the exchequer, harassed in finding his way between the need for maintaining incentives and his reluctance to impose physical controls, to finance rearmament in the form of higher prices.

The final point I want to raise, and I raise this with some diffidence, is the special position of the British export trade in relation to rearmament. I understand that Mr. Harrod will be dealing in a more comprehensive way with the question of our balance of payments, but there is one point in particular that I would like to examine for a moment.

In the previous wars of this century, Great Britain very early found herself in a very difficult balance-of-payment position. In the first World War, of course, we started with large foreign assets and therefore were in a relatively favorable position, but even then, by 1917, we were in a position in which I believe the war effort could hardly have continued but for the fact that at that stage the United States came in with full supports and credits to pay for the supplies that were being granted and really enabled the British war economy to carry on to the successful end of the war.

The same thing happened in the last war, although then we began with smaller foreign investments. As early as April, 1940, Mr. Churchill was stressing the point that the balance-of-payments problem, if no way could be found around it, would inevitably cripple or at least seriously limit the war effort. But there again providentially in March, 1941, the United States threw aside the cash provisions of the neutrality legislation which, in my mind, made possible a larger air force, a larger army, and an earlier date for the final invasion of Europe than could otherwise have been conceived of.

Now we are starting again, not on such a large scale, of course, but on a scale which is considerable, the same process of trying to build up military strength, and we begin with a position which is even less favorable now for two reasons. In absolute total our foreign investments are now smaller than ever. If we allow for changes in prices, I suppose that our foreign investments are now about a quarter of what they were in 1939. That is one change. The other change in our position lies in the character of our exports. The greater part of our exports in these days are engineering products. They come from the motorcar industry, the electrical engineering industries, and other minor engineering industries in which we produce specialty products. Fifty per cent of our total exports are now in those groups as compared with 30 per cent in 1939. Textiles and pottery and the rest are no longer nearly so important.

Now, it is quite clear from what the chancellor has been saying recently that he is determined to make an attempt to carry through rearmament and maintain that export trade. It is true he recognizes that some diminution in export trade may be inevitable, but he hopes to offset any reduction in the exports of engineering products by an increase in the exports of textiles and the like. One can understand why he wishes to maintain our export trade. He is anxious that Great Britain should continue to be able to stand on her own feet, and he recognizes that our chance of doing so depends upon our maintenance of a high position among the engineering exporters of the world.

I cannot help but feel that this attempt to do the two things —to rearm rapidly and to maintain engineering exports—is likely to break down. The point in time at which it would break down would depend upon the speed of rearmament, but I am assuming that speed is of the essence of the matter, and it may be that within the near future we may be confronted with a balance-of-payments problem again. It is true, of course, that our reserves in monetary terms have increased, but that in part has been due to a running-down of stocks.

At first sight, it might appear to be foolish that, at this critical time, Britain is in fact exporting a very large part of the production of her engineering trades. If we accept the diagnosis that the great danger from Russia lies within the relatively near future, a year or eighteen months, and if we believe that the speediest way by which a country can rearm is to use as quickly as possible the facilities provided by these engineering trades, then it seems very odd indeed that Great Britain should be busily exporting the output of these industries, very often in the form of luxury engineering commodities, luxury motorcars, to areas where that can have no possible advantage for the prosecution of the rearmament program and the placing of Great Britain, and with her the whole of the Atlantic nations, in a much more satisfactory posture of semipermanent defense.

The dilemma seems to me to be almost complete. On the one side one has the British attitude that, if we are to pay our way in the world in the long run, then clearly we must concentrate and export those things in which we have the greatest comparative advantage and that to sacrifice those exports at this time, serious as the crisis may be, would, when the crisis was over, land us once again in the position that we found ourselves after 1945.

The attitude of the American nation, I am sure, could be roughly summarized thus: The British have expressed a determination to take part in the rearmament program that is necessary for the defense of the Atlantic nations. If they have expressed that determination, they must be prepared to take the consequences of it. If they cannot both use the engineering trades for the purpose of rearmament and for the purpose of maintaining exports, then they must cut down their internal consumption further and devote the released resources to the development of their engineering trades. But that seems to me an extremely slow process, far too slow in the circumstances with which we are faced; and I think we are, or will ultimately be, faced with the choice between maintaining the export trade so that we can buy the things we need from abroad and carrying out rearmament expeditiously.

I will not go any further than to say that, in the desperate scramble for safety the Atlantic countries are making at the moment, a scramble which may be near to success if we can only put ourselves into the right posture for defense, it does seem to me odd that the second largest engineering industry in the world, the British, with its unique capacity for the production of specialty products, particularly in the field of aeroengineering, should to such a large extent be devoting itself to the sending-out to other countries of luxury engineering products which, at least for the next two years, seem to contribute nothing to the immediate task of rearmament.

I said I raised this question with great diffidence, and now perhaps I can explain the reason for that. If I were an American, I would always be very suspicious of plans and schemes that come from Europe. Experience of the last five or six years suggests that the first clause in most if not all of these schemes is that the American government will deposit a circulating fund of a billion dollars or something of that kind, and I can very well imagine that any suggestion that this difficulty should be overcome by direct aid would, and I think quite properly, be distasteful. But I put it to you as a problem that, if we are thinking of combined effort on the part of these two countries, the thought that we are devoting valuable resources to provide luxury motorcars for Egypt is almost intolerable.

CHAIRMAN BELL: Thank you, sir.

I have a hope that our next speaker will not be quite so delicate of our feelings and will tell us a little more about what he thinks we ought to do. I recognize that there may be some hesitancy about that, but I should like to assure him that we have told some unpleasant truths to one another and that there is no reason why he should not do the same thing with such guaranty as we can give that he will not be too cruelly treated by the press of the Middle West.

Our next speaker has recently written a *Life of Keynes* which I am sure the professionals among us have read. If not, according to the reviews—and I read reviews of such things—they should read it. He has also written an attractive little book with this appealing title: *Are These Hardships Necessary?* In addition, he has what we call "run for"—he has stood for—Parliament, which shows confidence on the part of certain persons in his discretion, but perhaps I should say, regrettably, there was not confidence of enough people. He is the joint editor of the *Economic Journal,* of which Mr. Keynes was the editor until he died. It is a real privilege to have Mr. Roy Harrod, of Christ Church College and University lecturer in economics at Oxford, speak to us about the facts of economic life. Mr. Harrod!

MR. HARROD: I thank you, sir, very much indeed, for your kind words and for the mention of certain publications. It is very regrettable that the title of one of them, *Are These Hardships Necessary?* is no longer applicable today. We will have to agree, unfortunately, that they are necessary.

I would like to say, to start with, that this is not in any sense a prearranged performance. I said to Professor Jewkes, "I don't expect we shall contradict each other, shall we?" and he said, "I don't think we shall," and that was really about all that transpired. I must apologize, however, if, on the contrary, there may be one or two points on which I shall be saying the same thing, perhaps in a slightly different way. That perhaps I ought to have foreseen. But, athough we may be thinking alike, yet, in certain respects, we seem to differ because, whereas Professor Jewkes preferred the material comfort of sitting down, I prefer the mental comfort of being able to see people over there to make sure that they are not barracking or anything of the sort.

He said he was going to spare you figures, and I have a number of figures here. That, I feel, is rather a decline from his standard, and yet I must try to put across a few figures. I shall cut the figures down to the utmost, but I think the figures do give a sort of reality to certain points.

Think of us as a nation with a national income of twelve billion pounds. I am giving it in pounds not from laziness but because I do not know what the rate of exchange from this point of view is. I rather think it is four dollars to the pound, if you ask me, so that our twelve billion pounds would give you fifty billion dollars.

Think of us for this purpose as about a fifth of you. I think that would be about right. But, unhappily, it does not mean that we have a fifth of the strength, because the income per head is not so very much more than half, and, of course, if we have a people with a lower income per head, the provision of necessities and those things which are needed to sustain morale must take a bigger fraction of the whole.

In the years since demobilization, I reckon we have engaged about 11 per cent for fiscal 1951–52. The other firm figure we boastful, but I think that is a bit higher than your effort after demobilization—it has been 7 per cent, or about 800 million sterling. According to the statement of January 29, 1951, which is liable to upward revision, because we are on the upward move now in these military plans, that is going to become 1,300, or about 11 per cent for fiscal 1951-52. The other firm figure we are given is for the three calendar years 1951, 1952, and 1953; we are to step up to an average of 1,600, or about 13 per cent, of the national economy, and that will be verging toward 2 billion sterling, or approaching 20 per cent toward the end of that period. The step-up, you notice, is not quite so steep as your projected step-up. In that sense, our problem of the hump is somewhat less acute. I should like to say at the very beginning that I think that there is an extraordinary similarity between our problems—up to a point.

One way in which we have a greater difficulty is that we have been absolutely fully stretched right up to the present moment. I was in Belgium only a fortnight ago and was talking to an eminent Belgian who is in the economic administration. I said, "How are you going to finance your rearmament?" He said, "Oh, well, you know, we are in a very lucky position here in Belgium because we have quite a lot of unemployment."

Well, our position is the opposite. We have an absolutely

fully stretched economy to start with. We have not had so far the rush of consumer buying that I think has been manifesting itself here, so that we have not been under any immediate pressure, such as came upon your economy, to think in terms of quick price and wage controls.

Professor Jewkes has described to you how we have been shaking off the controls. I should like to indorse what he says very strongly that it was particularly our fiscal policy of a heavily overbalanced budget that really made those controls unnecessary. I do not think that the government that we happened to have was particularly anxious to get rid of the controls as such, but, when by an overbalanced budget we very largely removed the inflationary pressure, these physical controls became unnecessary. There is no use going on allocating steel when there is enough steel for all. The allocator simply says, "Why go on with this?" and the controls drop away.

As regards the price controls and allocation of materials, we have moved very much away from them in the years following 1948. We still have, of course, our food controls, and we have very tight controls on the external side. I think there is hope, as Professor Jewkes has told you, and I should indorse that, that we will not have to go back in full measure to these controls which have been found so inefficient in the past.

On the whole, the belief is that we can do what is needed, always subject to one exception which I am coming to, by the kind of measures that we have been discussing the last two days here, by methods other than physical control, namely, by the budget and by control over capital expenditures. In the budget, consumers will be asked to release resources, to make sacrifices —we shall be told about that on April 10 [1951] by the chancellor of the exchequer, who will announce new taxation. As regards the investment side, we shall undoubtedly get a cutback there, too. I think that the present chancellor of the exchequer is not likely to stress that very much, perhaps for ideological reasons, but it will happen, and indeed it is happening. We have a certain amount of confidence in our grip on the situation in that we can by taxation get a reduction of consumption, in that we can by the controls over investment expenditure get what slice we want to there; and in that, anyhow in the early stages of this climb, which is, as I have to admit, a somewhat gentler ascent than yours toward our plateau, we can check inflation by this twin method.

Yesterday I ventured to say here that it seemed to me that in this country, too, it was needful, if you were going to avoid inflation, to have a reduction in nondefense capital expenditure; and I proposed a tax device which one or two of the people kindly took up and discussed, because that seemed to me to be in keeping with the general ideology of most people here, namely, that we want to avoid direct physical controls. But I have been told since I made that speech that there is the machinery in being here to enable the cut in investment to be brought about by direct control. If that is so, I believe it should be done.

I do draw an enormous distinction between the kind of direct control which says, "You can't do these things; you can't build these new factories; you can't build this road; etc.," and leaves it at that; this allows the private enterprise system and the market to function subject to the restrictions imposed. That does not kill private enterprise. It goes around and does all the other things it may do. That is a very different type of program from that of price control, which has to ramify out and multiply its staff and go into all sorts of details, or from the allocation of materials controls, which has to do likewise.

Now, if this were the end of the story, I should be fairly confident about the ability on our side to stop inflation by the methods of taxation in reducing consumer demand and of the limitation of investment expenditures by direct control. But I now come to the ground which Professor Jewkes has already touched upon, and that is our foreign position. There is where the great difference comes between our two countries.

You have to remember that something like two-fifths of the products of our factories go abroad to pay for the food and materials we must have; and, when you come to those engineering industries in which we have expert skills, the fraction may be higher. The statistics on this subject, I am afraid, are very tangled indeed, because of the peculiar position of Britain, which has to think about her own account but is also banker for the sterling area. The accounts of the two entities, Britain herself and the sterling area, get most terribly involved.

In passing, before I go on to the main point, I should like to say that we have in Britain been doing something for other countries in the way of capital provision. Last year we had a favorable balance—it is not going to last—on current account of £229 million, which is quite substantial in relation to our national income—about 2 per cent. It is a rather odd thing that this excess of exports was higher as a fraction of our income than the United States excess of exports in the same period.

In the two years before 1948 and 1949, according to the official statistics, which are not 100 per cent right, we broke exactly even on our over-all current account, which means that we passed on Marshall aid, plus £57 million of gold as well, to other countries by way either of a capital investment in those countries or of redeeming our debts to those countries. Not that the Marshall aid was not vital to us, because we had a dollar deficit. The Marshall aid paid our dollar deficit. But as against our deficit in our dollar trade, we had a surplus as against the nondollar area, and in that area we placed capital, not all of it necessarily well advisedly placed. That is a matter on which we may have controversies at home, but I think the feeling is that Britain has a part to play here, that some of the capital anyhow was well placed, and that it would be desirable for us to continue to place capital abroad if possible.

We have plans for the development of certain backward areas which many people regard as an essential part of the fight against communism in that part of the world. Britain, with her connections and good will there, can do useful work; and we ought not perhaps to say that we cannot send out any capital at all, though we may have to reduce the amount we have been sending out recently.

I now come back to the awkward problem which I approach in a slightly different way from Professor Jewkes.

Our trading position, in spite of that nice increase in our gold and dollar account which you may have noticed, has thrown great burdens on to us in the last two years—terrible burdens.

The thing began with devaluation. I was in the United States in March and April, 1949. I had the honor of addressing groups in the Federal Reserve Board and Federal Reserve Bank of New York, and I pleaded, "Don't think devaluation is a solution. We have this unfavorable balance, but the reason is that our economy is still congested." We were still suffering from that kind of inflationary pressure which takes the form of long delivery dates. I said, "No one knows how Britain will get on, how her trade will balance, if you eliminate those long delivery dates; if Britain could deliver promptly, she might be all right at a four-dollar pound. We don't know. Wait. Let us first have more disinflation internally." Unfortunately, our government did not go any further on those lines at that time, and, as the situation developed, devaluation became inevitable. But with devaluation the terms of trade immediately began to go badly against us. This is why I gave you those figures, because I want to emphasize the quantitative aspect.

I was talking about defense expenditures of £800 million being stepped up this year to 1,300, then to 1,600, etc. Already in the spring of 1950 I was able to calculate that the effect of the adverse turn in our trade would mean that we would have to export additional manufactured goods worth £220 million. This was before Korea, in the spring of 1950, and may be attributed exclusively to devaluation. The prices of our imports had risen, but the prices of our exports had risen very much less.

Since then the position has become worse again—very much worse. You have had Korea and the sudden development of great scarcities. Now, these scarcities and the high prices of certain products may be looked at from various points of view. The point of view that we have all the time very much in our mind in Britain is about the shortages in essential materials for the arms drive. For us, that is not a local problem. We cannot put any ceilings on those prices. They are world prices resulting from world scarcities, which are going undoubtedly to slow down our arms effort. That is one aspect.

Another aspect is that the term of trade became worse again. I am going to quote you some figures because they seem to me so beautifully simple. I take 1949 and compare it with 1950. In

1949 we had on visible account—I am talking about visible trade now—an unfavorable balance of £153 million. (With the "invisibles" added, there was a slightly favorable balance.) The next year we had an identical unfavorable balance on visible account of £153 million. The years 1949 and 1950 were identical, absolutely, so far as our balance of visible trade was concerned.

Our imports in 1950 were practically identical in volume with those in 1949. They did not go up. They probably ought to have gone up. Professor Jewkes has pointed out that we were running down our stocks in 1950. To avoid this, we should have had to let our imports go up, but we held them down. And in 1950 the imports were the same in volume as in 1949, and the balance of payments on trade account was identical. But our exports were up 15 per cent in volume. We were simply having in the year 1950 to send out 15 per cent more exports in volume, in actual goods exported, than we did in 1949.

Our trade balance in 1950 was exactly the same as it was in 1949, and our balance of payments was exactly the same as it was in 1949. We simply sent out 15 per cent extra exports, meaning something approaching £300 million worth of factory goods, for nothing. We got nothing back.

The combined effect of devaluation and the rising world prices due to the scarcities of certain materials had this effect.

We are dealing here with a strain, a burden on the British factory capacity, which is comparable to the burden of rearmament itself in its early stages. There is a double burden—the rearmament burden which we all know about and this trading burden in addition.

Things have become worse. I have given a comparison of 1950 with 1949. But if we take the February, 1951, figures, which are the last I have, the import prices were up 48 per cent, and our export prices only 16 per cent, and the terms of trade were thus 30 per cent worse than before devaluation. To buy the same quantity of imports that we were buying in 1949, we have got to export some £500 million worth of goods more. That is a bigger burden than the early stages of rearmament. (These extra exports take up some 12 per cent of the total factory capacity of Britain.) It is factory goods that we have to export. Happily, our invisibles are up by about £200 million, and it is thought that in this coming year they may be up another £50 million.

I myself believe—this is only my personal opinion, and I have had no recent contacts; in fact, I am not in the habit of having contacts, I am afraid, with our lords and masters in my country, and I do not know how opinion has been moving quite recently —and I am convinced that the time has come when we must think about revaluation. Devaluation has been really a very considerable failure. I think the figures I have just given you suggest that.

It may be that one cause of its failure is that there is a very strong tendency throughout the whole range of the British producers to charge prices which bear a relation to their cost of production. Some think that that is not the way businessmen behave at all, that businessmen try to judge their markets and charge the price that those markets will yield; but this seems to be contrary to the mental habits of the majority of British businessmen. They are in the habit of charging prices based on costs, retaining the old-fashioned idea that competition still exists in the world and that, if they begin charging prices above their costs, something will hit them sooner or later. Of course, there is a notable exception in the case of Scotch whisky, but in most cases the British exporters went on quoting sterling prices without trying to exploit the opportunity of putting up the sterling prices.

I think that devaluation has been, so to speak, proved a failure because it has certainly been a contributory cause of this portentous turning of the terms of trade against us. If there was a case for revaluation last year—which I think there was—it is much reinforced by the world rise in prices since. There is no reason why, if the British economy can get a grip on its own inflationary problems, along the lines which I suggested to you at the beginning, we should be drawn into the whirlpool of a world-wide inflation.

For that purpose, revaluation is obviously desirable. Revaluation would also help some of our associated territories. Australia is suffering from inflation rather acutely, and it would do her a lot of good, as all her experts realize, to have sterling revalued. It is politically impossible, I believe, in Australia to do this independently; but, if we did it, it would be very healthy from the point of view of the Australian economy.

That is just one thought I want to throw out; but what I want to emphasize in my talk is that this external position is absolutely essential to our problem. If mishandled, it may involve losses of value of the order of magnitude of rearmament itself and inflationary pressures of this same order of magnitude.

It is true that we have had a remarkable increase in our gold reserves, which up to a point is healthy; beyond a certain point it is not. I am told that gold is still flowing in. The latest figure is for the first quarter of this year when we got in 458 million dollars more gold. Up to a point it is useful; beyond a point it is a burden, because it means that our factories, instead of making arms, are making goods for export in exchange for gold. We do not want to do that. We simply cannot afford in our tight position to set a second Fort Knox up over on our side.

Now this gold import is the result of our being a banker for the sterling area. If I can only put this simply enough—the position before recent changes, let us say two years ago, was that Britain had a heavy adverse account on dollars. We had a heavy favorable account on sterling. The sterling area paid for their excess imports from us either by using up sterling balances or against investments made by Britain in the sterling area. We paid our deficit on the dollar side by Marshall aid. We hoped, of course, to be able to export more in due course to the dollar area, but still more did we hope that the sterling area would regain its earlier position of having an over-all favorable balance (including gold) with the dollar area so that the sterling area would pay us in dollars for our excess of exports to the sterling area and that we could use such dollars to pay our deficit to the dollar area. That was the pattern which we hoped would emerge instead of the other pattern by which we had to finance our deficit by Marshall aid and use our surplus to make capital investments in the sterling area.

It has come true. It has happened, but it has happened too much. It has come true because of the rise in prices of the scarce materials which the sterling area is selling to the dollar area. It has come true too much for our good because the sterling area is now paying in gold to us in large quantities. Getting gold is good for Britain as a banker; but as a trader and as a manufacturer and as a contributor to the effort of producing arms, she suffers because she also has to pay these high prices to the outer sterling area for her imports from it.

Just as the dollar area is paying higher prices for rubber, tin, etc., Britain is paying those higher prices, too; and our export surplus with the sterling area is tending to disappear. We shall soon be in the position in which we have no surplus with the outer sterling area any more, not because we are importing more or exporting less, but simply because the price of these sterling-area goods is rising against us.

Our surplus there is disappearing. Meanwhile, they are paying gold to us as a banker, and what they expect us to do against that gold which they are paying in—they are paying in the gold that we require to pay our dollar deficit and more gold—is to export more goods to them against that gold. This involves great pressure on us, a pull of demand from the sterling area to make us export more goods as against the gold that they are supplying us. Here is another extra pull, so to speak, coming on to the British manufacturing capacity. From whatever point of view we look at the position, we seem to be subjected to this appalling strain of having to produce more and more manufactured goods. During this winter, the last six months, our exports of manufactured goods have been running at 75 per cent above the level of 1938, and this strain is appalling.

Well, now, I have tried to give you a little more detail about this central problem. I think we could do our rearmament right up to our 20 per cent of national income without having inflation; but on top of that we have got to give so much more of our capacity to keeping pace with our external position that the problem does become appalling; that is where the danger lies.

I have already suggested one thing which I think would help us—revaluation. I think by revaluation we could get the terms of trade more in our favor.

Now, I wrote down in pencil on my paper—I have been talking too long, but I must have regard to this pencil note—"What ought the United States to do to help Britain?" Three things come readily to my mind. This is improvised—I did not get on my feet in order to say what the United States should do, but you asked me to say, and three things come readily to my mind.

One thing concerns these scarce materials. If you turn away for a moment from these internal problems which you have been discussing so much in the last two days to the broad international plane, and particularly think of Britain which is really making some rearmament effort and will, I hope, make a sizable contribution of arms to the common pool in proportion to her income and what she can afford to do, this question of the raw-material scarcity is vital, and, if something can be done to prevent further skyrocketing of these prices, that would be a very great contribution. In that connection, another thing occurs to me which I was almost going to say last night in our discussion on the level of expenditure here, but then I thought, "No, it is not for me to get up and say this thing," but, as I have been asked, I will say it now.

Much was heard last night about the economies of nondefense expenditures in this country. But I will also say, looking at it broadly and from the other side, is not economy in defense expenditure really a much more vital problem? By economy in defense expenditure, I do not mean planning to have any less divisions, any less squadrons, any less destroyers, or what-not. By economy in defense expenditure, I mean the scrutiny of what fighting services state as their requirements for reserve stocks. There, I believe, you can get a very large reduction in your budget. I am convinced that it is very difficult for the normal processes of administrative machinery to apply the necessary control; and I speak here with a little of our British experience in mind, because I think we were in a tighter corner than you, so far as the availability of resources was concerned, in World War II. Mr. Churchill himself took a great interest in the subject of limiting the requirements of the fighting services to the minimum that was really necessary for fighting.

When it is a question of having certain stocks, maybe of uniforms, maybe of spare parts, of all these things in reserve, reserves behind reserves, you mount up into very big figures. I believe that very special kinds of control are needed, because the ordinary administration finds it very difficult to stand up to the fighting services which say, "We know what we want and what is needed and what we have got to do." You have to have both interest in this problem at a very high level and thorough research by those serving that level before you can criticize those fighting services.

Well, that is a little parenthesis suggesting a method for relieving your inflationary problem here. But for this other world problem, obviously those reserve stocks, that piling-up behind, may have a very big effect on the scarcities of these materials in the world, so that, while perhaps in this country because you can afford it you have vast reserve stocks of some components or other, the British firms cannot make the first-line articles that are required because of the world scarcity of these materials. That, I believe, is a thing we have got to think about together, and it is a very important thing indeed.

Well, now, having dwelt on that, I have rather lost from my mind the other things that I thought the United States should do to help us, but I am sure it may be fairly evident. Do not suppose that, because this gold is piling up in Britain, things are becoming easier for us. They have become very markedly more difficult for us in this last year and are going to be more difficult in regard to balancing our external account. There was Marshall aid. The Marshall aid is now over (and perhaps it is well so) as far as we are concerned, but the problems still remain. They may take a different form, but they are still there.

I would indorse what Professor Jewkes says. Up to a certain point we must go on exporting, we must go on paying our way; but, if in the process of our adjustment we have, for the reasons which I have tried to explain just now, to devote still more facilities to producing more goods for export, that must reduce our arms effort. Foreign aid to us in some form or other that will relieve our external position is still very much to the point.

CHAIRMAN BELL: Thank you, sir.

We are not stretched tonight on a frame of Points I, II, III, and IV—even Point IV, these backward nations we have just been hearing about. We are instructed to take advantage of the situation to telescope a little the program for the balance of the conference that we slipped behind during the day. We are therefore, if possible, to proceed with the discussion of the long-run consequences for free institutions. Before I take that plunge, I would like to inquire whether there are any direct questions, not involving any speeches, may I say, to the gentlemen who have just spoken.

MR. MEYER: One of your exports is freight-rate income, is it not?

MR. HARROD: Certainly.

MR. MEYER: How much have these risen in the last year? You spoke of the rising cost of your imports.

MR. HARROD: I was talking about physical exports and imports, but I mentioned as a mitigation that our invisibles are up £200 million.

MR. MEYER: Of which freight rates are an important part?

MR. HARROD: Of which freight rates are an important element, and I can give them to you here if you give me a moment. They are an important element.

MR. MEYER: Thank you.

MR. CORTNEY: I was very interested in the remarks made by Mr. Harrod regarding a revaluation of the pound, but, if I am not mistaken, in his recent book he declares himself in full accord with Keynes against the revaluation of the pound in 1925. At that time the balance of payments of Great Britain was also favorable. How does he reconcile those two positions? I am quite intrigued.

MR. HARROD: I do not think there is any difficulty in reconciling them. The whole case was totally different. It is true we had a favorable balance of trade before 1925, but we wanted to have it. We were investing that abroad in what I hope were productive enterprises, worth while to ourselves and to the countries which were making the investments. We were in very nice equilibrium for two or three years before 1925, so far as the external account was concerned.

MR. CORTNEY: I beg your pardon—after 1925 you were in a more favorable position from the point of view of the balance of payments than before 1925. I have checked the figures.

MR. HARROD: I have not the figures. Mr. Cortney says that our balance of payments after 1925 was even more favorable than it was before 1925, but, unfortunately, our employment position was not more favorable. This revaluation caused serious unemployment. It also caused directly and without question a coal strike which lasted for six months and had a permanent effect on our coal export trade. It also caused a general strike which might have led to serious civil strife. We, happily, got over it fairly easily, but our export trade did not rise after 1925 to the extent of any of the European countries. Mr. Loveday has shown quite clearly in his book that our share in foreign trade was shrinking and that our unemployment was bad.

I regret to say when I look at this White Paper—a hateful thing; I just got the thing—that our shipping, according to this document, has only given us an extra £28 million out of the £200 million. I would have thought it would have been more, but, as it says that here, I have to believe it.

MR. TANNENWALD: I wanted to ask about one figure which I think Mr. Harrod should put out before the conference. He commented very briefly on the increase in the gold position of the British reserves. I would like to put this figure out and ask him to comment on it. I should also like to ask him a second question.

As I understand it, the British dollar reserves have risen or are expected to rise from 1 billion 6 million or 1 billion 8 million—I forget which it was approximately a year ago—to almost 4 billion dollars.

MR. HARROD: I have the figures here.

MR. TANNENWALD: I would like to ask him to comment on the significance of that. I would also like to ask him to give us an estimate, if he can, of how much economic aid he figures will be needed from this country in order to enable Great Britain to carry her fair share of the load.

CHAIRMAN BELL: You need not answer that second question.

MR. HARROD: A generous measure is all I am going to say. I should like to say that the idea that has been turning in my mind in the form of aid is that I think in some respects the European Payments Union has made a contribution to easing international payments in Europe, and I should like to see that Union broadened into an Atlantic Union and the whole clearance of positions facilitated by the United States being a partner, by a system of mutual credits, which, of course, no doubt, would mean some expenditure of dollars.

I believe that in defense one of the most potent ways in which dollars can be expended abroad, if they are to be expended abroad, is for facilitating payments and for relieving the anxieties of nations. I think what is holding Europe back—this applies to Continental Europe more strongly than to Britain—is the fear that, having gone through all these years of dollar shortage and privations of various sorts, the rearmament may exacerbate all those problems which people have been struggling with, which have meant hardships to them, and which they had hoped they were getting the better of. I believe that an Atlantic Union—always within the framework of the international co-operation; I have not forgotten that, and we hope that is the final consummation—but that at the next stage an Atlantic Union with dollars provided for equalization would be a good thing.

We are the bankers for the sterling area; the inflow of gold is due to the rise of the prices of sterling-area exports, together with a certain amount of postdevaluation capital movements. It is a most extraordinary thing that, whereas the foreign exchange control is one of our strictest and most difficult to evade by any ordinary citizen, yet, in spite of that control, there have been around that devaluation before and after such very large capital movements. It is a very extraordinary thing, and it is proof of the strength of will of a private individual in the face of tremendous obstacles. The inflow is due to capital movement partly, I think, but more it is due to the fact that we are a banker for the outer sterling area and are reaping the benefit of the rise of prices of the dollar sales of that area.

Mr. MEYER: Mr. Chairman, I do not want to monopolize the questions of Professor Harrod, but I seem to remember that at one time rubber in the twenties went to a dollar a pound, and your rubber holdings must have brought in large additional dollar income, did they not? Do you remember that?

Mr. HARROD: It may have gone to a dollar a pound after the war.

Mr. MEYER: Yes, in the middle twenties.

Mr. HARROD: In the middle twenties, I would not have said a dollar a pound because there was the famous Stevenson scheme to hold the price of rubber at a monstrous level which did Britain great harm because the Dutch undersold. Two shillings a pound was the Stevenson price.

Mr. MEYER: It went to a dollar.

Mr. HARROD: It may have gone to a dollar during the inflation period after the war, but I think the Stevenson scheme was to hold it to two shillings. That is my recollection.

CHAIRMAN BELL: You will now be rationed to two more questions.

Mr. OSCAR COX: Perhaps some questions to Professor Jewkes may help to illuminate the difference between the course of conduct for the United States and for the United Kingdom and also serve as a bridge on both the short-term and the long-term consequences of what may be done. The first question I would like to ask Professor Jewkes is: When was the last time that a major newcomer entered into any of the basic industries in the United Kingdom, such as steel, heavy chemicals, aluminum, or related fields?

Mr. JEWKES: British industry over the last twenty years has not been altogether stagnant. My own view is, and I have expressed it in many places, that the period between the wars was a period when monopoly was tending to paralyze British effort. But even if one accepts that, if one even believes that the beginning of the conditions which led to the nationalization of British industries was laid by such schemes as the Coal Mines Act of 1930, it has to be remembered that there has been a vast development in very many branches of the British engineering trades. I do not know whether you heard the other day of a

British airplane that crossed the Atlantic in four hours. I think that you will hear a good deal in the future of the British development in the field of artificial fibers. I think there is a great deal to be said for what the British motorcar industry has done recently. But I am not here to defend any of the consequences of the restrictive policies that were undoubtedly favored by all political parties in Great Britain between the wars.

MR. COX: Mind you, my point was not to add any adjectives or to be critical. I was trying to get a descriptive picture for purposes of deciding how you compare conditions in the United States and the United Kingdom and what lines of conduct should be followed. If I may ask you a few more questions, I think we can possibly illuminate the problems somewhat.

CHAIRMAN BELL: They are supplementaries, are they?

MR. COX: They are an extension of the same point. Approximately what has been the increase in the level of production in the same basic commodities, giving any illustrative examples, whether in steel or sulphuric acid or aluminum or similar products?

MR. JEWKES: Have you the figures there, Mr. Harrod, of the actual increase in industrial production since. . . .

MR. COX: Mind you, I am not concerned with industrial production of motorcars. I raised the question specifically in terms of the basic commodities which I mentioned, such as steel, aluminum, sulphuric acid, cement, etc. We might argue about what is basic, but I think on many of them we would all agree as to what are basic commodities or materials.

MR. JEWKES: The only figure I carry in mind is the output of steel, which is now 16 million tons as against a very fluctuating output before the war; but, I suppose, it ranged until four or five years before the war about 11. There was a substantial increase certainly in cement. The figures are not in my mind.

MR. HARROD: I think steel was about 8 million tons in 1936–37.

MR. JEWKES: I think 1937 was our peak. I think it was then about 11 as against the present 16 million tons.

MR. COX: Just using those illustrative figures, the two points which I think ought to be made are: (1), taking Professor

Harrod's point about limiting capital investment or nondefense expenditures, I think we have to be careful how we define nondefense expenditures; (2) that one should rapidly stimulate the production of basic items like steel because they are required for both defense and nondefense purposes. The second factor is important in terms of the joint problem of increasing the supplies required for the common pool.

With the development that has taken place in the engineering services in the United Kingdom, it is paradoxical that we are now sending, or contemplating to send, most of the aid under the United States military defense program in the form of finished munitions. This is quite a different thing from the full and effective utilization of the United Kingdom mechanical and engineering industries to produce munitions and defense articles with the raw materials supplied by the United States from its expanded production. If the United Kingdom utilizes its industries in this way, we should also take into account that the same machine and the same man in the United Kingdom that produce a gun cannot produce for export. So our aid has to be in a twofold form: One is the utilization of those capacities in the common effort, and the other aid is to supplement what you lose because you cannot supply the export market.

I think you are in the curious paradoxical position where, in terms of the Atlantic Union or the defense of western Europe, you have had a revolution since 1914 where the United States is saying, "When is western Europe going to get on the ball?" as against the experience in 1914–18 and 1939–45, when the United States was two years behind in the estimate of Europe in participating in the defense of western Europe in our own vital interest.

But look at the curious situation now where the United Kingdom and most of Europe is relatively, compared to the United States, lagging in the production of armaments. It is, therefore, quite understandable why the public in the United States is basically saying, "When is Europe going to get on the ball?"

MR. JEWKES: This takes us outside the field of economics, and it seems to me a very important matter if we believe that, in the present international crisis, as much as possible of the engineering capacity of our two countries and the capacity of the other Atlantic countries should be used for rearmament. It might be argued that the easiest way for the Atlantic nations to work together is to regard the fighting forces of the two countries as completely interchangeable and to think of British fighting men or American fighting men using British or American equipment indiscriminately. That is to say, that we would have a sort of two-way "lease-lend." I believe that while theoretically that seems to be highly attractive, there are, if we take into account the psychology of fighting men, some difficulties about it.

The first is that, if there is going to be production of the best kind of fighting equipment, it would be a very good thing if the American and the British munitions industries were competing to produce the best type of thing. I think there is a good deal to be said for emulation and rivalry there. That in the long run will mean that we both get better machines and equipment.

The second difficulty is that fighting men are extremely particular about the equipment they use. When a fighting force has to use equipment produced in other countries, it often finds that this equipment does not exactly fit its needs, its methods of training, etc. A good deal of time can, in consequence, be lost in designing and carrying out modifications. That was certainly the experience of the last war. There is a case for diversity of fighting equipment as well as for standardization.

Mr. Cox: I agree to a certain extent, but by what is being done now the opposite results are being produced. Out of the total military defense assistance program, by far the major part is now being allocated to produce arms in the United States of United States types for the use of the United Kingdom as well as the other countries in the North Atlantic Treaty Organization. I was not trying to solve the problem of standardization or to suggest that another armed force has to use exactly the same equipment in all cases as do the United States forces.

As you know, during World War II, in the early stages, the United Kingdom was producing a .303 rifle, and we were producing a .30-caliber rifle. Well, they worked that problem out. Now, presumably the other similar problems are somewhat soluble. I did not want to get into that. That is a completely different problem.

The fact is that, as you have described, so many of your automobile factories, your electrical engineering factories, and your mechanical industries generally, which have developed great skills, are, in the main, producing goods for export which, by any definition, would relatively be considered nonmunitions and nonessential items. It is only because of the foreign exchange requirements of the United Kingdom that these exports become items essential to the United Kingdom. All I am saying is that there are means for producing essential military items in the United Kingdom on a larger scale and that we should assist the United Kingdom in meeting its foreign exchange requirements where its manpower and resources are devoted to such military production and not to production of exports.

MR. JEWKES: Yes. I am sorry. I thought the question was leading to the other.

CHAIRMAN BELL: Have you a short question like that, Mr. Rostow?

MR. ROSTOW: I have a very short question. I ask simply, "Mr. Harrod, what ideas do you have about the proper way to organize a procedure for dealing with the raw-material shortage?"

MR. HARROD: Well, I do not know. I do not think I can give an answer to that. Many great brains are trying to focus their attention on it. I do not think I have anything specific to add except to underline that it is an extremely important thing from our point of view. I would like everyone here to feel it is very important, but as for my devising a method for international management of the raw materials. . . .

MR. ROSTOW: I meant simply whether you were thinking along the lines of a combined materials board that would do the allocation in order to reduce the pressure.

MR. HARROD: My idea would be that the United States would consider reducing the requirements for some of these materials on the lines I suggested. I believe that that is the root of the thing—that it may be that the United States requirement is somewhat padded and that the first line of help to us would be that some powerful organization here look at the raw-material requirements. That is a very tactless way to put it, and I do not want to dogmatize, but there is a very good chance that stated requirements on many of these materials contain padding. If that padding could be removed and a certain amount of self-denial exercised so as not to stockpile too far, for too many years ahead, that would be the most direct way of helping the British economy.

REPRESENTATIVE CELLER: Mr. Chairman, there is one brief question I have. I should like to ask either Professor Jewkes or Professor Harrod concerning the passage of the recent antitrust statute for Great Britain and whether that statute comes too late.

MR. HARROD: I will hand that to Professor Jewkes.

MR. JEWKES: As you know, under the Monopoly Act of 1948 we set up what is called a Monopoly Commission. It carries out, on a much smaller scale and with more modest resources, the kind of work that is being done by your Federal Trade Commission.

The Monopoly Commission is empowered to make a study of any industry which is declared by the Board of Trade as prima facie a monopoly. The Monopoly Commission has now been in operation for about two years, has presented its first report, and is dealing with other industries. In fact, the report already issued reminds me very much of the Federal Trade Commission reports on that kind of case. It is largely a case of resale-price maintenance. It looks as if we are going to have a law against resale-price maintenance. The difference between your system and ours is that we have not yet actually declared illegal any practice whatever. It is left for the government to decide in every particular case upon the report of the Monopoly Commission what is the appropriate action. In the case of the first report, the industry has discussed these questions with the government and has already agreed to desist from the practices that were objected to.

Whether it is too late or not, I do not know. I would say it is never too late. I hope, now that the Monopoly Commission has been much strengthened, that we will get some very good work done. The big difficulty always is that this has been put into operation by a government which has already set up monopolies in four or five major industries by nationalizing them; but perhaps that sort of paradox may resolve itself as people come to think further of these problems.

Mr. HARROD: May I add one thing. Professor Jewkes has just told you we may have a law against resale-price maintenance. Am I wrong in thinking that the United States has repealed its law against resale-price maintenance?

REPRESENTATIVE CELLER: We still have it, to our sorrow.

Mr. LAZARUS: The Miller-Tydings Act does permit resale-price maintenance. The effect of the antitrust laws which tended to prohibit resale-price maintenance prior to 1938 was repealed by the Miller-Tydings Act, and Professor Harrod is quite right.

REPRESENTATIVE CELLER: I misunderstood you.

Mr. ARNOLD: Anyway, we still have the Miller-Tydings Act.

Mr. LAZARUS: And therefore we have resale-price maintenance.

Mr. HENDERSON: This I know from experience—that we can never be truly strong unless England is strong, but let us suppose there is a complete unpegging of the pound. Professor Harrod has introduced the question of revaluation. The devaluation was accompanied by negotiation with various countries with which England had relations. What would be the effect of a complete unpegging of the pound and letting it find its true value in a free market? Would it be an increase? Would it be a decrease? If so, how much?

Mr. HARROD: I have no doubt it would be an increase. You have to make a provision that certain segments of our indebtedness which are still held in the liquid form of sterling balances remain what we politely call "restricted"—that is, blocked.

Mr. HENDERSON: Let us suppose you took the restrictions off. Let us suppose Egypt and India could utilize their balances.

Mr. HARROD: We cannot take those restrictions off, though we have now agreed with both countries to what I regard as a generous scale of relief, of transfer, from the restricted account to the open account. I have no doubt that sterling would rise, but my suggestion is not that; rather I should like to revalue by small stages with the consent of the International Monetary

Fund. I feel that we ought to try to keep in step with the ideology of that institution, which I suppose has the support of the United States Treasury. My idea would be to do it by stages, rather small stages at a time, working the way upward, feeling our way upward. I think we would go a long way upward.

CHAIRMAN BELL: Speaking on behalf of the management, they appreciate very much the fact that your interest has been such that we are now one and a half days behind schedule. Among the numerous suggestions for curing the situation is an inquiry as to whether you would be willing to meet tomorrow morning.

[There was discussion of the subject, and a vote was taken, the result being that it was decided to have a morning session.]

Unless there is violent objection, the meeting is adjourned until ten-thirty tomorrow morning.

VIII

A. THE LONG-RUN CONSEQUENCES
ON FREE INSTITUTIONS

CHAIRMAN LEVI: We now come to a session which of necessity must be somewhat brief, "The Long-Run Consequences on
Free Institutions." I will ask Dr. Stocking to speak on this point.

MR. STOCKING: In evaluating the long-run significance of mobilization for defense to free institutions, a person must resort
to conjecture. The sort of conjecture he resorts to will be influenced by his preconceptions. But, whatever his preconceptions,
a skilful person can find some support for his conjecture in logic
and experience.

Let me state briefly my preconceptions. I believe that the
type of controls which will do the least mischief to free institutions is that type that disturbs market mechanisms the least.
This belief is based on what I believe to be a historical fact
and a conclusion that I believe flows from it. The historical fact
is that there is a basic causal relationship between political democracy and its traditional freedoms and a system of free private enterprise; the conclusion is that the disappearance of the
free market as an institution for regulating economic activity
will eventually lead to a loss of liberty all around the place.
It would scarcely be appropriate here to go into the historical
relationships between the development of freedom in economic
affairs and freedom in political matters, but I would like to
make a few obvious and what I believe are common-sense and
relevant comments on the nature of the market mechanism.

A free market relies on decentralized decision-making to
guide production, to allocate resources, and to distribute the

social income. Concentration of power constitutes a threat to such a system. Direct controls substitute centralized authoritarian decision-making for the impersonal forces of the market. They put power over the market into the hands of governmental agencies. Direct controls by their nature interfere with someone's freedom in economic affairs. That they do so does not in and of itself make them bad. A free-enterprise system must have rules of the game if it is to work at all, but in making rules it is important to distinguish between rules designed to make the system work and rules designed to prevent its working.

How far the loss of freedom occasioned by direct controls will go will depend on how comprehensive they are and how long they last. But, as has frequently been pointed out in this conference, direct controls tend to be cumulative. One control leads to another. Price control without rationing will break down or create arbitrary or chance inequities. Wage controls necessitate price controls and lead to manpower allocation. If an emergency which provokes controls continues long enough and becomes severe enough, it is likely to lead to a comprehensive web of controls pervading the whole economy.

Because I reach this conclusion, I do not deny the necessity of direct controls in time of stress. For I do not believe that the market mechanism is well adapted to making, in a politically acceptable manner, major economic readjustments within a brief period of time. The impact of such readjustments may bring some confusion and some grief. To forestall such results a democracy in time of great stress is likely to resort to direct market controls. But because I regard direct controls as politically inevitable in times of great stress, I do not mean to imply that they should be lightly inaugurated, and to establish them without first trying to evaluate their long-run significance seems to me foolhardy. As do others at this conference, I believe that bold experimentation with indirect controls, supplemented by selective direct controls, as, for example, the curtailment of consumer credit and the control of private investment, might forestall the economic need of general direct controls. And I believe that the indirect controls offer a far better chance of preserving free institutions over the long run.

Indirect controls, more specifically monetary and fiscal controls, wisely used instead of constituting a threat to free institutions, are an essential apparatus for creating an environment within which the market mechanism can function well. And fortunately any skill acquired in using these controls in war or mobilization for defense perfects a tool useful in peace as well as war for the preservation of a free-enterprise economy. Direct controls, on the other hand, are a rejection of the market process. Authoritarian controls long continued may create habits of thought and patterns of behavior and, what is more serious, changes in the structure of markets and the organization and control of industry which may make it difficult to re-establish free markets once the emergency has passed.

I will try to be a bit more specific. But in doing so I must confess that sometimes it is hard to distinguish between the effects of economic mobilization itself and the effects of the authoritarian controls that are set up to direct it, and I shall not try to make this distinction in a meticulous manner. Economic mobilization with direct controls has tended to enhance private power, although temporarily it prevents its exercise for private ends. I will give two examples. In World War II when the government denied labor the privilege of commanding its market price and took over the control of wages, it was forced politically to protect and enhance union power by setting up and enforcing closed-shop agreements, the check-off, maintenance of membership, and similar union contractual arrangements. In some instances, notably coal, governmental control contributed directly to the enhancement of union power, indeed to the creation of a monopoly over the labor market. And the melody lingered on after the song had ended.

In a somewhat similar manner direct government control enhanced the power of big business as against moderate-sized and little business. In the allocation of materials and the letting of contracts, more or less inevitably controllers rely on the biblical principle, "To him that hath shall be given and from him that hath not shall be taken away even that which he seemeth to have."

As a result of World War II big business grew bigger, absolutely and in some cases relatively, and its power over the market was generally enhanced. One illustration will perhaps suffice. The United States Steel Corporation when organized in 1901 produced nearly two-thirds of the total steel ingot tonnage produced in this country. Between 1901 and 1939 it steadily declined in relative importance. By 1939 its percentage of total domestic output had been cut almost in half. World War II with its authoritarian controls reversed this trend. During and since the war United States Steel has grown as fast and at times and in some areas even faster than the domestic market for steel. That, of course, will be regarded by some as a blessing. And from one point of view it obviously is. War calls for more steel, and, to produce more steel, the steel industry must grow. But it is too easy to identify the advantages of a big steel industry with the alleged advantages of a giant steel firm. With proper controls, I believe it would have been possible to have created a big steel industry with economically more appropriate relations among the firms that comprise it than now exist. For the benefit of our British friends, let me say that the United States Steel Corporation is about as large as all the British steel companies, plus all the Belgian steel companies, plus all the French steel companies combined, and, in the language of a Supreme Court minority opinion, "It is big enough"!

On the significance of size to a free-enterprise economy, I will have to be dogmatic. Public policy, if its object is to preserve free enterprise, should aim at preserving as many business firms as is compatible with the economies of mass production and distribution. Markets of few sellers, or to use the ugly word the economists have coined, "oligopoly" markets, function differently from markets of more numerous sellers; and there is reason to believe that they interfere with the processes of economic readjustment which free markets facilitate. To establish that point would involve what a leader of American industry has characterized as a "jet-propelled flight into the realm of fancy," and, since I am sure that we all want to keep our feet on the ground, I will not do it. But, I repeat, direct controls substitute conscious deliberate teamwork under authoritarian direction for the automatic quasi-mechanical articulation of conflicting forces by which order is presumably established in a free market and, if long continued, I suspect, may destroy the free market and, what is equally important, the will to have it. A great deal could be said about how authoritarian controls lead to concerted action among business rivals and how they may permanently weaken reliance on market forces to control economic activity, but time does not permit my saying it. I will content myself in concluding by merely enumerating some of the ways in which they do this.

Under authoritarian controls administrators quickly learn that it is easier to regulate prices in industries of few sellers than in industries of many sellers. They therefore encourage associated activity to simplify the problems of control. Concerted action tends to become habitual. Direct controls, contrary to the confessions of our price administrators that their office offers no public career, tend to establish what has been characterized as a "power-hungry bureaucracy" that has a vested interest in perpetuating itself and that may eventually find the means of doing it. Direct controls may foster mergers among separate business units that wish to escape some of the adverse effects of control, and thereby they tend to reduce the number of sellers in a market. Direct controls lead to a softening of antitrust policy, if indeed they do not put it on ice, if for no other reason than that those who influence or make decisions in such matters under a controlled economy are not infrequently defendants in antitrust proceedings who have been called to the government to administer the controls.

But I have said enough to indicate a point of view on the long-run effects of direct controls on free institutions. I am reasonably sure that some will regard this brief excursion into the realm of ideas as an academic voice crying in the wilderness, and I am equally convinced that trying to persuade policymakers to shape policy in accordance with the implications of this discussion is like spitting in the wind. And the deeper the emergency, the stronger the wind will blow.

CHAIRMAN LEVI: I will now call upon Professor Hale.

MR. R. L. HALE: I want to talk a little about the background of this free-market concept. In the outline of the agenda, one of the objections to direct controls is said to be that they require the government to assume responsibility for the relative position of different groups. Now, as I see it, the government is accountable for the economic relations between groups, no matter what it does. Its rules, the rules of law, determine who owns what. That does not mean merely that the man who produces something becomes the owner. Many years ago John Stuart Mill observed that in protecting property the government has to do a great deal more than allow the producer to own what he produces and then protect him in it. In property, in land, and in all resources, he pointed out, the government has to have some kind of rules for determining who is to own these; and also in the case of the property of a decedent there have to be rules for determining who shall own that property after the previous owner is dead. Mill said it is not enough to say that the law merely gives effect to the wishes of the late owner. It does not always, and when we come to the case of one who has made no will, the law itself provides who shall be the owner. Now, I take it that Professor Hayek would say, "Well, yes, but these are general rules of law." He does not maintain that the government should not curtail anybody's liberty in any respect but that it should only do so by general rules of law.

Now, what is the great virtue of these general rules as distinguished from particular acts of authority? As I recall it, there were two chief virtues. In the first place, the general rules work impersonally and, second, the persons affected by these general rules would be able to know where they got off, how the rule would affect them. But we can phrase a legal doctrine in the terms of a general rule, and yet it may not be general at all. The general rule may be employed to delegate power to administrative officials, and Professor Hayek objects to such delegation. I think you might agree with me, Professor Hayek, on this point. We can say, for instance, as a general rule of law in the statute that the rates charged by public utilities should be just and reasonable. That does not tell any particular utility company whether its rates are too high or too low or just right. It takes an act of an administrator of some sort to decide what are just and reasonable rates.

Now, as I see it, the law does delegate power not only in these cases of administrative commissions. It delegates power to property owners; the very institution of property does that. The state, through the law, provides rules for deciding who shall own what, and then the state steps in to restrict the liberty of anybody other than the owner to use that particular thing. If I own something, if I own a piece of land, it is illegal, by virtue of the general rules of law, for anybody else to walk on that land; but I can change the law just by my own dictate and make it legal for you to walk on that land. The owner makes it either legal or illegal for the nonowner to make use of the property which the law assigns to him.

Mr. Viner: They cannot compel you to walk on it.

Mr. R. L. Hale: But you can compel someone not to walk on it.

Mr. Viner: That is legalese.

Mr. R. L. Hale: You can call on the state to keep an intruder out, and, having that power, you have a bargaining weapon. You will let me use this property if I will accept certain conditions which you lay down.

This does not mean that property is bad by any means. All it means is that we cannot avoid delegation of power to some people. The whole bargaining process, on which the price system and the market depend, is a system of mutual coercion of the different bargainers. Each one controls something which the other man would like, but the coercive power is not equally distributed, and it probably could not be and should not be. This delegated power determines the market relationship of the owner to the rest of the community. It affects the whole market. It affects the demand which is supposed to be so sacred for determining what goods ought to be produced. For instance, if the law assigns a large fortune by way of its inheritance laws to a certain person, the demands of that person will have a much greater effect on the market than if the law had distributed that fortune differently.

Now, all this pulling and hauling by various people to whom the law gives power accounts for the distribution of wealth among people. It may be a perfectly satisfactory distribution. If we scrutinize the results and think them economically sound, then we would not want the government to do anything to disturb them; but the government would still be responsible for continuing its distribution of governing power which accounts for the present economic relationships. We cannot pronounce them good just because they exist or because they exist without the help of government. They do not.

Now, if any of them seem bad, the next question is whether a governmental attempt to correct them would probably produce something worse. That is a conceivable attitude to take. One might agree that certain features of the bargaining system are bad but that they are not so bad as they would be if somebody tried to correct them. There may be cases where it is better not to have anybody use his own judgment as to whether the results will be good or bad. We apply that principle in the selection of a jury. There is no assumption that the twelve men chosen in any trial are the best-qualified men in the community, but we do not want to give any power to anyone to pick out favorites. So we choose them by lot. But, after all, in most things where the government's activity is going to have an effect, it seems wiser to take some account of the probable results.

Now, whatever we do, taxes are going to be necessary. Whatever scheme of taxation we adopt will have some effect on the market. Some taxes may impair the incentives to produce and thus affect the supply side of the market, while others may not. Must the choice of the tax be a blind one? Must we say, "Oh, a tax is just for raising revenue, and we must not try to use it as a means of social control"? We have unconscious control already, and the question is: Should we make it more conscious?

Take another case. It may be true that in industries like steel it would be better to break them up into small companies rather than try to regulate them, but I think almost everybody would admit that there are a few industries at least where a monopoly is necessary. Would not you agree to that, Professor Hayek, in the case of a public utility? I see you would not, and of course if you can have competing gas and telephone companies, with all of what some people would call the waste that that involves, then you may rely solely upon competition, and the government need take no further responsibility. But I think even members of the University of Chicago Economics Department would, some of them, agree that it is better to give a monopoly to some of these industries.

But if the government grants a monopoly and permits the company to fix its own rates, then the government is assuming responsibility for the relationships which may result from the company's unlimited power in this respect. If, on the other hand, the government regulates the rates, it is faced with the problem of how much the company should be allowed to earn. That problem cannot be intelligently solved without passing judgment on the desirable economic relationships between property owners in general and the rest of the community. Once that judgment is made, the question at once arises why the government should not readjust the relationships between the public and other property owners, not utility owners alone, whenever the present relationships seem to call for readjustment—the readjustment to take place either through control of the prices charged by those owners or by taxation of their excess incomes. Any such thoroughgoing readjustment, however, involves considerably more governmental concern with the distribution of wealth than we have at present.

Professor Hayek points out some very real dangers in concentrated government power. I am not blind to those dangers. Perhaps I am a little blinder than I should be, but we do not avoid these dangers by delegating concentrated government power to favored inheritors or owners of natural resources and letting them make rules which govern the economic life of those to whom less power is delegated. I do not know what the solution is. I merely raise this question because I should like to see Professor Hayek and others who adopt his general philosophy take a little more account of what the law does through the institution of property.

In the last chapter of Professor Hayek's *Road to Serfdom* he very properly, it seems to me, emphasizes the value of federalism in regard to international relations. Well, we have federalism in this country internally. When we give things to the government, it does not necessarily mean the federal government. It may mean the government of the United States or the government of a state or the city or county government. This fact seems to me to weaken the significance of the statistics. Mr. Gainsbrugh brought up the other night when he spoke about the danger of having so many jobs controlled by *the* government. There would be a danger if they were all controlled by one government and a person who offended that government might find himself out of a job; but a man who offends President Truman might be highly welcome to Governor Dewey. We have not got concentrated control just because it is "government" to which they owe their jobs.

Now, we have found it wise in this country to have a good deal of devolution. We have our states, and within a state we have municipal authorities. All those bodies we recognize as part of government, and we think we as individuals need safeguards against them. Safeguards can be divided, roughly, into two. We have certain constitutional rights which we can go to a court about. If the city of Chicago passes an ordinance which violates one of our constitutional rights, we may challenge it in the court as unconstitutional. That other organ of government, the court, will set it aside. Then, again, we have another safeguard in the ballot. The people most affected can have a voice in changing the administration. I know Professor Hayek thinks they would not have much voice left if the power got concentrated; but we do have these two theoretical safeguards

at least, which we do not have directly against private government.

Against a powerful private group that has governing power,
we have to rely on other safeguards. When the legislative
branches of state or national governments, responding theoretically at least to the wishes of a majority of those affected, intervene to protect people from the governing power of a private
group, the intervention may be quite as likely to spell a net increase in economic liberty as does the intervention of a court to
protect an individual from oppression at the hands of the legislature. There is still the danger that the legislature may not be
responsive to the wishes of the majority or that the majority
may itself oppress the minority. The problem of preventing oppression is a difficult one. But its solution is not advanced by
ignoring the fact that the government has endowed certain
private individuals with governing power which may be used
oppressively unless curbed by government.

CHAIRMAN LEVI: I will now call upon Mr. Knight.

MR. KNIGHT: For various reasons, and particularly to show
my appreciation of this delectable taste of upper-class life I
am enjoying at somebody else's expense, it seems appropriate
that I should say a word, at least, to express my loyalty to the
Chicago tradition about which you have heard something. And
I think there actually is a tradition in the economics group at
Chicago to lean in the direction of free enterprise and of freedom rather than the opposite direction. This does not, of course,
mean absolute freedom. We are not anarchists, and I think that
is really the main point. In matters of principle it is always a
question of how far and how; and it is a question which cannot
be answered by formula. We recognize as a matter of course
that the market system will solve some problems and not others,
at least by itself. Many must be handled in part or entirely by
governmental agencies and many burdens borne by these—
that is, through them, at the cost of private citizens.

Being about as much a philosopher as an economist, I am
always trying to get down to fundamentals, and I think there
are two fundamentals in this situation. The first has to do with

Russia and the Communist totalitarian system. It is a question for history to decide. If they can make their system as efficient as free enterprise, or more efficient, we are sunk. It *is* a competitive world.

The other fundamental issue of fact centers in the United States and the other remaining democracies—democracy defined by freedom of discussion and popular control of government. The question here is whether people want freedom enough to pay the price in the responsibilities and risks which freedom necessarily involves. And that again is very largely a question of whether they have the intelligence and the good will to judge how much freedom is possible. Good will, again, is, I think, largely a matter of sportsmanship. I believe it is sportsmanship that has made the English-speaking world the leader in liberalism—in fact, about the only regions in which free enterprise and democracy have ever "worked" in any thoroughgoing sense.

We lean to freedom (speaking for myself) mainly because the world seems to be moving in the opposite direction at an accelerating and, we think, a dangerous pace. This does not necessarily mean that our country has already gone too far, has passed that vague critical point at which totalitarianism becomes inevitable. But I, for one, do believe that the great problem now before the believers in a free society is to save it from saviors, that is, from reformers. It is to maintain among the free peoples a tolerable combination of freedom with order and unity, to prevent its political life from degenerating into squabbles over justice, which means largely the problem, as it was phrased by a former University of Chicago political scientist, of what gets what, when, and how. This, again, is largely a matter of how far any one interest or group may be the judge of its own cause, and how far pressure groups will insist in doing so—primarily labor unions and organized farmers, which are the really serious monopolies.

The trouble with people is, as Carlyle once said, they expect too much. If they realized that they deserved to be hanged, they would consider it a luxury to be merely shot. Once more we have to learn to live in the world, the kind of world it is;

and the danger now is, on the one side, grasping at an impossible justice to the sacrifice of possible freedoms, or conversely, on the other side.

Studying these things from a broad historical and sociological point of view, I am alway thinking of a saying, of, I believe, it was Edwin Wilson, that man is inherently a "Gawdsaker"—"for God's sake, do something." I think the social situation is fairly closely paralleled by the history of medicine down until at least very recent times. Not long ago I asked a student of medicine, from the standpoint of its history and social problems, at what date in history he would say that doctors began to cure more people than they killed; and he said, "Well you might give us another quarter-century or so." And political doctoring is still more a prey to romanticism and quackery.

Now, the drift of this discussion convinces one more and more that we are spitting in the wind, as Dr. Stocking has said. People are always going to believe in magic and miracles and are always going to patronize quacks. They are also going to believe that the cure for social evils is to punish or to liquidate some wicked somebody who is to blame for them. My stock reference in this connection until recently—and it has been the perennial theme of economists since the dawn of modern economics—is the tariff question. Here it is the foreigner who is taking advantage of us. Long ago someone observed that the free-traders always win the debates and the protectionists win the elections, and that illustrates the point.

Monetary policy is about as bad—the clamor to make capital cheap or free and to finance governmental largesse without anyone having to pay taxes, by eliminating the "money power" and creating money by fiat. And of late we confront arbitrary price-fixing; for example, the freezing of residential rents. Of course landlords as a class are rich and grasping and tenants poor and virtuous. This surpasses even protectionism and sets a new high for economic stupidity and indefensible justice.

However, I have been led to change my view on these and similar matters as to where the mystery lies. It is not that people are protectionists, inflationists, and price-fixers but that they do not carry these things out logically to a point where they completely wreck the economy. They do not protect American producers to the point of stopping, first, all international trade, then trade across state lines, etc., and finally stop "trade" and all specialized co-operation. Similarly, they do not put the resources of the country to manufacturing money or make housing completely free by prohibiting all charge for rent.

So I suggest that our hope in regard to primary or direct controls, in contrast with methods that are at hand which will preserve the free-market organization, primarily taxation and public expenditure, is indicated by these historical cases. We should strive to make the course of events take the line of our tariff history, that is, to keep price-fixing and rationing from doing *too much* damage. And if this conference and other efforts of the same kind can work just to keep these economic and political stupidities from being carried to the point where they become *too* destructive, we will have justified ourselves.

That is all I feel like taking your time to say in connection with the problem of the future of demoracy and free civilization.

CHAIRMAN LEVI: Mr. Hayek!

MR. HAYEK: Professor Hale has raised some very fundamental issues to the discussion of which we might well devote another conference. But, before I get to that, I should like at least to make a few remarks on some aspects of the issues raised under Items I, III, and V of this outline.

I feel very strongly that our division between the immediate and the long-run problems almost makes it look as if the immediate may be the most important. There has been some mention of the fact that the problem of mobilization may be a problem not of the next year or two but of the next decade or two, and I think we ought to pay much more attention than we have yet done to the question of what will be our war potential not in a year or two but in five or ten years, according as to whether we either change to a more or less planned economy now or whether we preserve the essentials of a freely working society. Of course, one's views on this are inevitably colored by one's general beliefs; but, contrary to what was argued yesterday, I, personally, am very strongly convinced that the flexibility and adaptability of a market system are infinitely greater than that of a system which has been made rigid by central direction.

There is at least a possibility that our military leaders may do again what generals have been supposed always to do in the past, to plan for the last war rather than the next, and then as soon as war starts we may find that the main problem is completely to readjust all the things we have been preparing to entirely new objectives. If that situation should arise, I am convinced that we shall be in a very much stronger position if we had not relied on directing our economy through direct controls but had preserved that ability for readjustment which free enterprise on the whole provides. I merely raise this issue. I would be talking far too long if I tried to elaborate it, but I think it ought to be one of our main considerations.

As to Item III, inflation, there again I can mention just a few rather elementary points. In the sort of attitude with which people entered the war of 1914 and perhaps still in 1939 or 1941, it was possible to argue, and it was very frequently argued, that the sort of temporary rise in prices which people imagined an inflation would mean was an evil which one might well take into the bargain and which was perhaps inevitable while new plans were prepared to meet an unforeseen problem.

Now the situation is different in two respects. First, we know beforehand that if war comes we shall have to mobilize for war purposes as much as we can possibly spare from civilian purposes, and we have a fairly clear idea of what magnitude this involves. There is no longer that excuse for resorting to inflation, that we had no other plans ready, but we can deliberately choose what to do.

The other consideration is that we know now that a rise of prices which has once occurred is going to be a permanent rise of prices. I think anything which is certain as a result of development of opinion in the last ten years is that no major general fall in prices will be permitted. Now, that surely ought completely to alter our attitudes or at least profoundly affect our attitudes about the dangers of inflation. Again, the conclusion will depend on whether one seriously believes that, once one starts on the inflationary path, one might get away with a minor inflation, or whether there are not forces inherent in the mechanism of inflation which make it almost inevitably progressive.

There, again, I only want to put on record what is rather an elementary consideration, which, however, has not been mentioned. That is that inflation achieves what it is meant to achieve only so long as it is greater than it has been expected and that for that reason anyone who wants to bring about by inflation what it is intended to do has to resort to progressive inflation. There is, basically, no limit which we will not sooner or later reach once we have decided to use inflation as one of the instruments of finance; once people expect a given degree of inflation, it ceases to be effective for the purposes. We have to inflate a little more. After a while people get used to that degree of inflation, and so on, indefinitely.

From a long-run point of view, an appreciation of the consequences of this would, of course, have to be based on a fairly detailed analysis of all those redistribution effects, change in the stratification of population, which inflation brings about. Therefore, we cannot generalize too much about it, because it depends to some extent on the structure of population, on the investment habits of the people, on their ability to change their habits of investment, etc. But I do not think anyone who has seen the effects not only of the catastrophic inflations of the Central European type or of the major inflation of the French type, but even the degree of inflation we have had in Great Britain in the last twenty years, can doubt that the elimination of the middle class, basing its position on some supplementary income from property, is probably one of the most serious shocks to the stability of the type of society we live in which could be conceived.

Again, I must beg your pardon if I just raise a few points on a subject on which one could talk for an hour, but I have to go on to Item V, where there are two different aspects to deal with. The one I mean to raise as the more fundamental one is the one which Professor Hale has raised. I had intended to turn first briefly to something which I thought could be taken for granted, namely, that, if as a result of war economy we abandon the free market and permanently retain the more or less planned system, then our other liberties are doomed. But, as time is short, I will merely ask the question: What chances are there of getting rid again of economic controls once we have them? Why is it, rather, that most countries have in the past found it exceedingly difficult to get rid of the system of controls once they came in? Everywhere in the world the two wars have undoubtedly greatly accelerated the tendency away from the market system toward permanent government control far beyond anything which the majority of people who advocated controls in the first instance had ever anticipated.

I think perhaps this is in a way the fundamental issue which this program raises: Can we adopt all these measures which may or may not be expedient for wartime purposes in the expectation and in the hope that, as soon as they are no longer required by the momentary emergency, they can be swept away and got rid of? Now, one reason, and I believe one of the major reasons, is that, in fact as soon as we get an economy no longer subject to the market as the guiding consideration, efficiency and productivity are reduced. We are then faced at once with that basic issue between alternative economic systems. At once people who have control of what incomes will be will insist that people should not be remunerated according to the actual value of their services to the rest of the community but that an attempt should be made to remunerate the various classes of people according to the majority view about what the merit of these classes is. Such a remuneration, according to imagined merit, is inevitably very different from the relative value of these services to the society and results inevitably in a system of remuneration which no longer provides incentives or makes people produce what is wanted. The result is that we get a position in which the position of many classes is determined to a much greater extent even than in our present economy by more or less direct subsidies and that the perpetuation of the existing position of these classes depends on the maintenance of that system.

Perhaps the most permanent effect of all economic controls in Europe on the economic systems has been that of rent controls. So far as I know, no country which was a belligerent in Europe in 1914–18 has since then got completely rid of the system of rent controls. Those countries in which rent controls were then introduced had a major inflation following. It meant that housing in general was transformed from a private industry into a kind of public service where additional housing could be provided only by the government or by government subsidy and where the direction of the new building was no longer determined in any way by a market for rents. In consequence, the whole field of building for housing purposes was taken out of the market completely, and a whole large section of economic activity was permanently removed from the market mechanism.

I think this is probably an extreme instance, but it illustrates a very general problem. I doubt very much whether, once we have, as a result of war planning, achieved a price and income structure which is very different from that which would exist under a free-market system, but which is also in its recognizable aspects much more clearly dependent on the deliberate will of the community than any result of the market, we are likely ever again to get completely rid of it. That is the one part of the problem, one of the aspects, which I wanted to mention.

There was one other aspect which I thought I must not pass over. However, it is extremely difficult to put convincingly in a short exposition. It is the sort of psychological aspect of wartime controls on the future leaders of business. In the short time at my disposal I can only give you an impression and not the full supporting argument, but I might just from memory quote something which I said nearly ten years ago.

When I wrote the book to which Professor Hale was so good as to refer, I put in somewhere a footnote saying that, when I first came to England in the early thirties, what was regarded as a typically German view, that is, the government determining the whole aspect of economic life, was, on the whole, still very foreign to British thinking; but that I had once or twice experienced the feeling of being suddenly returned to what I regarded as the German atmosphere, and that was when I came into the company of the ex-planners of World War I who were thinking in exactly the same way in which some of my German friends had been thinking.

I do not think there can be any doubt that the moverment for planning in Great Britain in the postwar period has been led and advanced very largely by men who had been in charge of war planning during World War I, had tasted the pleasures of the job, had been so persuaded by their success that they thought it ought to be preserved for peacetime. I think the most remarkable thing was that the most ambitious planners among them were not the academic people who had gone into planning but were the business leaders who had been called into a planning activity and had found that in directing a whole industry they were saved so many of the troubles they had as individual enterprises that they were greatly attracted by the idea of preserving centralized direction of monopolized industries. I should at once add, I think, that the experience of this war in some respect has been slightly different. The reaction with which, so far as I can judge, the war planners returned from their jobs very largely depended on their previous backgrounds. The noneconomists among them, I think, have shown very much the same reactions as the planners of World War I. They were fascinated by the delectable task of running a big thing, and, if they had views favorable to it beforehand, they had only become more convinced planners by their experience. It is very different, I ought to add, with the economists who went into wartime planning. It was not surprising that those of them who beforehand were believers in free enterprise were confirmed in their experience. What was more remarkable was that a great many of my friends who before their experience in a war planning agency were rather favorable toward a centrally planned system came back on the whole thoroughly cured from this particular ambition. I am not sure what the reaction has been in this country. I rather fear that in this respect you have been more like Great Britain in World War I, where to a large extent, in spite of the great number of economists on which they could draw, they relied to fill their leading posts on people from the business community.

Again, I am discussing a particular aspect as an illustration of a very much wider question of how far the experiences of a planned economy are likely to affect attitudes of the people who will guide affairs and shape opinion after the war. I am sorry, but this is a subject on which I had hoped to talk at greater length. However, if I am not to remain on my feet unduly long, I must turn at least briefly to this very fundamental issue which Professor Hale has raised, the possibility of retaining freedom, assuming that we abandon the system of free markets and rely permanently on government direction for the organization and direction of our economic activities.

In one respect, Professor Hale has made my task easy because I think he has picked on what is the central issue in this connection, the possibility of preserving in such a system what is a first approximation, as we might describe it, of the rule of law as distinguished from specific orders and commands.

CHAIRMAN LEVI: Mr. Hayek, I am afraid we will have to give you an allocation of, say, five more minutes, because we are running a time-rationing system.

MR. HAYEK: If you will ask me to sit down now, you will greatly help me because an adequate reply in five minutes for what one could hardly do in an hour is almost more than I can manage.

CHAIRMAN LEVI: That is a problem of freedom and control, and you will have to work that one out.

Mr. HAYEK: May I suggest that, important as is the issue raised by Professor Hale, I will have to try to give you my answer in private conversation rather than here.

CHAIRMAN LEVI: I regret that I will also have to ask the rest of the speakers who have been allocated time to be somewhat brief, since we are running on a tight schedule. I will now call on Mr. Ford.

MR. FORD: I would like briefly to speak of two things. One is I feel that, when we speak of the probability of direct control, we are speaking somewhat after the fact. When the attorney-general testified before the enactment of the Defense Production Act, in July, 1950, he was asked by Senator Sparkman if he anticipated it would be necessary for direct controls to be invoked; and his reply was that if we had an adequate taxing policy and an adequate fiscal policy, and given the power of priorities and allocations, that would not be necessary. Well, we do not have that, and therefore we do have direct controls. If this conference could recommend what would be adequate taxing and adequate fiscal policies, I am sure that it would be helpful to Mr. Leventhal in mitigating the necessity for direct controls.

I think there was some disagreement yesterday between Judge Arnold and Mr. Garrison on the question of voluntary agreements or voluntary controls. I think Mr. Garrison was speaking to the point that it is helpful in a period of mobilization if the agricultural and labor leaders, for example, would agree that wages would be stabilized and there would be no strikes, if industry would agree there would be no lockouts, etc. Judge Arnold was speaking to the point of the danger of voluntary agreements as against the adequate enforcement of the antitrust laws and how, during this peoriod of time, it is the duty, particularly of the antitrust division, to watch voluntary agreements, to watch where they may lead, to have the right to attempt to break up such agreements, to supervise and insist that advisory groups have certain controls.

In that connection, I want to emphasize, as Mr. Morison did in a speech before the New York Bar Association recently after he took his office, that there will be continued vigorous enforcement of the antitrust laws. There will be certain situations where we may have to modify or postpone our request for relief, our method of relief, where it would do damage to the defense effort, but, short of that approach, we do not intend to abandon the vigorous enforcement of the law.

Following the enactment of the Defense Production Act and in accordance with Division 708E of such act, the attorney-general made on December 7, 1950, a comprehensive report of what our activities had been since the enactment of the act, what we felt our duties were in relation to that act. We are now, for example, in constant communication with Mr. Harrison's office, the National Production Authority, and we are constantly asking, and they are glad for the Antitrust Division to ask, "Let's know the economic facts back of the particular industry vis-à-vis the demand the military is making for goods and matériel before we categorically say that any one company is to have tax amortization."

We can and should go further. We say that before we try to make these determinations, the basic responsibility which any businessman would feel in a similar situation would be to know all the facts; and we are constantly doing our best to impress this point—that, since we are not in the situation we were in World War II, where we had suddenly overnight to expand and double our productive capacity (although I have no doubt that we would have to increase yet again our productive capacity but certainly not to the extent that World War II required), we survey and carefully survey every scrap of production facility that is available in the United States. Why do I say that? Maybe because I am essentially a lawyer and not an economist I want to use every tool I can on my side, and I point this out, that General Marshall has sent out a directive to all the defense establishments saying, "You must decentralize and disperse this production effort of ours." Why? Because even as laymen you and I know that the defense program must be dispersed.

Briefly, I think the problems are twofold. One is that we must, so far as we can, insist upon a broader basis of procurement than that followed during World War II, when approximately 51 per cent of the contracts went to thirty-three of the largest corporations. If we are to maintain our competitive economy, particularly in the concentrated area it is in now, we cannot permit that pattern to be repeated. Second, in connection with tax-amortization certificates, I think there must be very detailed and definite planning before they are granted to any large extent. The granting of those can have a very definite impact upon further concentration and the further deterioration of our competitive economy.

Mr. Morison is here. He can tell you, since the speeches are limited to five minutes, what his specific efforts have been with Mr. Leventhal on the judicious application of price controls to try to prevent any whittling-down of antitrust concepts and with Mr. Wilson's office, Mr. Harrison, and the defense establishments.

CHAIRMAN LEVI: Mr. Morison!

MR. MORISON: Mr. Ford has summarized the objective of the Antitrust Division during the current period of mobilization. Let me just footnote what Mr. Ford has said.

We operate not only under the Defense Production Act of 1950, which definitely enjoins all defense agencies to accomplish their objectives, as far as practicable, within the framework of the American system of competitive enterprise, but also under presidential directives which require the defense agencies to consult with the attorney-general to determine and eliminate factors in our military buildup which may tend to promote monopoly or undue concentration of economic power. Now, we conceive that our responsibility is not that we should become a pariah and beat the drums and insist that everything that is being done is wrong. Rather, our attitude is that we are partners with the officials who are charged with responsibilities in this defense effort, enormous and complicated as it is. We propose, in so far as it is humanly possible, to work with those officials to attain the fundamental objective which underlies everything that all of us do, that is, to deliver the materials required by the Joint Chiefs of Staff, in the quality and the quantity and at the time that they need them. I have very definite feelings about this. I think that you economists and you businessmen who are here recognize that a defense mobilization, even of 15 or 20 per cent, may have the effect of cutting deeply into our concept of a competitive, free-enterprise system.

I want to point to the differences between World War II and our present defense effort. At the outbreak of World War II we were faced with a lack across the board of the facilities for production. We had gone through a fifteen-year period of economic stress which left the country without machinery and machine tools and the brick and mortar to accommodate expansion of facilities even approaching the urgent demands imposed upon us by Pearl Harbor. Our industrial mobilization then was a terribly confused effort, directed at creating industrial plants by the quickest and most direct route. The result was to concentrate production facilities into the hands of a few to the greatest degree in the history of the country.

The extent of the concentration of economic power which went on during World War II has been pointed out in the first report of the attorney-general to the President and Congress submitted under the Defense Production Act on December 7 of last year. As Mr. Ford stated, that report sets forth that the impact of our defense procurement was to place more than one-half of the billions of dollars that went into World War II contracting into the hands of the thirty-three largest corporations in the country. The result of this distortion was the elimination from the industrial scene in the postwar period of large numbers of small and medium-sized enterprises who found it impossible to compete with the tremendous facilities built up by the dominant corporations during the war.

Now, mind you, I am not a stark idealist who has lost sight of the practical needs presented by a national emergency. I recognize that we must pay a price for everything that we do, and if the price to defend our country from aggression may prove to be concentration of economic power, and if the need is demonstrated, then I think we must take the risk. Our position, however, is that in this period of accelerating mobilization we have an opportunity to plan our defense procurement program with the care and deliberation which will serve both to hasten our defense expansion and to preserve all segments of business, large and small alike.

In this period of expanding military production the efforts of all defense agencies are directed toward the same end of procuring our needs within the framework of our competitive enterprise system. Thus, we are in constant consultation and communication with Mr. Leventhal's office to assist in the formulation of price ceilings which will be equitable to all. Frequently we can draw on the files and records of the Antitrust Division to disclose pricing evils brought about by monopolistic practices. Those evils should not be perpetuated in our economic structure through the freezing of monopolistic prices. I can say that the Office of Price Stabilization has recognized its mutuality of responsibility with us and has worked in harmony with the Department of Justice.

In the field of tax amortization, although we have no responsibility under the law and no veto power, we certainly have been in constant communication with Mr. Harrison's office, and have constantly asked, "Let's examine the economic facts in this particular industry vis-à-vis the demands of the military for goods before we say which company or companies shall finance their expansion of facilities from the public purse through tax amortization." There, again, the officials in the Defense Production Administration have been appreciative of our interest and of the facts which we have given them.

We uniformly insist that, before determinations are made which affect our economy, all the facts shall be gathered and reviewed as a basis for decision. Certainly that is the procedure which any sound businessman should follow in a similar situation. We have constantly pressed the point that our present position is completely at variance from World War II, when we faced the necessity of increasing our productive capacity almost overnight. Now, although we must expand our facilities, we may proceed carefully on the basis of a survey of every scrap of the production facilities in the United States.

As a lawyer, I want to use every tool that I have available to me. For that reason, I insist that we utilize careful planning to meet our defense needs. Through this planning, I believe we can successfully carry out the directive of General Marshall when he said, "You must decentralize and disperse this production effort of ours." As laymen, you and I know that we can take an industrial map of the United States and draw red circles around Pittsburgh and Detroit and certain areas in the Southwest where there are tremendous concentrations of industrial capacity. These would be prime targets if we were attacked.

CHAIRMAN LEVI: Mr. Morison, we are operating on a five-minute rule. Will you please summarize if you can?

MR. MORISON: Thank you, sir. I am glad you brought that admonition. I get on my favorite subject, and I lose all sense of time.

Let me summarize. There is military significance in the dispersal of our production machine. Further, as a practical consideration, we must utilize our entire production capacity, not only to enable us, if need be, to meet the needs of total war but also to preserve our competitive economy for the peacetime future. In my opinion, if we do not proceed with our expanding military buildup on the basis of careful planning and if we have a 15 or 20 per cent strain on our economy for ten years or more, we shall forever lose medium and small-sized business as an element of serious competition.

CHAIRMAN LEVI: Congressman Celler!

REPRESENTATIVE CELLER: I thoroughly agree with what Dr. Stocking has said—that we must be more vigilant in these times of mobilization to give some modicum of protection to small business. I am not going to give you any figures, but there is no doubt that, as a result of the mobilization of the last war—and the portents indicate the same situation now—the huge concerns become mastodon in size and the demise of small business increases. One would come to the conclusion that small business is a casualty of war. It should not be so, and I hope that those in charge of procurement, the allocation of military orders, will act differently in this present era of mobilization than they did in the last.

But the same pattern apparently that was woven during the last mobilization effort is now being woven again. For example, I have before me a statement from the Munitions Board entitled, "Military Purchases from Small Firms," dated March, 1951. For the period from July to December, 1949, the amount of military purchases directed to small firms was 23.8 per cent of the total; the period January–June, 1950, it was 24.8 per cent;

July–December, 1950, it went down to 21 per cent; January, 1951, it is down to 16.6 per cent. So there has been a diminishing stream of military procurement orders for small business, a small business being defined as an entity employing less than five hundred persons.

Now, when we contemplate the magnitude of the orders that are being placed, we certainly, and you economists certainly, must be most vigilant in trying to help in this regard. The defense orders are flowing at the rate of nearly fifty billion dollars a year. Defense spending, which is a better measure of actual output, has reached an annual rate of twenty-four billion dollars and at the end of the year will match the rate of orders, namely, fifty billion dollars. Unless we watch out, big business will get into the position that was stated before the Committee on the Judiciary in the House through one of its subcommittees: "Every man for himself," said the elephant, as he danced among the chickens.

Now, one other item I want to dwell upon briefly concerning mobilization is the dollar-a-year man. The Truman Committee made the following report in part: "The Committee is opposed to a policy of taking free services from persons with axes to grind, and the Committee believes that the government should not continue to accept the loan of dollar-a-year and without-compensation men by companies with so large a stake in the defense program." I have lists of all the industry advisory committees, and I can assure you (and I would be very happy to show those lists to anyone) that a major portion of all the members of the industry advisory committees that have been appointed were and are involved in defense orders in the mobilization effort; they thus have undoubtedly large stakes in those defense orders. For example, I note that included on a list of the current personnel of the National Production Authority so-called dollar-a-year men are at least thirty persons without salary who are employed by companies which number among the one hundred largest corporations in the United States. Seventeen of the thirty of these nonsalaried workers are otherwise employed by companies in the steel industry or their subsidiaries, and interestingly enough every one of the steel companies was a defendant in an antitrust suit. The United States Steel Corporation or its affiliated companies has four persons working for the United States government on a noncompensatory basis. One employee on the list is otherwise employed by an industry trade association, the American Iron and Steel Institute. There is a regulation which precludes the employment without compensation of anyone who is in an executive position of a trade association for fear that he might have an undue influence on policy-making.

The President by executive order has provided that, in so far as without-compensation employees are concerned, "appointment to positions other than adviser or consultant may be made under this order only when the requirements of the position are such that the incumbent must personally possess outstanding experience and ability not obtainable on a full-time salaried basis." Whether this prescription is being carried out is indeed a subject for detailed investigation, and I shall endeavor to conduct an investigation along those lines. I know, for example, that many of the without-compensation personnel on the roster of NPA, far from having special technical skills which may not be obtained elsewhere, are merely sales managers of companies or concerns. What special service they can render that cannot be obtained elsewhere, I have not been informed, but certainly pitfalls in such a picture are manifest.

If I have just a half-moment yet, Mr. Chairman, I would like to point out some of the defects of the activities of the so-called industry advisory committees. I will say that small business is not properly represented on these business advisory committees. Under the rules and regulations prescribed, a government agent must be chairman of all these committees. That rule thus far is more honored in the breach than in the observance. A government agent must initiate and prepare the agenda of the committee. That is not followed. The minutes must be full and complete, and there must be full and complete minutes of subcommittees, full and complete minutes of so-called task forces. That rule thus far is more honored in the breach than the observance. The committee must be established under statutory authority. That is, in many instances, not the case. Many of them are so-called voluntary arrangements and have not been cleared by the constituted authorities. And in these cases of voluntary arrangements, I am informed—not as yet with conclusive proof—some of the members of the committee (and this apparently is the case with the Rubber Advisory Committee) actually determined where defense orders are to go and what shall be allocated when and to whom. They dictate questions of policy, quite to the contrary of the rules and regulations, and that is a very serious situation, and our attention must be directed to it.

Now, the signals are all set. What are we going to do about those signals? Are we going to disregard them, or must we follow them up religiously and rigorously to see that the acts that we have passed in Congress, the rules promulgated thereunder, are observed?

Mr. COHEN: Mr. Chairman, I have only a few general observations to make. I take it that we are all concerned here with preserving freedom against the threats that assail it. On that ground there is unanimity among us.

But the problem is to find the most appropriate means of preserving our free system. I am reminded of a meeting of a learned society that I attended two years ago. I listened to a couple of eloquent but depressing addresses on the prospect of freedom in the world. The speakers feared that the prospect of freedom was not very encouraging in Europe because the free system would not be able to meet the stresses and strains that would have to be met there. They believed the free system would continue in this country until it had to meet the stresses and strains of a severe depression.

Now, my conception of freedom is of a much more robust institution, an institution that can live and function in rough as well as calm weather. It is the problem of all of us who believe in freedom to inform ourselves of the conditions under which freedom can live and survive. I would venture to suggest that, as long as we preserve our political democracy in this country, the long-term effects of controls which are imposed in order to enable us to meet our defense needs are likely to be influenced much more by the economic pattern of American life which will exist at the end of the defense emergency than they will be by the interest or desire of power-seeking bureaucrats to preserve their power. Therefore, I think it is most important, as has been emphasized by other speakers here this morning, for us to bear constantly in mind the effects of particular controls and of the standards governing their exercise on the pattern of our economic life—on size and competitive character of business enterprise. It seems to me in the present discussion we have given too much consideration to the theoretical question of controls *vel non*—controls or no controls—rather than the practical question of what types of control and what techniques of controls are most likely to help us to perform our necessary defense tasks and to preserve the greatest practical degree of freedom during the period of control and thereafter.

We have discussed and have found general agreement that there are advantages in fiscal and monetary controls over direct controls. But, I think, if we review the lessons of the last fifty years, we will find that those advantages are in no small part due to the fact that we have learned more about the exercise of fiscal and monetary controls than we have about so-called direct controls. Just let me give you one example in the fiscal field. Sometime back, I believe that it was the dominant thinking in the fiscal field that the primary if not exclusive purpose of taxation was to raise revenue and that all sorts of dire results would follow if attempts were made to use taxation for other economic or social purposes. It should be remembered that, just before the close of the last century, Mr. Joseph Choate in successfully assailing the constitutionality of the federal income tax argued that the income tax was the beginning of an inexorable march toward communism. It is significant to observe that in the discussion here we have all discussed without apologies the types of fiscal controls that are most likely not only to help us raise revenues but to restrict nondefense spending.

I am convinced that careful study and constructive thinking

may reveal possibilities of developing standards and techniques in the exercise of direct controls that we have failed even to consider in our discussions here. I am no more persuaded by the discussions here that all forms of direct control are bad than I am that all forms of fiscal control are good.

None of us in this room can tell how long the defense emergency will last or whether before it is passed we will be plunged into all-out war. We should therefore not be content with the hasty improvisation of crude controls or an obstinate rejection of all direct controls en masse. But we should give much more attention to the specific problems which confront us and the specific means which may assist us in their sound solutions. We lawyers have learned that broad generalizations do not decide concrete cases. Too often, I fear, we exhaust ourselves in debating whether controls are necessary or not rather than patiently and constructively considering the standards or techniques which we can develop to meet a situation with the least inroads on our freedom of action. In practice, in meeting the stresses and strains of an abnormal situation, laissez faire may restrict and not preserve freedom. Traffic rules may be as necessary for a congested market as for a congested highway. But poor traffic rules may be as bad or worse than none.

We should carefully consider the effects both of policies of control and of policies of laissez faire upon freedom not only during the defense emergency but thereafter. Defense production with or without direct controls may profoundly affect the economic pattern of American life. Big business and big unions may exercise a greater control over the so-called free markets than big government. Even with improved laws and procedures to check monopoly and oligopoly, large-scale business enterprise and comparable large labor organizations will continue to exist. Without destroying the efficiency of mass production in our interdependent society, we must be eternally vigilant to see that enterprise is kept free and competition is not allowed, by the action or inaction of government, to become stratified and feudalistic. The gates must remain open in practice as well as in theory to newcomers, or our system of free enterprise will cease to exist. Economic freedom and political freedom are one and inseparable. In a free society the individual's freedom and livelihood must not depend upon his willingness to follow the line laid down by any political party or any large aggregation of economic power.

I, for one, do not want to live in a world where I have to follow in goose-step a party line dictated by government or by any large aggregation of business or labor power.

CHAIRMAN LEVI: I wish to remind the conference that we are operating under a five-minute rule, because otherwise the chairman is in the position of operating with selective controls, which is not something he desires to do.

MR. LEVENTHAL: I am somewhat disturbed by the fact that Dr. Stocking introduced the subject of his discussion today, or concluded it perhaps, by stating that he felt his remarks were merely spitting in the wind. I take it he meant that there were forces at work so vicious, so uncontrollable, that really nothing could be done about them once you started on a system of direct controls.

It seems to me that in this conference we have had too much discussion in the field of economics, and not enough discussion in the field of political science, or public administration, together with the field of economics, which I take it makes up the field of political economy; so that we could have more profitably considered the framework of direct controls which preserve freedom to the maximum extent, and I underscore Mr. Cohen's observations on that point. Some of the speakers have assumed that government controls inevitably mean a loss of freedom or immediately and necessarily mean a loss of freedom. On the other hand, we are all familiar with a system of government controls in this country which have had as their purpose the maintenance of economic freedom and the maintenance of a maximum degree of decentralized decision. I refer, of course, to the antitrust laws.

We operate, in general, under a system of schizophrenia, I suppose, in which we ask for government controls in that regard, in order that we may have maximum freedom in the ultimate from forces that would otherwise be at work. And I think, in that connection, it is interesting to see that those controls have been the most effective in achieving maximum individual freedom at decentralized levels as they have become more detailed. So long as the courts were enforcing the antitrust laws under general rules of law, very little was done except in the opening cases. Much more is done now that the Antitrust Division of the Department of Justice through the operation of the consent-decree section undertakes to work out with the courts rather detailed rules to achieve individual freedom.

It is also interesting that the Public Utilities Holding Company Act, whose draftsman we are honored to have with us today and which set forth a relatively detailed system of government administration, has perhaps been the most effective statute, underlying the most effective program that has been developed for obtaining maximum decentralization of decisions in a field which was becoming increasing centralized. Those who fear that bureaucrats always perpetuate themselves may take some heart from the fact that the public utilities division of the Securities and Exchange Commission is actively engaged in liquidating itself.

We fall, I think, into an error of loose thinking when we use the word "controls" and assume that all types of controls are the same. Let me give as an example the differences in possible rationing controls. Rationing, in general, is a direct control, of course. But it seems to me there is a significant difference between the type of rationing control which was developed in Great Britain, and which required each individual to register with a particular grocer, and the type of rationing control that we had in this country, in which an individual had his own ration coupons and had freedom to choose the grocer with whom he was going to do business. One is set in a sphere of regimentation, if you like, or certainly enforced continuance of a particular pattern of business, and the other maintained maximum freedom of choice. There is a vast difference between the two.

It is noteworthy in that regard that the system of rationing inaugurated by Mr. Henderson rejected, for the most part, the proposals of so-called downstream rationing, in which the supply would be made available to the first source of supply to distribute down to its regular channel of trade, and instead used the so-called upstream rationing, in which the coupons were made available to everybody to patronize, say, the filling station of his own choice. As the filling stations sent the ration coupons into their suppliers, they got the supplies appropriate for those coupons. I say it is important and basic in the administration of direct controls that those who are phrasing and framing the particular controls emphasize a system of application which maximizes competition and freedom, or at least interferes less with freedom while it is in effect.

Mr. Ford and Mr. Morison have been kind enough to advert to the co-operation which exists between the Office of Price Stabilization, among others, and their division. It may be interesting to comment that, while Dr. Stocking was the administrator of the Fuel Division of the OPA, there was in effect a maximum price regulation governing the wholesale prices of oil products. That regulation provided that if a company could not determine a maximum under one or another of a set of formulas, the company should select as its selling price the selling price of a certain group of reference sellers. This was a mechanical device in the ceiling regulation which reflected the system of market leaders that was known in the oil industry.

Within the past few weeks, when the problem of oil regulation came up again, I took up this question with Mr. Morison. Our experts consulted with each other. We decided that the use of the provision for a reference seller, or representative seller, had such implications as to the market leader practice, which in turn had unfortunate implications from the point of view of the antitrust division, that it should be omitted from this regulation. This story recently came out in the newspapers, but with some errors. This is a mere detail, but it is the kind of detail which shows that, in the day-to-day work of administration of these direct controls, there are choices. There are choices between those which preserve freedom, as I said before, and those which do not. There are choices between those which promote centralization and those which promote competition to the maximum extent.

Finally, I should like to call attention to certain aspects of direct controls, as administered by the Office of Price Stabilization, which should alleviate fears of bureaucratic tyranny.

The Office of Price Stabilization has in certain regulations adopted a system of so-called gross margins, for example, in the restaurant regulation. These, to the extent that we can use them, provide maximum freedom to the person subject to the controls to set individual prices and preserve some measure of freedom for the operation of the price function. That is an important factor to be taken into account in analyzing the kind of direct controls we have. We also have regard for the rule of law in the administration of our controls. No individual adjustments may be made in prices, except pursuant to a general standard which is announced. That general standard is publicly incorporated into the regulation, and there is no possibility of individual or capricious action granting an individual adjustment price increase to one person and not to another. The fact of the congressional review to which we are continually subject is also an important element in preserving freedoms.

Finally, I would say that the Office of Price Stabilization is aware from the beginning that it must, at an early date, start planning a decontrol policy as well as a control policy and that we will be administering the controls for the temporary period when they are in effect in such a way as to make possible an early decontrol.

SENATOR BENNETT: Ladies and gentlemen, I am very grateful for the opportunity of coming to this conference, and, because I am neither an economist nor a lawyer, I should like to devote my five minutes in the interests of the person we seem all to have forgotten—the individual American citizen whose destiny we are blithely disposing of in these three days. I should like to remind myself, and I hope you, that freedom belongs to the individual. It is not ours to dispose of or operate with; and I am happy to be told that the objective of these various procedures we have been discussing is the preservation of the freedom of the individual to operate as he pleases.

I wonder what the objective of this conference is. It seems to me many times that we are like a group of learned doctors gathered around the bed of a patient discussing the technicalities of his disease without being very much concerned about whether he survives or not. Is this just a dry run? Is this in fact a jet-propelled excursion into the stratosphere of higher economic theories? If it is not to be, we have to be concerned with some kind of process by which the ordinary citizen can exercise his freedom more effectively in the light of these various economic conditions we have discussed.

So I would hope, probably vainly, that out of all this discussion we can distil a point of view, or several informative facts, which will enable the individual citizen to preserve his own freedom against the bureaucrat, against the big-business monopolist, against anybody, because in the last analysis freedom is meaningless unless he is so able to preserve it. I am distressed by the realization that, unless something definite is done, all the effort of these three days will have been negated in the end.

The American people are greatly concerned with this problem of inflation. They want to know how to live under it. They want to know what they can do effectively to get rid of it, and they want to know how to operate wisely in the face of these theoretical conditions that seem to operate on them. We are apt to talk blithely about the process being an educational one. It certainly is, and here is the pick of the educators in this field. Are you going to be content with an intellectual exercise for your own amusement, or somehow out of such a meeting as this can something be done which will enable the citizen, when he votes next time, to express himself effectively for the preservation of his own freedom? I hope the latter can be undertaken.

B. SUMMARY STATEMENTS

CHAIRMAN LEVI: We now turn appropriately enough to the final topic, so you will see why the Chair has been trying to limit the statements.

The final topic is put in terms of a question—"Can we agree on a program for economic mobilization?" I should like to state what I had in mind to state on the first day of this conference, namely, that in the minds of the committee which arranged this conference it is not imperative and perhaps it is not important that we agree on a program for economic mobilization here. It is perhaps equally important, or more important, that if we disagree there be clarity as to the disagreement. The distillation, in other words, would not be a distillation of such a jet-propelled flight as to be above the disagreement. We have therefore asked various participants to state a program for economic mobilization which would presumably be a statement both of agreement—but I think perhaps more important—and of disagreement, and any distillation which may occur after that, at least, will have those clear statements before us.

MR. STOCKING: The statement that I made about power-hungry bureaucrats who have an interest of perpetuating themselves in office would, I think, be appropriate if it were modified to read: "so-called power-hungry bureaucrats who have the desire to perpetuate the ideas upon which the controls rest." One of the things that disturb me about the system of controls is that those of us who administer them find it so easy to identify the public interest with our own interest, and we find it easy to conclude that the economy will be better off if people like us are making the decisions about it.

MR. HENDERSON: I had intended to begin this Sabbath meeting with a few kind words for Adam Smith.

I would like to start with what I consider a vital contribution by Fred Lazarus, drawing attention to Mobilizer Wilson's first report, which indicated the planning for the period ahead and emphasized the possibility of sufficient growth within the productive system, in perhaps two or three years, so that given no larger program than assumed, sometimes spoken of as fifty billion dollars, it would be possible to carry the defense load out of the increased productivity that would result. I consider that something which is very worthy of support. For that reason I believe that some attention must be given to the amortization question. I believe that, as I said in the first session I attended, we do not need to be too exacting as to these grants, that these are not necessarily a giving-away of something by the government.

I recommend the suggestion of Congressman Celler that there be a negotiation, if possible, as to the future use of the facilities. But I should certainly want to see that made firm and certain at the very beginning. As I think Hensel will remember, that was one of the main considerations we had in the first five-year amortization plan, that anybody entering that contract, and with the hazards ahead, would know things for certain. I think the government has to lead the way in maintaining firmness and sanctity of contracts.

Next, as to the facilities, I think that we will need both direct and indirect controls for an intelligent guidance of this expansion, and I place emphasis on the defense-related industries as much as I do on the expansion of armament-producing industries. In my opinion, transportation, both by rail, pipelines, and ships, and the increase of facilities such as for cement are also important.

I should like to say that I believe we will need the direct controls in order to whittle down somewhat building within the private area which could be postponed until a later time. We have gone into a fairly high degree of regulation already, with a limitation of 50 per cent of credit, for example, for a business building; and yet, as the recent vigorous surge of expansion plans shows, there has been practically no diminution resulting from the controls as they have been exercised to date.

Again, I feel that we have not paid enough attention to the

potential within debt management and savings as a means of heading off inflation. As I recall, since I have been here, only Martin Gainsbrugh mentioned it, and I have a very, very distinct feeling that this needs to be emphasized. Nor do I think that we should abandon a study of the possibilities of further withdrawal of consumer income, either by the nasty term "compulsory saving" or the much more enlightened term of "increases" in the social security withholding.

I see no reason why a spending tax should not be studied. One of the reasons why it has been opposed has been the supposed difficulty of administration. I submit with the expansion of social security coverage, with the expansion of the income-tax-filing requirements, and the experiments that we are having with regulation of all retail stores, the administrative difficulty has been considerably reduced.

I think that there ought to be further consideration given to the suggestions made by Lloyd Garrison for coming to some kind of a harmonious bargaining arrangement with labor. I have a feeling that the Knudson-Hillman arrangement, and later the use of the Wage Board, gave us tremendous hidden advantages in that we had less stoppages. For that reason I think that there needs to be some harmony there.

As to the indirect controls, I am sometimes reminded of my son, when he was in the hospital with a very painful earache; the doctor always selected for the injection of penicillin some place in the anatomy that was far removed from that point where the ache was taking place, and my son had a natural wonderment as to how that penicillin was going to find its way to the ache. I think in the argument as advanced by both Hitch and Stein, and others, there is a recognition of the need for more immediate action on the allocation of resources.

With my hand very firmly on the *Wealth of Nations,* I hold that in time of crisis the government is the better judge as to what is needed than the market. I think that we tend to over-emphasize price and wage controls, and I went to some length to try to say that the architects were certainly in a frame of mind to recognize other potentials. I still subscribe to what Stocking has said of the danger of getting into a position of defending your own children.

Now, as to price and wage controls, I think we run a danger that the lull that is taking place here now, which may run perhaps another three to six months, has, you might say, moderated the necessity for controls. I regard that as a period for using great intelligence in the selection of the controls. I think the margin controls that Leventhal spoke about represent as good technical mechanisms as intelligent people can apply. But certainly with an increase in the volume of spending and with a rise in incomes, there will be a resumption of price increases which would make controls necessary.

While I am not clear whether or not the amount of inflation that is deferred is the same amount as it would be if it were entirely in the open or whether some of it does pass into savings and stays there—I am quite sure that it should not be allowed to enter into the course of prices. The price level—if George Stigler will let me use the index—was somewhere in the 90's when the first real impact of mobilization in World War II began to be felt. It was around an unrealistic 112 when the OPA was abandoned, and went up to something like 168. I remember debate with Senator Taft as to whether or not we could ever expect to go back. I felt that the adjustment to long-term debt and other forces meant that we might have a recession. The index fell to 152 and has gained about 30 points since that time. I think that if we can pick out some of the spiral inflation that was spoken about yesterday and make the appropriate fiscal and monetary adjustments, we can render a great service.

Now, as to a program on what to do: I think we have got to consider that the 1952 requirements on a cash-consolidated basis are likely to be around seventy-five billion dollars, and they may be more. I think the Committee for Economic Development ought to be proud for having established the concept of a cash-consolidated budget as a means of judging the impact on the economic system.

The Treasury is asking now for ten billion dollars. My own

judgment would be that seven and a half billion dollars of revenue, based on the anticipated increases, would probably take care of that particular situation.

There were several proposals about getting a tax levy which would give us more substantial overbalance. I have a great deal of difficulty with that, because I find it impossible to imagine the size and type of tax program which could really offset a flight from the dollar, considering what liquidity there is.

In Forrestal's administration there was a requirements review board of some sixty people who were constantly reviewing the requests of the military chiefs, and, in addition, since they cannot fire me as they did Lou Johnson, I can mention that the studies on which he relied for cutting down on the administrative costs certainly indicated the possibility of a billion or more in that direction. I should like to re-emphasize the suggestion that there ought to be a civilian committee review of the federal expenditure. As far as balancing the budget is concerned, I feel that in the immediate time ahead there is a possibility of a tax program which would not be of extraordinary impact, and, as Mr. Kestnbaum said, and I think also Mr. Steinkraus, this is the first time that we have had business saying, "Yes, we accept the emergency and the necessity of budget balancing," and it is refreshing, considering that, when we had the fight for a larger percentage of the war to be covered by taxes, we had no help either from the fiscal authorities or from business or from labor.

Now, as to a tax program I would suggest that the CED is probably as near correct as anybody on the matter of an increase in the personal income rates. I believe, however, we need to consider some higher exemptions for the extremely low-income groups. I would like to see the curve flattened at the executive salary range, on account of the inducement, and that would be executives of all kinds, including those of labor unions.

As to the corporate tax, I suggest the repeal of the mischievous excess profits tax. I think that Beardsley Ruml in the next week will make a speech calling attention to some of the dangers that are inherent in the cheap dollars that result. I would like to see a higher corporate rate. I think I would go a point or two higher than the CED did, and that would be particularly so if there was a repeal of the excess profits tax. Certainly, there is some point at which your corporate taxation begins to lose a lot of its vitality.

So, today, I hope my friends on the labor side will see what a punitive rate the rate on corporate taxation is as to their own low-income people who are holders of stock. I hope they may join me also in advocating the complete repeal sometime of the corporation tax and substituting a tax on profits as they accrue to the income-tax recipients at their appropriate brackets. I think that in the search for revenue we should not overlook the possibilities of what there is in retained profits—thirteen billion as of last year. Of course, only a liberal like myself would dare suggest that. I do not think labor or the Treasury ever will.

As to excise taxes, here I depart very strenuously from my friends in the CED. I think they made an impromptu proposal, and they associated themselves with the administration too vigorously. The rates suggested are higher than wartime rates, and on a few commodities, consumer durables, they are high on the phony idea that they are needed for control and diversion, and I insist that the control mechanism under Fleischman is adequate for that purpose. Also, these are items that are in all the low-income budgets, and therefore it offends my sense of equity to have it rationed by pocketbook.

I also think that the tax—if we need excise taxation—should not be at the manufacturing level, because it is pyramided. It gets bedded in and bedded down for eternity as a hidden manufacturers' tax. I would substitute a retail rate, and we have just completed a study which shows that, even with all the exemptions that people customarily think of on goods and services, there is a base of 135 billion dollars, exclusive of alcohol, tobacco, and gasoline, at which a 6 per cent rate could be applied.

Finally, I would say in summary that I do not share with a number of the observers here the idea that the present controls existing as they do for 20 per cent of effort going to the military means a complete surrender of private effort. There is still a lot of room for ingenuity there. We should have an emphasis on the long-term or medium effects, as Mr. Hayek has pointed out, certainly incentive for expansion, more consideration for debt management and savings, a scrutiny of the budget, and a monetary policy.

In closing, I should like to thank my host, the University of Chicago, for keeping the flame alive and letting the term "free market" not disappear; and, also, I feel that it will engender not only impetus toward the indirect controls which I favor in peacetime but that it will maybe produce some close study of what the possibilities and potentials are of indirect controls at the fiscal and monetary level.

MR. DIRECTOR: To build and maintain our armed forces requires labor, land, machinery, and materials that we would prefer to use for the purpose of our normal pursuits. We may hope for a prompt end to this necessity, but we must be prepared for its indefinite continuance. We must therefore meet the emergency with an economic policy that we could continue indefinitely, if necessary—an economic policy that will increase our basic sources of strength, that will distribute the burden of rearmament fairly, that will permit the maximum realization of our economic potentialities.

Existing economic policy for the emergency does not satisfy these requirements. It is a patchwork of improvisation and expediency. If maintained, it will impair our productive strength and gravely weaken our free institutions. A satisfactory economic policy for the present emergency will aim at the following goals.

1. Ordinary government expenditure should be reduced. We cannot usefully specify the nature of these reductions, but it is important that the periods when citizens are asked to give up a portion of their income should not be periods when the welfare activities of the state should be increased, but rather should be periods when those who receive benefits from the state should also give up a portion of these benefits. Welfare activities bear some relation to the aggregate resources available for con-

sumption and to the distribution of income. The aggregate will clearly be reduced, and the distribution of income is not likely to become more unequal than it is now. Specifically, government programs conceived under depression conditions, such as subsidies to agriculture, are clearly inappropriate during the mobilization period.

2. Inflation should be prevented. The consequential distributions of the cost of mobilization are by no means of a desirable type, to put it mildly. Its advantages for maximizing output and diverting output to the military program are of minor importance. There is significant danger of destroying an important class in the community, as has been amply demonstrated by the experience of other countries. Wartime inflation develops bad habits of monetary management. To rely on a moderate amount of inflation is dangerous; the emergency may be of long duration, and it will then become increasingly difficult to contain the inflation within moderate limits.

3. Government expenditures should be financed largely or entirely from current taxes. In this way, the inflationary effect of government expenditure will be offset by the taxes levied to finance them. The physical reality that economic resources are being diverted to rearmament is thereby matched by the financial reality that monetary resources are so diverted.

As to the form of taxation, I need only say that I can see no reason why the main reliance should not be on the personal income tax. The objection to such reliance is mainly in terms of incentives and is consequently mainly an objection to more progression in the system and implies that additional amounts should be obtained via an increase of basic rates and the lowering of exemptions.

I see no occasion for a general sales tax, or for particular excise taxes as additional revenue producers. Individuals are as good judges of what is good for them in extraordinary times as in ordinary times. If they want to spend given fractions of their income for tobacco and other "necessities," I can see no reason for an endeavor to get them to spend more on "luxuries," and this use of terms is not a slip.

As to differential taxes of the excess-profits type, the justification in terms of comparison between those who stay at home and those who do the fighting cannot in fact be made. As to those who stay at home, there appears to be nothing odd about rewarding workers and enterprises who do make an effort to meet the changed requirements. If, at any time, it is found that there are proper windfalls not only in terms of past events but in terms of influencing supply and allocation during the whole emergency period, and if they can be properly isolated, then excise taxes can be used to divert such windfalls to the government. As to reforms in the system of taxation, they should be of the same kind as are appropriate in ordinary times, namely, to include all income, to apply the same rates to all types of income, and to treat persons in the same income classes alike.

4. Monetary policy should be directed exclusively at preventing inflation. Inflation can develop only if there is an increase in the supply of money, or if widespread expectations of inflation lead people to increase the rate of use of money. Inflation can be prevented at its source by preventing an increase in the supply of money or by reducing the stock, if necessary, to offset increases in rate of use.

It is useful to think of a proper budget policy—all taxes, or some noninflationary borrowing—as having the function of preventing government activities from being inflationary. With such a budget policy, the reserve system has ample powers to control the stock of money through open-market purchases and sales of securities. The function of monetary policy may therefore be looked upon as primarily designed to prevent private activities from being inflationary.

Changes in the rate of use of money cannot be predicted. Increases are now being fostered by price control and threats of rationing; the probability of further increases in the rate of use of money can be minimized by an announced policy of preventing an increase in the supply of money. Should increases in the rate of use develop on a significant scale, their effect can be offset by monetary means. Up to now monetary measures have caused rather than curbed inflation, because they have been dominated by a policy of keeping down interest rates on government securities. This policy should be stopped immediately, if necessary by congressional direction to the Federal Reserve System to adopt the prevention of inflation as the overriding goal, despite its effect on the level of the rate of interest on government securities. Keeping down government interest rates is and for some time has been inflationary.

5. Direct price and wage controls should not be used during the emergency. If inflation is stopped at its source by monetary, budgetary, and tax measures, no general rise in prices will, in fact, take place. If it is not so stopped, then inflation is mainly postponed. There are no obvious advantages in such postponement. It is not clear that it will be easier to remove the source of inflation after the emergency than during the emergency.

The function of wage and price control as a psychological factor to persuade the community that something is being done can readily be provided in other ways. There is Professor Stigler's suggestion that monthly income-tax bills should be sent out—and I hope he will not object to the mailing of duplicates each week.

If inflation is not stopped at its source, price control can keep particular prices down only at the expense of disorganizing production and distribution. Prices and wages are the means employed in a free economy for adapting the productive system to changing requirements. The only qualification that I would make to this general point derives from the existence of private restraints which keep prices and wages from rising sufficiently to conform with the changed circumstances. But this circumstance calls not for price and wage control but for allocation control, and this only in order to expedite the diversion of resources to the military program and not as an aid in distributing output in general. As I do not wish to fall into the class of reformers designated by Professor Stigler, I will only note that the emergency is no occasion for increasing the amount of private restraints, even if effected in rooms where the assistant attorney-general is present with a copy of the antitrust laws in his pocket.

I am familiar with the claim that controllers will in fact do what the market would do in setting the right prices and wages. I do not regard this as a very likely possibility. Hence, if prices are prevented from performing the function of adapting the productive system to changed requirements, as they will be if they are controlled, other means will have to be found for balancing the amounts that buyers are ready to buy and sellers are ready to offer. The only other methods that can be used over a long period are administrative allocations of raw materials, the direction of labor, and the rationing of consumer goods. These, I submit, are wasteful economically, impractical administratively, and dangerous politically. But, above all, a nation using such controls frequently and extensively cannot very long remain a free nation.

MR. VON MISES: What is needed in wartime is to divert production and consumption from peactime channels toward military goals. In order to achieve this, it is necessary to tax the citizens, to take away from them the money which they would otherwise spend for those things they must no longer buy and consume. At the breakfast table of every citizen sits in wartime an invisible guest, as it were, a G.I. who shares the meal. In the citizen's garage stays not only the family car but besides—invisibly—a tank or a plane. The important fact is that this G.I. needs more in food, clothing, and other things than he used to consume as a civilian and that military equipment wears out much quicker than civilian equipment. The costs of a modern war are enormous.

The adequate method of providing the funds the government needs for the conduct of war is, of course, taxation. Part of the funds may also be provided by borrowing from the public, the citizens. But if the Treasury increases the amount of money in circulation or borrows from the commercial banks, it inflates. Inflation can for a limited time do the job. But it is the most expensive method of financing a war; it is socially disruptive and should be avoided.

There is no need to dwell upon the disastrous consequences of inflation. All people agree in this regard. But inflation is a very convenient makeshift for those in power. It is a handy means to divert the resentment of the people from the government. In the eyes of the masses, not the Administration, but big business, the "profiteers," the merchants, appear responsible for the rise in prices and the ensuing necessity to restrict consumption.

Perhaps somebody will qualify what I am saying here as antidemocratic, reactionary, and economic royalism. But the truth is that inflation is a typically antidemocratic measure. It is a policy of governments which do not have the courage to tell the people honestly what the costs of their conduct of affairs are. A truly democratic government would have to tell the voters openly that they must pay higher taxes because expenses have risen considerably. But it is much more agreeable for a government to present only a part of the bill to the people and to resort for the rest of expenditures to inflation. What a triumph if they can say: "Everybody's income is rising; everybody has now more money in his pocket; business is booming."

Deficit spending is not a new invention. It was during the greater part of the nineteenth century the preferred fiscal method of precisely those governments which were not called democratic and progressive, of Austria, Italy, and Russia. Austria's budget showed yearly a deficit from 1781 on until the late eighties of the nineteenth century when an orthodox professor of economics, Dunajewski, as minister of finance restored the budgetary equilibrium. There is no reason to be proud of deficit spending and to call it progress.

If one wants to collect more taxes, it will be necessary to burden more than was done hitherto the lower-income brackets, the strata whose members consume the much greater part of the total amount consumed in this country. Up to now it was customary to tax predominantly the corporations and the individuals with higher incomes. But even the outright confiscation of these revenues would only cover a fraction of the additional funds the country needs today.

Some experts have declared that it is necessary to tax the people until it hurts. I disagree with these sadists. The purpose of taxation is not to hurt but to raise the money the country needs to rearm and to fight in Korea. It is a sad fact that the evolution of world affairs makes it necessary for the government to force people who used to buy nylon stockings and shirts to shift, as it were, to other Du Pont products, namely, munitions.

Kant in his book, *Eternal Peace*, suggested that government should be forbidden to finance wars by borrowing. He expected that the warlike spirit would dwindle if all countries would have to pay cash for their wars. However, no serious objection can be raised against borrowing from the public, from people who have saved and are prepared to invest in government bonds. But borrowing from the commercial banks is tantamount to printing additional bank notes and expanding the amount of deposits subject to check; it is inflation.

There is nowadays a very reprehensible, even dangerous, semantic confusion that makes it extremely difficult for the non-expert to grasp the true state of affairs. "Inflation," as this term was always used everywhere and especially also in this country, means increasing the quantity of money and bank notes in circulation and of bank deposits subject to check. But people today call inflation the phenomenon that is the inevitable consequence of inflation, that is, the tendency of all prices and wage rates to rise. The result of this deplorable confusion is that there is no term left to signify the cause of this rise in prices and wages. There is no longer any word available to signify the phenomenon that has been up to now called "inflation." It follows that nobody cares about inflation in the traditional sense of the term. We cannot talk about something that has no name, and we cannot fight it. Those who pretend to fight inflation are in fact only fighting what is the inevitable consequence of inflation. Their ventures are doomed to failure because they do not attack the root of the evil. They try to keep prices low while firmly committed to a policy which must necessarily make them soar. As long as this terminological confusion is not entirely wiped out, there cannot be any question of stopping inflation.

Look at the silly term "inflationary pressures." There is no such thing. There is inflation or the absence of inflation. If there is no increase in the quantity of money and no credit expansion, the average height of prices and wages will by and large remain unchanged. But if the quantity of money and credit increases, prices and wages must rise whatever the government may decree. If there is no inflation, price control is superfluous. If there is inflation, price control is a sham, a hopeless venture. It is the government that makes our inflation—the policy of the Treasury and nothing else.

We have been told a lot about the necessity and the virtues of direct controls. We have learned that they preserve the individual's liberty to choose the grocer he prefers. I do not want to examine what value has to be attached to direct controls from any metaphysical point of view. I want only to stress one fact: as a means to prevent and to fight inflation or its consequences direct controls are absolutely useless.

CHAIRMAN LEVI: We would like to conclude with two speakers, asking them, for obvious reasons, to be brief. First we will hear from Mr. Feller and then from Mr. Viner.

MR. FELLER: I wish the opportunity were available here that is available in Congress, and I could ask permission to revise and extend my remarks for the record. Then I would not say anything.

CHAIRMAN LEVI: I hasten to say that all remarks can be revised and extended.

MR. FELLER: Taking that opportunity, I will attempt to avail myself of it and limit myself to about three minutes if the chairman will permit me.

I have disagreed with a great deal that has been said here. I will not give you my conception of what the program for economic mobilization should be, because it is obviously impossible in the time limits. I will simply state the considerations which I think are relevant.

What we have is the impact of a sudden shift of our productive resources which will impose sacrifices upon the community. My position is, in direct opposition to the position of Mr.
Director and of some other people, that in that period efforts
must be made by direct controls and otherwise to insure that
the burden upon the community is not allocated in the way
in which it would be allocated on a free market to those who
happen to hold strategic positions. We are not talking about
an equilibrium period. We are talking about a shift from one
period to another.

A great deal of the burden of the labor movement is the
slogan of equality of sacrifice. I will not go through the provisions which we think are necessary to accomplish that equality. I will simply state here that the consideration is not simply
one of efficiency; we are not dictators, and we do not look at
social policy as something which we must bow to because we
cannot do otherwise. We should bow to considerations which
should govern us even if the economists could run the economy
without the ballot box. They cannot, and the economy will not
run that way even if they could try to run it that way, because
the people who operate the economy will not operate it that
way. The important thing is that we have to consider the impact of the changes required by the imposition of a mobilization program on the various classes of the community in terms
of our social values.

The only other thing I want to say, because remarks have
been made about labor, is that the labor organizations which
believe in this kind of program have offered to come in on a
wage stabilization program, though it is difficult sometimes to
persuade our members that we ought to do it.

Mr. Viner: Mr. Chairman, your putting me at this spot has
only one explanation that I can imagine, and that is that you
feel sure that, if at this stage I can find any ideas that have not
already been expressed, they will not be respectable ideas.

I am going to try honestly to speak as I now feel, without
regard to how I felt when I first came here. I believe I have

profited from this conference and that I have been changed a little. I think that some others have also been changed a little and that that is the proper function of a conference such as this.

What I will say may disturb some old friends and new enemies here. If you will accept an interjection of a few theological terms—and they are not wholly inappropriate—there have been three levels of discourse in this discussion. One is the one Leon Henderson referred to and attributed to Adam Smith. It is not quite correct, historically, but it is as close as historians need to get. There is an invisible hand which does all the regulatory work needed without any apparent machinery. I think we have heard that view at least implied. Another one is, I think, substantially Leon Henderson's own position; he has a lot of belief in the invisible hand, but, like Isaac Newton, he wants an intermittent providence with the right to interfere overtly whenever the invisible hand does not suffice. The third is the belief in the need for continuing providence, where everything is decided by superior authority for every individual because they are judged to be too incompetent or too selfish to do anything right by themselves.

I believe in Leon Henderson's intermittent providence, particularly when changes have to be quick and abrupt. However, this is an opportunity for self-exposure. We have heard freedom treated as if it were virtue and control as vice, and that is where I stand. But I, unfortunately, do not believe in an excess of virtue. The only thing I know that we cannot have to excess, and I am not too sure about that, is moderation. Elmer Davis, in his early days, wrote a novel, and there was one good thing in it. One of the chapters started with this motto: "If the prophets ever get the upper hand, God save Israel." I need not explain, however, that I also believe that there can also be an excess of vice. I hope you will concede to me that belief.

Where I stand now is not in kind different, I believe, from where I stood as I came here, but it is different in degree. I would like to rely as much as possible on the indirect controls, to get them into effect as vigorously and quickly as possible.

I would not bet on their being adequate, but I would test their adequacy. I would support them by direct controls preferably only at strategic points, except that even there I would yield further. I would like to see more general controls organized, the administration set up, ready to operate, and possibly even operating. They would not have to operate, I believe, until next September [1951]. But they may be necessary for a period when quick transfer of resources is needed. I would like to have them provided with easy, self-operating provisions for their early termination.

I would also select controls with a view to their being of a noncontagious type. They should be carefully studied in terms of their rationale and their character, to see that they are not the kind that breed associated controls needed in order to protect the original ones. This will require great ingenuity, great knowledge of facts, and direct contact with the firing line, and we from the ivory towers ought not to say too much about it except to state the general principle.

I repeat that I would also make needed concession to public opinion. It will be very important that we have as united an American people as possible. We must respond to the desire the public will undoubtedly have that there shall be no gross profiteering from the country's peril, even if we can prevent it only at the cost of a certain measure of inefficiency.

Now, a word on the reference which a preceding speaker made to bureaucrats. Despite my free-economy convictions, I have never been able to get seriously afraid of American bureaucrats. I have seen them in close action. The young ones are more dangerous than the older ones. They come in with a stock of vigor and ideas and principles and one-sidedness and the liking for pulling levers which it takes longer for Washington to squeeze out of them than out of the older men. A good many bureaucrats, I think, after their first few weeks of enthusiasm, are looking mostly for a system which will enable them to sleep at night rather than for one which involves the constant issuing of orders to avert imminent crises. I do believe there is often a lust for power on the part of bureaucrats, but it is a lust for the possession of the symbols of power. I have sometimes seen less zeal than was desirable for its actual exercise.

In any case, the public is there; it includes persons with a sense of humor; it has speaking for it newspapers with very sharp editorial tongues. Any general control that begins to work obviously badly begins to obsolesce almost before it starts to operate, and we then get the sick buzzard that dies quickly even without the aid of the Supreme Court.

What does not die so quickly is the payroll that these agencies build up. They have developed a technique whereby they can maintain themselves even if their functions have gone, with the aid of the lawyers who are monopolizing too much of the real brains of the country. One way is to issue general prohibitions, very carefully and elaborately drafted at great expenditure of legal thought, and then to issue general licenses permitting wholesale departure from the prohibitions. That takes a lot of time and a lot of staff.

The real danger to our economic freedom comes, I believe, not from the bureaucrats, but from Congress and the people. Our freedom will not be wrenched from us, but we may give it away.

One issue which was important for this conference has been given discussion, much of which was to me enlightening. I know this is an important issue, but I know little about it, and that is how to organize the administrative offices in order to carry out efficiently the mobilization program. I have no views on it. My general impression, as an ignorant outsider, is that the organization setup even now, and I am sure it is still unfinished, is much better than we had in the last war.

But there is another angle of organization for efficient administration, and for the preservation of as much of the values we cherish as possible, that has not been touched in the least in all this conference, although I think it is important, and that is the mobilization of Congress for an emergency period. I know of no change it has made in its procedures, which never were good, to adapt itself to the emergency needs. I know of no sacrifice it has made to the needs of the situation. One of the essentials, I am sure, in the situation we are in is the capacity for speed in making decisions by what passes for the congressional mind, including flexibility, reversibility, the possibility of retreating quickly if they find out that they have made a wrong decision. I think that in the discussion of the organization and public administration aspects, those who know about public administration should not forget that the administration itself will not be able to work well, no matter how sound its principles, how good its organization, if it has to face the slow procedures, the seniority rule, the bargaining for power between committees, and the unwillingness to cease even for a moment to do some vote-gathering associated with Congress.

MR. MORRIS: Before I am deprived of my luncheon, I do not want to be deprived of the opportunity to express my appreciation of our host and sponsor and financier of this extremely interesting conference.

CHAIRMAN LEVI: Let me express our thanks to the participants in this conference who have all been very patient. The conference is adjourned.

INDEX OF NAMES

341